ETHNOCIDE: A CULTURAL NARRATIVE OF REFUGEE DETENTION IN HONG KONG

Ethnocide: A Cultural Narrative of Refugee Detention in Hong Kong

JOE THOMAS
La Trobe University, Melbourne

LONDON AND NEW YORK

First published 2000 by Ashgate Publishing

Reissued 2018 by Routledge
2 Park Square, Milton Park, Abingdon, Oxon OX14 4RN
711 Third Avenue, New York, NY 10017, USA

Routledge is an imprint of the Taylor & Francis Group, an informa business

Publisher's Note
The publisher has gone to great lengths to ensure the quality of this reprint but points out that some imperfections in the original copies may be apparent.

Disclaimer
The publisher has made every effort to trace copyright holders and welcomes correspondence from those they have been unable to contact.

A Library of Congress record exists under LC control number: 99075540

ISBN 13: 978-1-138-70729-0 (hbk)
ISBN 13: 978-1-315-20148-1 (ebk)

Contents

List of Figures, Photos and Tables

Preface

The present study is an ethnographic inquiry into the socio-cultural dynamics of the Vietnamese asylum seeker detention centers in Hong Kong during the period of 1988-1995. This book essentially deals with the British asylum policy towards Vietnamese refugees and its outcome in Hong Kong; the British policy of a prolonged administrative detention (detention without a legal procedure) of a large number of children, women and men. The refugee administrators managed to solve the Vietnamese boat people crisis in Hong Kong through a series of refugee policies. However, very little is known to the world about the nature of these policies and their consequences. This book, based on the author's first-hand field experience as a camp worker in Hong Kong, argues that the administrators managed to solve the crisis by perpetuating horrendous human rights violations and subsequent ethnocide of the asylum seekers trapped in the detention centers.

When the asylum seekers are betrayed by the refugee protection regimes, what do the asylum seekers do; how do they cope with such a betrayal; what are the consequences of such a betrayal; and how such a phenomena was allowed to happen, are some of the themes of this book. Ethnocide is not an accidental or unavoidable consequence of cultural contact between two cultural groups with unequal power. In Hong Kong such a phenomenon has occurred through a carefully planned refugee policy and programme, executed by an efficient bureaucracy with the blessings of the global refugee protection regime - the United Nations High Commissioner for Refugees.

It is a pleasure to acknowledge the indebtedness to several individuals for helping me to write this book. I would like to thank all of them. Without their care and consideration this work would not have been possible. However only I am responsible for the views expressed in, and any shortcomings of, this book.

Dr. Michael Lanphier, at the Refugee Study Center, York University, Toronto was kind enough to accept me at his center with valuable suggestions. He also patiently read the first draft of this book and made substantial suggestions and criticisms. Dr. Harrell-Bond, Director of the Refugee studies programme at the University of Oxford helped me immensely in developing **a theoretical framework for this study.**

With great pleasure, I would like to acknowledge the support offered by my colleagues, Dede Farrell, Nigel Priece, Senoo Rawat and Ravi Lulla. Several of my friends in Hong Kong detention centers helped me in many ways. Mr. Thu, Mr. 'Big' Hung, and Ms. Van helped me in data collection.

I would also like to acknowledge the encouragement and guidance I have received from Dr. K.S. Nair, Dr. S.Parasuram and Mr. G.AA. Britto.

Thanks to the South China Morning Post Publishers Ltd for granting me **permission to reprint the article, 'Why I weep for Hong Kong', SCMP, 27-09-**1992.

Finally, Mridula, my companion and friend for encouraging me to complete this work.

Joe Thomas

List of Abbreviations

AI	Amnesty International
AMS	Auxiliary Medical Services
AVS	Action for Voluntary Services
BBC	British Broadcasting Corporation
CAPO	Complaints Against Police Officer
CD	Community Development
CFSI	Community and Family Services International
CISD	Critical Incident Stress Debriefing
CMA	Christian Ministers Alliance
CPA	Comprehensive Plan of Action
CSD	Correctional Service Development
DRV	Democratic Republic of Vietnam
EEC	European Economic Community
ESF	Ecole San Fronte
HIDC	High Island Detention Centre
HK	Hong Kong
HKCAR	Hong Kong Christian AIDS For Refugees
HKCAS	Hong Kong Civil Aid Society
HKFPA	Hong Kong Family Planning Association
HKHSR	Hong Kong Housing Services for Refugees
HKID	Hong Kong Immigration Department
HKRC	Hong Kong Read Cross
ICCB	International Catholic Childrens Bureau
ICCPR	International Covenant on Civil and Political Rights
IOM	International Organization of Migration
ISS	International Social Services
JP	Justice of the Peace
JVA	Joint Voluntary Action
MIA	Missing in Action
MOU	Memorandum of Understanding
MSF	Medicine San Fronte
NEZ	New Economic Zone
NGO	Non Governmental Organization
NIMH	National Institute of Mental Health
ODP	Orderly Departure Program
POW	Prisoner of War
PRC	Principal Refugee Claimant
PRPC	Philippine Refugee Processing Center
PTU	Police Tactical Unit

RCHK	Refugee Concern Hong Kong
RKHP	Royal Hong Kong Police
RSRB	Refugee Status Review Board
RV	Republic of Vietnam
SCF	Save the Children Fund
SCMP	South China Morning Post
SCVP	Special Committee for Vulnerable Persons
SKDC	Shek Kong Detention Center
UĀM	Un Accompanied Minor
UDHR	Universal Declaration of Human Rights
UK	United Kingdom
UN	United Nations
UNHCR	United Nations High Commission for Refugees
US/ USA	United States of America
VOA	Voice of America
WHDC	White Head Detention Center
WHO	World Health Organization

1 Introduction

Hong Kong has had a long history of association with the Vietnamese asylum seekers. It began with the arrival of a Danish container ship 'Clara Maersk' on May 4, 1975, in Hong Kong. This container ship had an unusual cargo of 3,743 Vietnamese refugees who were rescued from the South China Seas. At a short notice camps were set up to house the refugees until they could be resettled abroad (this task was completed only by 1978). By then new asylum seekers began arriving in Hong Kong. The government's declaration of 'port of first asylum policy' in 1979 solemnised the Colony's initial flirtation and valour with the Vietnamese refugees. This was an open invitation to all Vietnamese seeking refugee status to use Hong Kong as a transit point for resettling in another country. This was an indirect result of USA and it's allies' futile war against Vietnam and their subsequent defeat at the hands of the Vietnamese army. This book traces the history of Vietnamese refugee issues in Hong Kong from its initial honeymoon period through various phases. The various stages includes the thawing of relations, chilled tolerance, irritation, separation, segregation, downright hostility, violence, and finally a 'divorce', scrapping the 19 year old 'marriage' with the first asylum policy for the Vietnamese refugees in 1998 by the Special Administrative Region (SAR) Government of Hong Kong. The core theme of this book is an analysis of the strategies adopted by the refugee managers to clear the so called 'refugee problem' in Hong Kong.

Background

Research for this book was conducted during a momentous period in the history of Hong Kong, the years leading up to the return of the territory to Chinese rule. It details and covers the experiences of detained Vietnamese refugees between the period of 1988-1995. One of the conditions of the transfer of power in 1997 between Britain and China was that the problem of the Vietnamese refugees/asylum seekers should also be 'solved'. Ironically, during the same time it was forcibly repatriating the Vietnamese, Hong Kong was also importing skilled and semiskilled persons to meet its labour requirements.

What is in a name? The Vietnamese refugees who came to Hong Kong and other South East Asian countries to seek asylum have been described under various names during different periods of time. During the early part of the refugee saga all Vietnamese who managed to reach Hong Kong were called refugees. The popular media labelled them as 'Boat People'. The administrators often used the acronym VBP (Vietnamese Boat People). In 1988, the government unilaterally 'discovered' that not all asylum seekers were genuine refugees implying that some of them were fleeing Vietnam due to economic reasons. They decided to implement a refugee screening procedure in Hong Kong to identify the so-called 'genuine refugees'. This was the first sour note of the colony's relation with the Vietnamese refugees. The Vietnamese who were identified as 'genuine refugees' were released from detention and were moved to another camp pending resettlement to another country. In early 1990, the Hong Kong government began referring to all asylum seekers as Vietnamese migrants. In this book I have used the term refugees and asylum seekers interchangeably, without particularly referring to their official status of refugee or non-refugee.

When hostilities between the United States and North Vietnam came to an end and Vietnam was unified in 1975, many former South Vietnamese political activists, administrators and soldiers left Vietnam to seek political asylum in other countries. They landed in many of the neighbouring South East Asian Countries, which served as a transit point for their subsequent resettlement in Western countries. Hong Kong was a 'harbour of hope' (Philpot, 1980) for many and provided refuge to thousands of asylum seekers from Vietnam since 1975. During the initial phase of Vietnamese asylum seekers exodus any Vietnamese who arrived in Hong Kong was automatically assigned refugee status. Most of the asylum seekers during that time were from the former South Vietnam. This arrangement continued for 13 years, till the midnight of June 15, 1988.

As the years passed, Vietnamese of Chinese origin also joined the ranks of asylum seekers because of reported persecution and the ongoing power realignments within the united Vietnam. In 1988, many former North Vietnamese also began fleeing the country. There was a massive surge of humanity trying to escape Vietnam by any and all available means. Clandestine departures often resulted in extreme sufferings, breaking up of families and loss of lives. Such an influx of Vietnamese asylum seekers precipitated detention of asylum seekers in various camps across South East Asia. The social and political consequence of such a detention is one of the key phenomena explored in this book.

The first UN conference on Indo-Chinese refugees

For the first time in history, at the initiative of the USA and Britain, a special UN conference was held in Geneva to address the situation of the Vietnamese fleeting their country. Its agenda, which reflected cold-war politics, was to decide how to continue to 'facilitate' this outflow; to lay down the rules for the rescue of people at sea, who were increasingly in danger from un-seaworthy craft and pirates; and to convince other allies to accept a quota for resettlement in their countries.

The Voice of America (VOA) and the British Broadcasting Corporation (BBC) were 'in charge' of broadcasting information to Vietnam on the west's resettlement policy and of the existence and location of the mercy ships. This open policy of encouraging the exodus of Vietnamese continued for 17 long years. The US ships were specially positioned at the South China Sea at the time to try and save the 'boat people' from pirate attack at sea. Even international humanitarian agencies like Medecins Sans Frontieres (MSF) chartered boats (L'ile de Lumiere) to rescue the boat people.

Because of the political temperature which had been raised all over the world during the Vietnam War, the response in the west to this 'humanitarian crisis' (a crisis fuelled for the benefit of cold-war objectives) was overwhelming and the media attention was intense. At the same conference, different countries established quotas for the number of Vietnamese refugees they would accept from the countries of first asylum.

The second UN conference on Indo-Chinese refugees

The second International conference on Indo-Chinese Refugees was also held in Geneva (13-14 June 1989) by the United Nations General Assembly. The mood of this meeting was quite different than the earlier one. By this time, with some exceptions, attitudes towards the 'boat people' had hardened. Hong Kong was already detaining refugees from 1982 and the automatic granting of asylum had ceased a year earlier. The agenda was to develop a framework to deal with the continuing influx of Vietnamese 'boat people'. The Vietnamese 'boat people' were no longer described as a humanitarian crisis, but as a 'boat people' crisis. It was agreed that since Vietnamese were no longer automatically considered to be refugees, each and everyone would have to be 'screened', that is, to be put through a refugee determination status procedure in the countries where they sought asylum. Vietnam was asked to take back all those who were 'screened out'.

This conference provided the framework of a 'Comprehensive Plan of Action' (CPA) to deal with this large influx of refugees from Vietnam. In addition, the Orderly Departure Programme (ODP) was established. It was designed to allow people to legally migrate from Vietnam, mainly to the Unites States. Under the CPA agreement, UNHCR was asked to monitor the procedures and a special monitoring committee was set-up. However, the implementation of the CPA varied from country to country.

Not every country detained Vietnamese asylum seekers, as did Hong Kong. Moreover, across the region, the refugee determination procedures were differently applied. In Hong Kong; the Immigration department under very minimal supervision of the UNHCR handled the refugee determination process. In Malaysia and Indonesia, the military took the primary role, although in Malaysia, the process did involve UNHCR staff. The issue of children without their parents also received different treatment depending on the country they were in. For example, the age of a child in Hong Kong was determined as anyone 16 or below at the date of their interview with an immigration officer. Others defined 'children' as those under 18 on the date of arrival in the camps. Around this period, with the gradual rapprochement with Vietnam, a separate agreement was reached to allow 'Ameriasians', the children (but not their mothers), who had been fathered by servicemen during the war to leave Vietnam for the United States.

The CPA was a bureaucratic solution for a humanitarian crisis. However, the authors of the CPA failed to anticipate the prolonged detention of a large number of asylum seekers. They also did not suggest any concrete measures to protect the best interest of the detainee's by protecting their rights and privileges. Under the CPA, an agreement was reached concerning who was responsible for paying the cost of continuing to host the asylum seekers in the countries where they had landed to claim asylum. This responsibility explicitly fell on the United Nations High Commission for Refugees (UNHCR) in the case of Hong Kong. Later this became a bone of contention because UNHCR was reluctant to be seen to be paying for prison facilities in which asylum seekers were being detained.

UNHCR being an inter-governmental agency was expected to monitor the daily management of the asylum seekers and refugees. It's other functions included searching for durable solutions and offering social services to the detainees. The Hong Kong Civil Aid Society (HKCAS) was the agency initially assigned by the government to deal with the refugee situation. Another local agency, 'Caritas', offered assistance for resettling the refugees in another country.

The British-Hong Kong Government subsequently passed specific immigration laws to determine the refugee claims of the asylum seekers of Vietnamese origin. These asylum seekers often waited up to four to five years to present their refugee claim to an immigration officer. Those waiting for the screening to determine their refugee status as well as those who had been 'screened out' and deemed as 'non refugees' were detained under the same legal framework and under the same conditions.

Detention camps for the asylum seekers in Hong Kong

The Vietnamese detention camps were situated in remote islands faraway from the urban centres (Figure 1.1, Location of Vietnamese Detention Centres). These centres were inaccessible to the preying eyes of millions of tourist who visit Hong Kong every year, and also from the eyes of the local population. During the peak of the refugee saga in the late 1980s to early 1990s, the detention centres were home to some 50-60 thousand Vietnamese men, women, and children (Fig 1.2, Vietnamese Asylum Seeker Population in Hong Kong). This unique social condition has led to several questions being raised related to the contemporary refugee policy, such as the role of international power relations in shaping the refugee movement, and the psycho-social

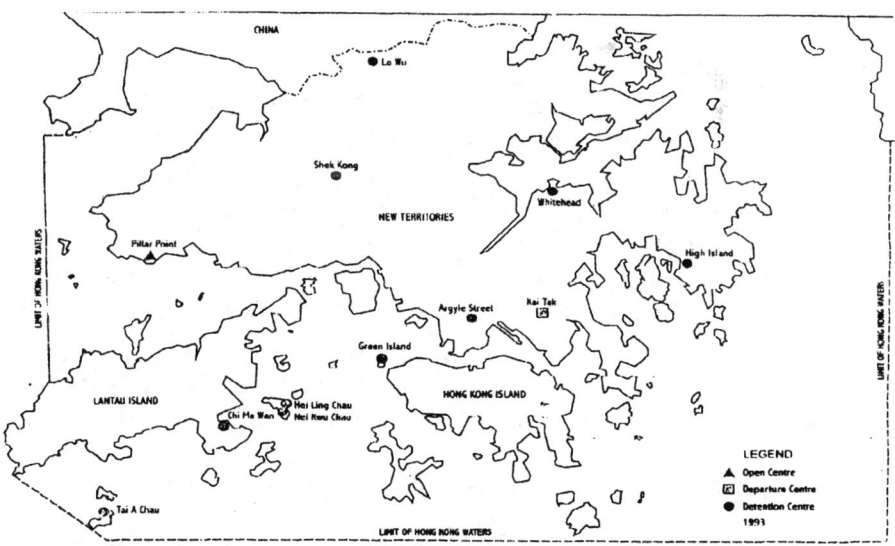

Figure 1.1   Location of Vietnamese Detention Centres

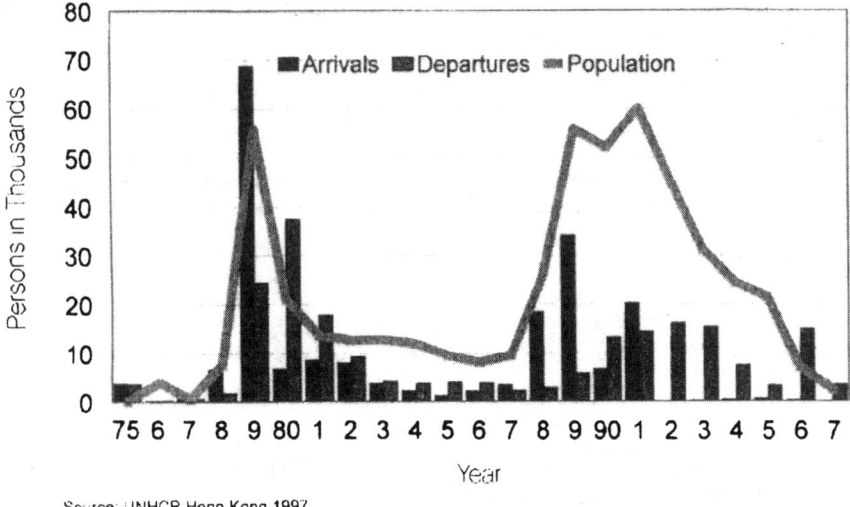

Vietnamese Asylum Seekers in Hong Kong
Arrivals, Departures & Population

Source: UNHCR Hong Kong 1997

Figure 1.2   Vietnamese Asylum Seekers Population in Hong Kong

consequences of detaining large numbers of people, including disabled, elderly, orphaned and abandoned children in appalling conditions. A descriptive ethnography of the socio-cultural conditions experienced by the Vietnamese asylum seekers detained in Hong Kong camps, and various other issues related to this phenomenon are the core theme of this book.

The Vietnamese asylum seekers were under the administrative custody of the British-Hong Kong Security branch which passed the responsibility of daily management of asylum seekers to the Correctional Service Department (CSD), Royal Hong Kong Police and a private company called the Hong Kong Housing Services for Refugees Limited. Since most of the asylum seekers came to Hong Kong in boats, an ambiguous term 'Boat People' has been used to denote all Vietnamese asylum seekers who arrived in Hong Kong. They were detained under what is known as Immigration (Vietnamese Boat People) Detention Centre Rules, which is essentially an adapted version of the British prison rule.

The detention centres where the Vietnamese asylum seekers lived was a different world by itself. Women, new-born babies, men, elderly, physically and mentally disabled, youngsters and children were barricaded within tall barbed wires. Some stayed on for six to seven years. Surrounded by the high security fence and observation towers, they walked around aimlessly like trapped animals inside the camps, or idled away their time by lying down in their bunks doing nothing in particular. Each family was assigned a bunk in a three-tier sleeping space. They were expected to sleep on a wooden plank without a mattress. The physical conditions in the camps provided very little privacy. The searchlights were always on. There was no partition to separate the bed spaces except for some cloth curtains for those who managed to get it from the camp charity workers. The food was centrally cooked and distributed. The role of the mother as the one who provides nourishment was watered down, as her caring role was minimal. The father was robbed of his authority as he was no more a bread winner and provider of the family. There were innumerable queues for everything, for food, drinking water, and the use of the toilets and washing facilities.

None of the asylum seekers were entitled to any special facilities or privileges. Despite this, the 'Big Brothers' formed an alleged collusion with the camp administration staff and enjoyed certain special privileges such as occasional food from outside the detention facilities, a can of beer or a cigarette. The elderly, the physically disabled and the children faced the same hurdles in their day-to-day life within the camp. They queued up for medical treatment or for an appointment with the agency staff for presenting any genuine request. Camp rules were often interpreted according to the whims and convenience of the low ranking functionaries. Most asylum seekers had never seen a copy of the rules under which they were detained.

Sense of betrayal

According to Leonard Davis (1991), the Vietnamese issue in Hong Kong can be divided into four periods:
1. May 4, 1975, when the first group of 3,743 refugees rescued from the South China Seas landed in Hong Kong until July 2, 1982, when the 'closed camp' policy was introduced;
2. The initial six years of 'closed camp' era that witnessed a steady flow of refugees leaving for resettlement countries;
3. The period from June 16, 1988 (the day on which the screening and repatriation policy came into operation) until the beginning of 1990 when it seemed that the Comprehensive Plan of Action endorsed by the international community was breaking down because of the inability of

the British and Hong Kong governments to continue with mandatory repatriation, and the pressure from the Chinese government to abandon the policy of first asylum; and

4. The subsequent apparent disintegration - with the exception of voluntary repatriation - in the first six months of the new decade of many policy initiatives and earlier coping strategies.

This book also deals with another phase of the refugees, namely, the so called 'non-refugees'. A large number of asylum seekers deemed as non-refugees (screened out) were reluctant to go home. They felt betrayed by the international community for changing the rules of the game by instituting a screening procedure, that many were unaware of when they left Vietnam to seek refuge in Hong Kong. Many refugees and refugee commentators believed the process of refugee status determination was riddled with flaws. The UNHCR suggested that it's role with a 'screened out' population was limited and scaled down the social service facilities, citing resource crunch as one of the main reasons. However, most of the independent observer's felt that it was a ploy to use cutbacks as a leverage to send the unwanted Vietnamese back home.

Scope of this book

Volumes are being written on Vietnamese refugee issues' but very little on the socio-cultural consequences of prolonged refugee detention and the strategies used by the British government in Hong Kong to solve the 'refugee problem'. Refugees are often understood as a product of forced uprooting, economic changes, ethnic violence, war, famine and natural disasters. There is very little discussion or data on the dynamics of international geo-political considerations in producing and sustaining refugee phenomena. The human misery and the consequences of such a policy is also often overlooked by the refugee administrators and refugee researchers and many human rights and social service agencies. This is essentially because of the policy of the refugee administrators to deny independent access to the camps for researchers and the mass media.

It is generally understood that the process of becoming a refugee involves several stages. Imminent danger or perception of danger, the process of taking a decision to leave, the process of flight, the stage of initial asylum and resettlement or repatriation. Each stage has its own issues, tasks and particular experiences. It appears that the issues and concerns of resettlement and adaptation to the host countries dominate the global literatures on South East

Asian refugees. Very little data and experience exists on issues related to initial asylum, particularly about the asylum seekers who are detained for a long time. Such a literature bias is a significant indicator of the nature of global geo-political considerations in academic research and its impact on production of knowledge itself.

This exploratory and descriptive case study of Hong Kong's experience with the Vietnamese refugees has its implications for theoretical paradigms that have hitherto governed planned intervention for refugees all over the world. The objective of most social service intervention is to assist the asylum seekers to adapt with the local conditions as quickly as possible. In the Hong Kong case it appears that planned social service intervention was used as a tool to force the asylum seekers to go back to their country of origin, despite apprehensions of the asylum seekers to do so. Because of it's own internal mechanisms, plain omissions or through deliberate decisions, the office of the UNHCR failed to protect the 'best interests' of the Vietnamese asylum seekers detained in the Hong Kong camps raising serious questions about the role of UNHCR in the post cold-war era. Such case studies cannot by their nature propound a universally applicable theory but proposes a set of hypotheses for further testing and validation in different context for refinement. Several such case studies would contribute to the evolution of a theory as an alternative to the dominant theories to date.

Aims and objectives

This study focused on the following specific themes
- The social context of motivation to seek refuge and the process of escape from Vietnam
- The socio-political context of international initiatives related to asylum seekers detained in Hong Kong
- The specific policies of Hong Kong government towards the asylum seekers and subsequent violations of their rights
- The day to day socio-cultural conditions of the asylum seekers detained in the camps,
- The cause and consequences of violence in the camps and
- The role of social service intervention in detention centres.

It also examines the impact of detention in the following areas. Family organisation and family control, religious organisation, social organisation, group control, co-operation and conflict, and social change and integrity of the group in general.

This book also looks into the life situation, as of post June 1988, of asylum seekers detained in Hong Kong detention camps in general and specifically certain non-humanitarian outcome of the Comprehensive Plan of Action (CPA) developed by the international community to deal with the large influx of refugees from Vietnam.

Method of data collection

Harrell-Bond (1986) in her study of refugee assistance in Sudan adopted an anthropological participatory, action oriented and consultative approach to data collection. However, considering the political sensitivity of the issues under investigation, such an approach was impossible to implement in detention camps. This study is an enquiry into a unique social process; an effort has been made to utilise a series of appropriate tools to assess this social process. The following are the main methods used for data collection. Personal interviews, field observations, life histories, participant observation and informant interviews. The most important source of data was from purposive group discussions conducted with the camp leaders based on thematic issues. These discussions were carried out during the my work as a 'community worker' in the camps between November 1990 to July 1993. Such 'clandestine' anthropological fieldwork has it own limitations. One of the main problems was that a specific theoretical framework did not guide the initial data collection. Another important problem was obtaining permission to do a study on refugee conditions in detention camps. I tried to get an 'official permission' from the agencies and the camp authorities, which did not materialise. In fact the message clearly given was that if the research agenda were pursued, I would loose access to the camps as a camp worker. However, according to the honoured tradition of an anthropologist in the field, I started keeping 'camp notes' quite regularly. There was a therapeutic effect in keeping such a notebook. It was a way to cope with the stress of working in the camps as a community worker by distancing oneself from the day to day events of the camps and recording it as an observer. But while presenting an interpretation of the data, I reluctantly used the method of presenting myself as the narrator of the 'study'.

Purposive group discussions have been used as a serious method of data collection in this study. The usual method of recording data was by means of a daily activity report book where observation notes and interview reports were recorded. Some of the meetings were tape recorded, which was edited and transcribed during the weekends. The asylum seekers wrote their own case studies presented in this book. The case studies have not been formally edited except for the sake of clarity. The camp regulations did not permit cameras to be taken into the camps and the handbags of all the staff were regularly checked. Yet, on several occasions I managed to 'smuggle' a camera into the camp. Various photographs and videos recorded by me by the means of a hand-held video camera to record the daily life activity within the camps were also reviewed at a later stage while writing this book.

As a part of my fieldwork, I visited all the camps in the territory several times. Through a net work of community leaders and a group of sympathetic staff, I kept an active contact with the camp community leadership and kept abreast with all the developments in each camp on a regular basis. Most of the data for this book evolved from the two camps where I worked regularly as a community worker; the Tai A Chau and Sek Kong detention centres.

The objectivity and positionality

Objectivity is the cornerstone of any scientific endeavour. A view or form of thought is more objective than another if it relies less on the specifics of an individual's makeup and position in the world, or on the character of a particular type of creature he is (Nagel, 1986). Many of the anthropological contributions to knowledge are often subjected to deep suspicion of observer's personal prejudices. The title of this book itself may attract such a suspicion. It is indeed difficult to accept the fact that in the late 20th century, in an era of great progress in the area of negotiated norms of civility and respect to the rights of human beings, a phenomenon such as 'ethnocide' might be a subjective interpretation of a social reality.

In this context, even though, I tend to agree that ethnographic knowledge is never impersonal (Kleinman, 1994) it is important to explore the issue of objectivity of this study further. The data for this book has been mostly derived from a series of anthropological methods. A discussion on the objectivity of anthropological method is beyond the scope of this book. However, I agree with the idea that the concept of objectivity requires explicit acceptance and extensive use of variability of observations (Sen, 1994).

Positionality of objectivity is understood as a state of recognition and acknowledgement of the influence of observational positions and willingness to scrutinise its impact on objective assessment. Positional objectivity is also a claim regarding the objectivity of observations from certain positions. Sen (1994) proposed the need to take the positionality of objectivity a step further to transpositional objectivity. Such an endeavour is essentially a decision of the researcher on what best to take and present. In this instance, the preferential access I enjoyed with the study population and the freedom I undertook to prioritise issues are the two main factors that influenced the transpositionality of this book.

Access as a positional parameter in this study has a wider meaning, which includes physical access to the population under study and an intellectual and emotional access to the people under study, which is essentiality the level of acceptance of the researcher by the community. I had an unique opportunity to access the refugee camps on a day to day basis for a prolonged period of time. Such an access facilitated in observing a wide range of activities and experiences of the refugees, which are generally not known to others. I can safely claim that I was sufficiently accepted by a large number of 'study population' who were willing to share their stories with me. Some of my personal characteristics also contributed to the issue of emotional and intellectual access to the population under study. Being from a South Asian background, my position as a 'migrant worker' in the camps was much similar to the experience of the refugees I was trying to study. This factor struck a common denominator in my interaction with many respondents in the camps. My lack of clout and access to resources as a camp worker was often a standing theme of discussion between the respondents and myself. Unlike a traditional anthropologist (often from a developed country), who can descend into a community with trappings of power, influence and an image of endless access to resources, I presented myself as a 'native anthropologist', who lacked resources, clout and influence. In addition, I could closely identify with the vulnerability of the population I was trying to study. This approach had certain advantages. I am sure that the stories they shared with me were genuine. Most of the respondents knew that they had nothing to gain by telling an exaggerated story to me. Almost all the respondents knew that the study was self-financed and I had no financial sponsorship to do this study. Some others thought that I was just an over enthusiastic camp worker who kept extensive notes on the meetings and conversations. Though, I was unable to speak Vietnamese, I managed to acquire a basic Vietnamese vocabulary. Besides, I had constant access to staff-interpreters in the camp as part of my privileges as a camp worker.

A researcher's scope of prioritising the issues to be presented in the final analysis is an important trasnspositional parameter. A research priority could be an external priority, priority of the sponsoring agency, or it could be a priority of the subjects under study. The initial approach for this study on refugee detention was generalised without any specific priority largely based on an element of an intellectual curiosity. The priorities of presentations came at a much later stage. The prioritisation of research issues was largely based on an empathetic effort to understand the phenomenon of refugee detention mostly from a refugee perspective.

Presentation of Chapters

This book is divided into nine chapters. Chapter two reviews the literature on refugee issues in general. A number of typologies and analytical frames are reviewed in this section. Berry's integration theory has been critically analysed and rejected due to his overemphasis on the individual adaptation process of the refugee/asylum seeker to the host culture. In modern times refugees are to a large extent pawns in the international power games. This chapter has contributed towards a more adequate typology to apply a scheme to analyse the refugee context in Hong Kong.

The socio-cultural consequence of the detention of asylum seekers is explained with the assistance of the concepts of 'total institution' and 'Ethnocide' along with other theoretical constructs. Ethnocide is defined as a process of a community losing all its' internal cohesion, community structures, networks and direction. A community may lose its ability to influence its direction and affairs due to the direct intervention of a dominant group. Ethnocide is the product of a process of an extreme community reaction to an extreme external stimulus of segregation and separation of that community from a broader society. This is the conceptual parting point of this book.

Chapter three discusses the socio-cultural and political conditions in Vietnam, which might have contributed to the exodus of the asylum seekers, and which might also act as distant determinants of the camp conditions. This chapter also describes the flight of the asylum seekers from Vietnam and the life experiences of the asylees while they were fleeing from their own country. It also discuses the relationship between the process of exodus and the process of ethnocide taking place in the detention camps in Hong Kong.

Chapter four reviews the context of international relations and the role different government's play in shaping the life situation of asylum seekers detained in Hong Kong. It especially reviews the role of the 'super power' United States, and how the American foreign policy in South East Asia contributed to the misery of several asylum seekers. Careful international monitoring is a factor, which could contribute or lessen the consequence of ethnocide in the camps. However, this chapter explains how such monitoring mechanisms fail to deliver positive results in the Hong Kong context.

Chapter five is divided into two parts. The first part analyses the socio-political context of Hong Kong and it's role as a first asylum country in receiving a large number of asylum seekers and what made it a favourite temporary destination amongst the other South East Asian neighbours for most of the asylum seekers. The second part of this chapter gives a detailed account of the human rights violation of the asylum seekers in Hong Kong. International instruments for the protection of Human Rights are used as the yardstick for assessing the extent of violation of the asylum seekers detained in Hong Kong. This chapter contributes towards the growing area of knowledge in anthropology for the rights of individuals, especially, when they are facing difficult conditions. 'Individual disorientation' which is a contributory factor in ethnocide is directly related to the level and extent of human rights violation of the asylum seekers in the camps.

Chapter six is also divided into two parts. The first part of this chapter deals with the personal concerns of women in the camp. The second part presents a descriptive ethnography of the camp life. It presents data on the day to day living conditions in the camps and the survival strategies developed by the asylum seekers to cope with detention. It also describes the process of community disorganisation, another contributory factor of ethnocide, taking place within the camps. In addition, it graphically describes the ongoing struggle between the asylum seekers attempt to preserve the integrity of their culture and way of life and the attempts of the camp administration to break such community bonds and linkages through various means.

Violence in the camp is an external manifestation of ethnocide. Chapter seven describes the nature and pattern of violence in the camps. Detention camp in itself is a symbol of structured violence by a civilised society to the refugees who arrive seeking asylum. This chapter analyses the root of structural violence and the intra-camp violence which in itself is a coping mechanism for a few of the detainees to exercise control over their immediate environment at the expense of the mental and physical health of several women, children and the disabled. Camp violence is a product and consequence of individual disorientation and community disorganisation. An asylum seeker with reasonable level of personal resources can cope better with the demands of the camp conditions. Asylum seekers with few personal resources and people from vulnerable groups such as children, elderly and the disabled suffer more due to the process of ethnocide.

Chapter eight is a critical descriptive account of the social service facilities available in the camps. Often the social service agency staff are the only sympathetic listeners and channels of contact for the asylum seekers to the outside world. The pattern of services available in the camps has a link to the overall quality of life of the individuals detained in the camps. Besides, the service intervention can also reduce the consequences of ethnocide to a large extent.

Chapter nine offers a conclusion highlighting the main themes under discussion. The overall social process that went into the detention camps was a planned ethnocide as a direct consequence of the refugee policy of the British government in Hong Kong. The international community and social service agencies were mute spectators or silent collaborators of this crime against humanity.

The 'refugee managers' and British diplomats in Hong Kong claim success in sending all the asylum seekers who are determined as non-refugees back to Vietnam. They succeeded in doing so only because of a successful implementation of an administrative practice and a set of policies that led to a process of 'ethnocide' of asylum seekers. Under the pressure of detention and subsequent ethnocide the detained community lost its' internal cohesion, community structures, networks and direction. The findings of this study has far reaching consequences in the area of ethnic relations, refugee rights, refugee assistance programmes, refugee policy, international relations and the role of UNHCR in refugee protection in the post cold-war era.

2 Understanding Refugee Detention: Conceptual and Methodological Issues

Introduction

This chapter presents a brief review of literature and theoretical frame of reference to explain the issues under study. Most importantly, it narrates issues of personal dimensions in conducting refugee research in detention centres. It also examines the experiences that could influence the decisions to explore further for conceptual and methodological clarity in doing anthropological fieldwork. A number of typologies and analytical frames are reviewed in this chapter. During the initial preparation of the data collection, much emphasis was placed on Berry's (1991) theory of 'refugee integration'. However, when the data started accumulating, many issues were beyond the explanations of an 'integration approach'.

Berry's integration theory has been critically analysed and rejected due to overemphasis on the individual adaptation process of the refugees resettled in a host culture (Berry's theory has been discussed in detail elsewhere in this chapter). In modern times refugees are to a large extent pawns in the international power game and product of a complex socio-political process. Therefore, a rigorous approach is necessary to identify various typologies of refugees. This chapter also presents a typology of such diverse refugee groups.

The concept of 'ethnocide' is introduced as a theoretical construct to explain the consequence of refugee detention. Ethnocide is the process of a community losing its internal cohesion, community structures, networks and direction on account of the policies of segregation and separation introduced by the British government in Hong Kong. In addition, a conceptual framework is presented to analyse the cause and consequences of refugee detention in Hong Kong.

The landscape of developing a theory

Efforts to develop a theory to understand the issues under study have taken different twists and turns. According to Richmond (1988), theories of international migration can broadly be classified as macro and micro in their level of analysis. The macro level theories deal with issues related to immigrants adaptation process, economic and social integration, assimilation, etc. Whilst, the micro level theories deal with issues related to socio-psychological factors, issues related to motivation, decision-making, satisfaction and identification, mostly away from the broader societal consequences. Review of literature available in the area of refugee studies reveal that most of the studies have been focusing on mental health aspects of the refugees and the individual psychological aspects of adaptation to the host culture (NIMH, 1991).

Earlier studies primarily concentrated on the psychosocial aspects of refugees in a resettled context. Much of the data for these studies came from the refugees resettled in the United States and Canada (NIMH, 1991) and mostly in the context of adaptation of refugees to the developed countries. Refugees resettled in a third country or assimilated in the host society and culture get more attention from academicians and refugee policy makers. Several studies have been conducted on the issues related to resettled refugees or the refugees integrated into the local culture (Adelman, 1979, 1980, 1982; Ahern and Athey, 1991; Harrel-Bond 1986; Lanphier 1981, 1982, 1983, 1984, 1985, 1987, 1988; Berry 1990, 1991, 1992).

Nonetheless, these studies have contributed useful information about the psychosocial adaptation in general, and mental health situation in particular. However, limited number of studies have been done on the socio-cultural aspects of the 'refugee sojourns', or on asylum seekers who are detained in the first asylum countries like Hong Kong (Leonard, 1991; Hitchcox, 1990; Refugee Concern, 1991; Asia Watch, 1991). Moreover, a serious 'gap' exists in studies and in our understanding the socio-cultural consequences of asylum seeker detention centres and the role and impact of 'social services' in the process of social change in detention centres.

An accurate number of refugees incarcerated all over the world is not available. However, during the peak of the Vietnamese refugees' arrival in Hong Kong, about 65,000 refugees were incarcerated in Hong Kong detention centres alone. The United States government incarcerated several thousand Cuban and Haitian refugees in it's Montana Bay naval base for a short period of time. Several countries incarcerated or assigned refugees to geographically inaccessible regions with almost the same effect of 'segregation' from the host culture and the culture they fled from or left behind.

The populations of concern to UNHCR in the region (covered by the Regional Bureau for Asia and Oceanic) as of 1 January 1996 are some 1.5 million people. This population comprised of 887,800 refugees, 357,500 returnees, and 249,700 internally displaced persons and 46,800 asylum-seekers. Of the refugees, the largest caseloads in 1995 were in China (288,300), India (274,100), Nepal (126,100), Thailand (101,550) and Bangladesh (51,100). Among the assisted returnees, significant caseloads were in Myanmar (196,300), Sri Lanka (54,000) and Vietnam (18,200). The largest group of asylum-seekers were some 36,500 Vietnamese in ASEAN first asylum countries, and in Hong Kong, who did not fulfil the refugee criteria under the Comprehensive Plan of Action (CPA) for the Indo-Chinese Refugees and were expected to return to their country of origin (UNHCR, 1996).

Refugee detention in Hong Kong caught the attention of several researchers. The earlier writings on refugees were about how they were taken care of in Hong Kong (OXFAM, 1986). Separation and loss (Loveridge, 1985) were the main themes of 'refugee studies' at the earlier stages of refugee experience in Hong Kong. Chan (1987) described the refugee experience in Hong Kong as 'refugees in transit'. Fozzard (1986) and Bousquet (1987) described the refugee situation as a state of 'being in limbo'. Morgan and Closon (1987) described the situation as one of 'people in upheaval'. For some, it was just 'another impossible situation' (Donnelly, 1992). Knudsen (1990) and Salisbury (1992) described the refugees detained in Hong Kong as 'political prisoners'. Chan (1990) noted that in Hong Kong, the humanitarian response to the refugees was ambivalent and hostile. According to Wolf (1990, 1991) detention was a subtle form of 'inhumanity' and a 'betrayal', and was an 'unjust policy' (Feinberg, 1993).

Leonard Davis (1991) offers an introduction to the issues of the asylum seekers in Hong Kong. His primary focus was to analyse the growing social policy concern towards them in general. Though Davis discusses about camp life, he mostly focuses on the rampant violence and the hardships of children in particular. Davis made use of a unique methodology. Using the 'letter to the editor' column in the local newspapers he tried to fathom the public opinion towards the asylum seekers. He contributed a series of 'letters to the editor' to influence the course of the discussion and to elicit public opinion.

The main objective of 'Refugee Concern' (1991) study on camp issues, especially, on children was to generate material for an international campaign against detention (which never materialised). The main drawback of this study was that it was devoid of a basic theoretical framework. Even though the discussions were on the condition of the detention centres; religion, tradition, culture, family structure and its role in detention centres; education and health; it was not conducted with any methodical rigor.

Barbara Harrell-Bond (1986) in her monumental analysis of Ugandan refugee assistance program, highlighted the impact of refugee assistance on the recipient population. Even though Harrell-Bond's study is based on the overall framework of refugee integration - adaptation to the host country, she has not made any specific attempts to develop a conceptual model to explain the issues she studied. The issues in Harrell-Bond's work were carried out in an entirely different social and political context far removed from the Hong Kong situation. Ugandan refugees were settled in a more or less rural context and refugees in Hong Kong were detained in detention camps in an urban area.

Personal experience and theory building

Search for an appropriate theoretical and conceptual framework is a key endeavour in any research. Often selecting a theoretical construct is an act of serendipity. Very little is written on factors affecting the selection of an appropriate theory for a study. Some of my personal experience in dealing with the politics of refugee research made me aware of the need to explore deeply for an appropriate conceptual frame of reference in understanding the nature and impetus of refugee detention. Such experiences also encouraged me to comprehend the macro structural dynamics that sustained refugee detention and the role of various humanitarian agencies involved in refugee assistance in Hong Kong.

In this context Margaret McCallin's (1992) review entitled 'the psychological well-being of Vietnamese children in Hong Kong Detention Centres', deserves a closer look. This study is an interesting example of the politics involved in doing refugee research and the 'real reasons' for commissioning refugee research. My interest in this study has three reasons. In a curious twist of events, my employment with CFI, which facilitated my access to the refugee camps as a community workers was terminated because I expressed certain concerns about the recommendations of this study in a private letter to the author. And the second, this is the only large-scale study ever to be conducted in the camps with the official permission of the management, service agencies and the UNHCR Hong Kong office. Most importantly, this study managed to pull together the support of a large number of community representatives, professional staff and children.

The data for this study was collected from 301 girls and 297 boys with the help of a questionnaire. But this study is critically flawed in several aspects. One of the major drawbacks of McCallin's study was the lack of a framework in analysing the social conditions of the Vietnamese asylum seekers in general and the situation of refugee children detained in Hong Kong without their parents (in the refugee bureaucratic parlance they are called as 'unaccompanied minors').

McCallin's inability in developing a theory and her inherent bias against refugees de-railed her objective of enquiry. Hence, the study ended up making recommendations which were not based on the findings but were based on certain preconceived notions and superficial understanding of the social conditions in the camps. McCallin's reluctance to address the question of *institutionalised violence* in the form of prolonged administrative detention is also noteworthy.

The research tools used for the data collection in the study itself was highly biased against the asylum seeking community. Despite her probing questions on alleged gang warfare as a *source of traumatic experience* only 14 such incidents were reported. McCallin assumed that community protest witnessed by children was a source of trauma. Community protests' in the camps was a way of life for the asylum seekers to collectively exercise control over their life. It was a collective cathartic exercise in a hopeless and oppressive situation. McCallin however, completely ignored the traumatic experience of being subjected to 'teargas shelling' by the police, the so-called 'weapons search', and forcing children and the entire community to squat outside their huts for long hours (during cold winters, rain and hot summer) for frequent 'head counts'. In addition, she entirely disregarded crucial points like, the total disregard shown by the camp regimes for the well being of children; reluctance in facilitating community participation in children's well being; and fragmentation of services that are inadequate for the children living in the camps without their parents.

Even though MacCallin offers birds eye view of the psychosocial conditions of the asylum-seeking children in the camps, her study does not offer any methodological or theoretical insights into the holistic socio-cultural process-taking place in the asylum seeker detention centres. McCallin's project was basically commissioned to develop a case to advocate the need for the unaccompanied minors to go back to Vietnam. This was in the children's 'best interest' according to her study.

Most importantly this study is an example of how refugee research is used as a tool to justify the oppression of refugees. None of the research-stakeholders were willing to take a stand on the structural root of violence and the role of detention as structural violence. Nonetheless, the operational definition of *violence in the camp* suffered greatly due to the conceptual poverty of the study.

Most ironically, the agency that was instrumental in aiding the MacCallin survey was asked to close down it operations in Hong Kong camps by the UNHCR. MacCallin, was hired as a research consultant as a last ditch by the CFSI to resurrect its image as an expert agency in dealing with 'refugee children without parents' detained in Hong Kong camps. The research and the findings were to be the first step to encourage and counsel children to go back to Vietnam.

Key conceptual issues

Acculturation and adaptation: an inadequate theoretical framework

Some other authors have also tried to evolve a theory of refugees, for example, the concept of 'Bereavement' (Harrell-Bond, 1986; Joao Boavida, 1991), and migration adaptation model by Ruben Rumbaut (1991). Perhaps Berry (1990, 1991a, 1991b) has approached the issue of theorising on refugees in a more systematic manner. Berry (1991) described what he termed 'refugee career' as a 'process of acculturation and adaptation'. He maintains that the refugee individuals and groups must somehow deal with this process in all its dimensions: political, economic, cultural, social and psychological (Figure 2.1).

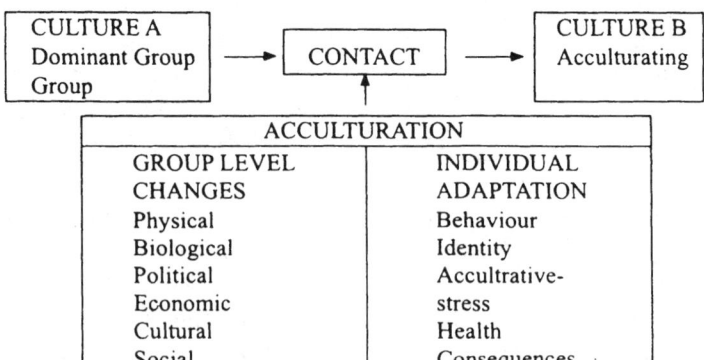

Figure 2.1   The Process of Acculturation and Adaptation
Source: John W. Berry, 1991

Berry employed the concept of acculturation and adaptation to explain the process of socio-cultural changes, which takes place among the refugees in their new host situation. According to Berry, all refugee individuals and groups must somehow deal with this process in all its dimensions. Berry observed that dominant groups or the power of host culture exert a very overpowering influence over the powerless refugees.

..... group level changes, including physical conditions (housing and safety), malnutrition and sanitary conditions, political isolations, economic loss, and cultural and social disintegration are likely to be much worse for refugees than any other type of acculturating groups (Berry 1991).

Berry suggested six phases of events to explain the experiences during a refugee career:
1) Pre departure: The time before the escape from the situation.
2) Flight: The process of escape from the country of origin.
3) First asylum: Acceptance in a first country for asylum.
4) Claimant: Claiming to be refugee hence seeking refugee status and establishing it.
5) Settlement: In a third country or in the first asylum country and
6) Adaptation: Adaptation to the host country.

However, Berry's theoretical abstracts are unable to sufficiently explain the process of socio-cultural changes taking place among the refugees detained in Hong Kong detention camps. The major drawbacks of Berry's theories in the Hong Kong context are enumerated below:
1) Berry approached refugees as a homogeneous entity. He did not notice and elaborate on the typologies of refugees. However, in the Hong Kong context there is a need to elaborate on the typology of refugees. There are asylum seekers and others who are determined as non- refugees.
2) In the Hong Kong context refugee is a general term that embraces three typologies, asylum seekers, and asylum seekers determined as non-refugees and refugees waiting to be resettled in a third country.
3) Berry explains the refugee carrier as a linear change of pre-departure to adaptation in the host country, moving from one phase to another. This is not true of the asylum seekers detained in Hong Kong. A large number will have to return to the first phase of refugee carrier or to a very similar situation.
4) The relation between the host culture and the refugees/asylum seekers is not of a continuous contact which could contribute towards a process of

acculturation. The pattern of contact in Hong Kong is separation and segregation from that of the host culture.

5) In modern times the refugee and asylum seeker situation operates in a political context, both at the micro and macro political context (national and international political context). Berry fails to explain the political context of refugee issues and does not trace the linkages, mechanisms, and the role of political interest in sustaining, perpetuating detention and affecting the quality of life of a large number of refugees under detention.

Community and social institutions

Some administrators are reluctant to accept that the asylum seekers are a cultural community and they consider the asylees' as an aggregate of independent individuals. This demands a brief discussion on the nature of community and social institution to develop adequate conceptual clarity to the issues under discussion. Do the asylum seekers in Hong Kong qualify to be considered as a community or are they just a group of strangers put together? Refugee administrators often ask this question. During the initial phase of the saga of Vietnamese refugees in Hong Kong, some refugee administrators were willing to refer to the asylum seeking population as a community. But when the asylum seeking population increased in volume the administrators were reluctant to accept them as a community.

> A large number of social anthropologists, sociologists, social workers, and other students of social life made comprehensive studies of communities, nevertheless, it is difficult to find agreement even within each of these groups as to what a community is (Young 1956)

In general, a community always occupies a territorial area and is characterised by common interests, common patterns of social and economic relations. Furthermore, it derives a common bond of solidarity from the conditions of its abode, and has a constellation of social institutions and is subject to some degree of group control (Young, 1956). Young argues the need for defining and designating the community in order to understand the community. According to Young, the assumptions behind the study of a community are:

(1) that it represents a basic unit by virtue of the relative homogeneity of its members who have strong cultural and traditional ties with the social interests and institutions of the area;

(2) that the unit is undergoing certain processes and changes which can be identified and;

(3) that these changes are occurring in every phase of the community's physical and social life;

(4) that changes have created new problems, new social situations, new institutions and modes of contact;

(5) that a new understanding of these conditions are essential in order to see in what way they are affecting the life of the group;

(6) that it is possible to compare the findings of one community with those of others and to establish social and personal types of behaviour sequence and process;

(7) that it is possible to learn trends of community life and changes;

(8) that it is possible to direct, organise and control forces of community change and;

(9) that control can be according to a plan, that is, it can be rational, scientific controlled by purposive action (Young, 1956).

Social institutions are a highly complex phenomenon. For a practical purpose, they can be defined as a set of social relations that are regularised and consistent. Those relationships are apparently stable and ruled by certain norms and values. Institutions may exert a stabilising influence on customs, norms and values. Social institutions are the regulatory systems that control and regulate the behavioural values of the individuals during the phase of socio-cultural transition. They are also a complex set of concepts and attitudes regarding the ordering of a particular class of unavoidable or indispensable human relationships that are involved in satisfying certain elemental individual wants and social needs.

Social institutions

Any classification of social institutions are subjected to criticism of overlapping, but the underlying principle in classifying social institutions is the predominant interest and activities of the institutions under study. The patterns of daily interaction with the clients who are linked together through the institutions are also taken into consideration when the institution is defined.

Pauline Young speaks of six types of social institutions:

1. Basic cultural institutions: the family, the church, and the school.
2. Economic institutions: commercial and economic enterprises, labour unions, and real estate boards.
3. Recreational institutions: settlements, athletic clubs, art clubs, parks and

playgrounds, theatres, cinemas, dance halls, and swimming pools, etc.
4. Institutions of formal social control: government and social service agencies; police.
5. Health institutions: hospitals, clinics, elderly and children's homes.
6. Communication institutions: transport, postal services, telephones, newspapers and periodicals, radio and television.

It is clear that the asylum seekers' who share common language, cultural traits and links can be considered as a community and the nature of their residence is tantamount to institutions and their day to day life in the institutionalised detention camps. Before an appropriate conceptual paradigm is developed it will be useful to elaborate on the concept of community disorganisation, as this concept may give clues to the socio-cultural process that is taking place in the detention centres.

Community disorganisation

Social or community disorganisation is conceived of as a failure of rules. Three major types of disorganisation are formlessness, cultural conflict, and breakdown. With formlessness, no rules exist on how to act. The root cause of social disorganisation, broadly speaking is social change. As change occurs, the parts of the social system get out of tune with one another (Rubington and Weinberg, 1989). Community disorganisation is a process of a community losing or disintegrating its socio-cultural network or social relations, inability of social institutions to meet their social function and the lack of general cohesiveness of the social structure. This process can be a response to a situation or an external stimulus, for example, the ecological changes or a result of a collective experience of the community, like mass displacement and continued uncertainty regarding its future. Economic distress, dependency, crime and general delinquency are often associated with community disorganisation. This study examines social control in the community, means of social control, family organisation and control, social organisation, co-operation and conflict within the community for the purpose of assessing the level of community disorganisation.

The concept of social disorganisation itself presents a weak candidate in selecting an apt conceptual framework to understand the dynamics of refugee detention. Refugee detention in Hong Kong presents a unique challenge to social theories as it operates in a multi-layered, complex, social and international political context. An apt theory which could explain the complex situation under study could be a theory as complex as the problem itself.

Total institutions

Goffman (1961) in his study on 'mental asylums' observed that the social world of 'asylees' has to be approached subjectively as it is experienced by the asylees themselves. He adds

> ..... any group of person, prisoners, primitives, pilots or patients - develop a life of their own that becomes meaningful, reasonable, and normal once you get close to it and that a good way to learn about any thing of this world is to submit oneself in the company of the members to the daily round of petty contingencies to which they are subject (Goffman, 1961).

Goffman's methodological approach and theoretical constructs, particularly, the concept of 'total institutions' was the parting point of enquiry for an appropriate theoretical framework for analysing the determinants of social conditions of asylum seeker detention centres in this book. Goffman's concept of 'total institutions' was proposed as one of the most appropriate model to explain the social conditions of the asylum seeker detention centres in Hong Kong during the early period of refugee detention (Fozzard, 1986). However, no serious effort was made to use the concept in explaining the nature of refugee detention in Hong Kong.

> 'Total Institutions' may be defined as a place of residence and work where a large number of like-situated individuals cut off from the wider society for an appreciable period of time together lead an enclosed, formally administered round of life (Goffman, 1961).

According to Goffman the 'total institutions' of our society can be classified into five categories:
1. Institutions established to care for persons felt to be both incapable and harmless.
2. Places established to care for persons felt to be both incapable of looking after themselves and a threat to the community.
3. Institutions organised to protect the community against what is felt to be intentional dangers to it, with the welfare of the persons thus suggested not the immediate issue.
4. Institutions established to pursue some work like task and justifying themselves only on these instrumental grounds.
5. Institutions designed as retreats from the world and often serving also as training stations for religious persons.

According to Goffman, the central features of 'total institutions' are:

> All aspects of life are conducted in the same place and under the same single authority. The member's daily activity is carried on in the immediate company of a large batch of others, all of whom are treated alike and are required to do the same things together. All phases of the day's activities are tightly scheduled, with one activity leading at a pre-arranged time into the next, the whole sequence of activities being imposed from above by a system of explicit formal ruling and a body of officials. The various enforced activities are brought together into a single rational plan designed to fulfil the official aims of the institution (Goffman, 1961).

The political compulsion of the British-Hong Kong government to control the influx of the Vietnamese asylum seekers into Hong Kong and to segregate them from the general Hong Kong population gave rise to another form of 'total institution' detention centres for asylum seekers in Hong Kong.

A purposely designed and enforced inactivity under the line of authority is also a shared character of the 'total institution'. In Hong Kong, a large number of 'asylees' (inmates) aimlessly mill around without any purpose. 'Case workers' are employed to do counselling to help the individuals to cope with the system (a contribution to fulfil the official aims of the institution) rather than to question the system or to transform the system.

The size of Hong Kong detention centres is enormous. During the data collection for this book, the Whitehead Detention Centre (WHDC), was holding about 22, 000 asylees. It was dubbed as the largest prison in the world. Tai Ah Chau (a remote island) held about 8,000 asylees and High Island about 7,000 asylees. The population of major Hong Kong detention centres was equivalent to the population of a small township in a modern society.

The handling of many human needs by a bureaucratic organisation is the key factor of 'total institution'. In Hong Kong detention centres the basic human needs like food, shelter and clothing, was taken care of by the bureaucratic organisation. Food was centrally cooked in each of the detention centres and distributed. The menus for Correctional Services Department (CSD) managed centres and non-CSD managed centres were different and were decided by the British-Hong Kong government.

The Shelter for asylum seekers consisted of metallic Nissan huts, which usually held 250 families. Each 'inmate' was given a 6 x 3 x 4 bunk bed in a crowded three-tier sleeping bunk system. Asylees were expected to sleep on these wooden planks. Sometimes, even within the camps the families were separated. In some camps these huts were locked from outside by the camp authorities during the night to prevent escapes.

The camp management provided clothing. This was often collected through the Hong Kong charities 'old clothes donation' drives. The quality and quantity of sanitary needs of the asylees was also determined by the bureaucratic process, including the quality and size of the under garments. Asylum seekers were supervised by the police, Correctional Services Department (CSD) staff, private Security Companies, or by 'regulators' employed by the camp management, whose chief activity was not guidance or inspection but 'surveillance'.

In 'total institutions' the basic split is between inmates and supervisors. In Hong Kong detention centres other group of players had a role - the social service providers. In Hong Kong, a three dimensional role was played by the 'inmates', camp management and the service providers. In the ultimate analysis the role of the camp management and the service agencies were in the same spectrum (Fig 2.2).

A variety of roles were played in this triangular relationship. The common ground between the camp management and the service providers was that both took special care not to upset the other. However, the objectives of the total institutions and the desire of the asylees seem to run in opposite directions.

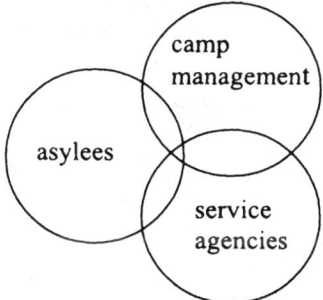

Figure 2.2   Relation between Service Agencies, Asylum Seekers and Camp Management

A delicate balance of equilibrium had been worked out between the asylees, service providers, and the camp management. Mostly this balance was brought about by the intervention of the UNHCR as an intergovernmental agency, the major financier for the service programs and the asylees as the beneficiaries of the programs (Fig 2.3).

The delicate balance between the asylees, service providers and the camp administrators was brought about at the expense of the asylees. The asylum seeker was weakened in this equilibrium due to the process of 'atomisation of the individuals'. Several factors forced the asylees to act only for their own well being. The anxiety and the pressure of the detention centre and the imminent refugee status determination procedure drained all altruistic tendencies or characteristics of the 'social man'.

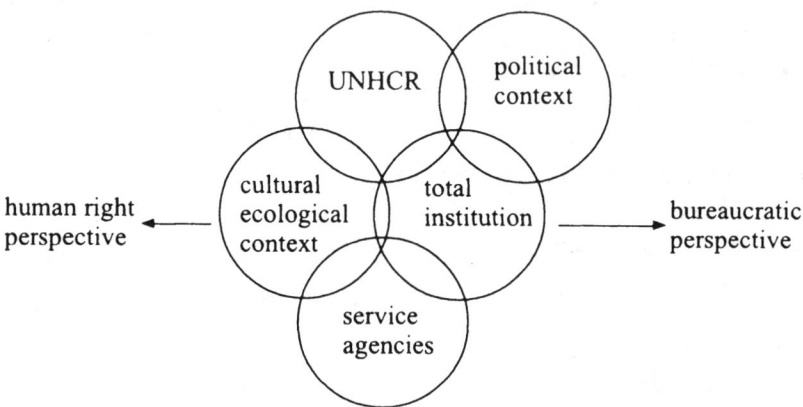

Figure 2.3   An Equilibrium between Asylum Seekers, Camp Management and Service Agencies

The asylees and the camp management staff were at opposite ends of each other's interest. They viewed the other as typical stereotypes. The camp staff (both the service providers and the camp management), felt that the asylum seekers were secretive, liars, untrustworthy, bitter and ungrateful, economic migrants. While the asylum seekers maintained that the staff were mean, arrogant, and unable to understand the 'Vietnamese way'. The staff tended to feel superior, self-righteous, generous and full of expertise.

Mobility and social intercourse between all the groups was restricted. The communication between the asylees and the camp administration, between the asylum seekers and the service providers was also restricted and limited. Information often flew from the higher to the lower levels. The detainees were told what to do, when to seek assistance and when to receive services.

The camp management and the social service staff operated an eight-hour shift in all the camps. The camp management staff were present 24 hours, except at Tai Ah Chau camp. The service providers were not expected to, nor had any facilities to stay overnight in the camps after the normal office hours.

Plans about any imminent movement of the population from one camp to another, and also within the camp, refugee status determination interview dates, the procedures of the interview and other information about the 'fate' of the asylees was withheld from the asylees until the last minute. They were excluded from the decision making process of their service needs. The service staff and the camp management collaborated and developed service plans that were later communicated to the asylees.

The principles of work, sanctions and rewards, in the camps were different from the outside world. The asylum seekers worked as paraprofessionals, health educators, teachers, interpreters, camp aids (to the service providers), they worked in the kitchen, as car cleaners (management or service agency staff cars), office assistants, hut representatives, food distributors and in general as errand boys within the camps.

Unlike other 'total institutions' family life was allowed in the detention centres for those who had a family, or one who could establish a new family, if one could locate a spouse or a willing partner. But lack of privacy and space made it impossible to have any meaningful family life. The camp environment restricted the moments of exclusiveness, solitude or meaningful domestic activities for the couples or for the other family members.

The asylum seekers came to Hong Kong detention centres with their 'presenting culture' from Vietnam (next chapter presents a detailed descriptive account of an example of presenting culture). The detention centre culture could not substitute the culture they had already brought in. Yet the detention centre acted as a 'crucible of culture'. The patterns of cultural changes occurring in the detention centres forced the asylees to remove certain behavioural opportunities which enabled them to keep pace with the social changes in the outside world.

The asylum seekers came to Hong Kong with various expectations and hopes. Some with a clear picture of hope for the future, but many did not. People fled Vietnam for various reasons. They escaped from re-education camps, from new economic zone, some did not want to go to new economic zone, some deserted draft, and some avoided military draft, or had general political disagreement with the government. Others were unable to pursue education, to practice religion, or carry on with their profession. Few escaped because of difficult living conditions, some were unable to manage economically or wanted to rejoin family abroad, whilst others were seeking a better life, and some asylees had no personal reason to leave Vietnam but their family encouraged them to get out of the country.

The detention shattered the hopes and expectations of a good number of asylees. This shock was the first impact towards changing their inner world. It upset their mental framework, as they had expected a different kind of reception in Hong Kong. The resentment and anger along with the detention centre conditions gradually forced the asylees to change culturally socially and individually.

The longer the duration of asylees' stay in the detention centres, the greater was their possibility to get 'disciplined' (a term originally used by Robert Sommer in 1959, to explain the process of patients who grow old in a mental hospital). This 'disculturation' tended to make them temporarily incapable of managing certain features of daily life 'outside' if and when they went back to it (Goffman, 1961).

The full meaning of the asylees being 'in' or 'out' of the detention centres in Hong Kong has a wider meaning than just being inside the detention centre or out of it. For being 'out' of the detention centre, one has to be either 'screened in' or has to go back to Vietnam, either voluntarily or involuntarily. In case of going back to Vietnam the asylees are likely to get a glimpse of Hong Kong on their way to the Airport. Escaping from the detention centres into the Hong Kong mainstream society was also of no great help, because Hong Kong is a place where, all the members of the society, by law are expected to carry their identification papers at all times and are subjected to frequent identification searches. Just escaping to 'Hong Kong' society was in effect a continuation of another form of social exclusion. There are cases of 'escaped' asylees, especially women, approaching the service agencies in assisting them to go back to the detention centres. This aspect of Hong Kong society is a strategic leverage for managing asylum seekers. While being taken out of the detention centres for medical and other reasons the asylum seekers were aware of the futility of escaping from the custody unless prior arrangements with friends or relatives was made.

The concept of 'total institution' alone does not explain the process related to the social phenomenon of asylum seeker detention and subsequent consequences. Yet, it provides sufficient clues to look for other concepts, which can help in clarifying the theme under study.

Ethnocide: The nature of socio-cultural process taking place in the detention centres

To explain the relationship between the modern societies and tribal, ethnic minorities, anthropologists use the concept of ethnocide. Even though the concept of ethnocide has two principal aspects, economic and cultural; the cultural aspect of ethnocide is more relevant in explaining the socio-cultural process-taking place in the Hong Kong detention camps.

According to Stavenhagen (1987), the cultural aspect of ethnocide means that all sub national ethnic units must disappear to make way for a nation state. In this frame of reference all the ethnic aspirations of any group of population could be repressed. The perception of the dominant cultural group is that the cultural aspirations of any 'unwanted groups' such as refugees, ethnic and tribal minorities are a physical obstacle to the goals of dominant culture. Stavenhagen defined ethnocide as the loss of territory, resources, cultural identity and the capacity of an ethnic group to ensure its own biological and social reproduction.

The concept of ethnocide is also often used to explain the nature of relationship between the indigenous people (minority culture) and the state (majority culture). However, it may be applicable in any situation where an exploitative relationship exists between the majority culture and the minority culture. According to Gneerre Maurizio (1987), the state may practice ethnocide simply by refusing official acknowledgement that a minority exists, in the case of Vietnamese refegees, even though the British-Hong Kong government acknowledged their presence in the territory, but as unwanted guests. Even when the presence is acknowledged by defining the ethnicity of the group narrowly, the government can actually shape the course of ethnocide. Gneerree further elaborates that even when acknowledged, an ethnic group often finds itself within a nation administered by completely unknown people. Such a description is very apt to explain the Hong Kong situation.

According to Moore-Thomas (1979), ethnocide can be defined as the destruction of a traditional culture, with or without the destruction of the people living in it. This takes place in the context of an economic imperialism and an unequal exchange. Ravis Giordani Georges (1973) relates ethnocide to the denial of those cultures of that vision of the world that makes life worthwhile. Ethnocide is essentially linked to ethnocentrism. Ethnocentrism, arises from the idea that the other, the one who is different, is bad (Clastres Pierre, 1974).

One of the important aspects of culture is that it is a dynamic process. All the members of a cultural community have the right to pick and choose the cultural traits of the community at reasonably broadly defined parameters. This process is enriched by the capacity of the individuals to make conscious decisions and to live with the consequences of their decisions, often with chances to modify their decision based on an unpleasant consequence. The underlying theme of enquiry of this book is what happens to the community when their cultural freedom (along with other freedoms) is curtailed because of their situation for a prolonged period of time. The concept of ethnocide is introduced along with other theoretical constructs to explain this phenomenon.

In this study ethnocide is defined as a process of a community losing its' internal cohesion, community structures, networks and direction due to the direct intervention of a dominant group. Ethnocide is the product of a process of an extreme community reaction to an extreme external stimulus of segregation and separation of that community from a broader society. More appropriately this process takes place as an ongoing contradiction between the forces (policies and programmes) which perpetuates ethnocide and the effort of the detained community to maintain their integrity, networks and direction. The process of ethnocide takes place in a community context rather than at an individual level. But in the ultimate analysis the individuals, particularly the younger generation of the community have to live with the consequence of ethnocide, something akin to being socially and culturally handicapped.

The socio-cultural changes taking place within the Hong Kong detention centres are changes without constant and continuous contact with the host culture. They are also effectively cut off from their own 'home culture'. In the detention centres all that the Vietnamese were trying to do was to reproduce an image of the culture they had left behind to give some meaning to their daily existence in the camps.

Any attempts at segregation and separation of the asylum seekers creates severe stress on their desire to recreate a culture image. This triggers, of community disorganisation and individual demoralisation. The following model is proposed as a first step to explain the socio-cultural changes taking place in the detention centres (Figure 2.4).

The above discussions bring home the point that there is a need to develop a more appropriate framework for analysing the determinants of social conditions of the asylum seekers detained in the camps. In the proposed frame of reference various issues related to the theme under study are clubbed into four groups. They are
1) a set of distant determinants;
2) a set of immediate determinants;
3) intermediate outcome and;
4) ethnocide as the potential outcome.

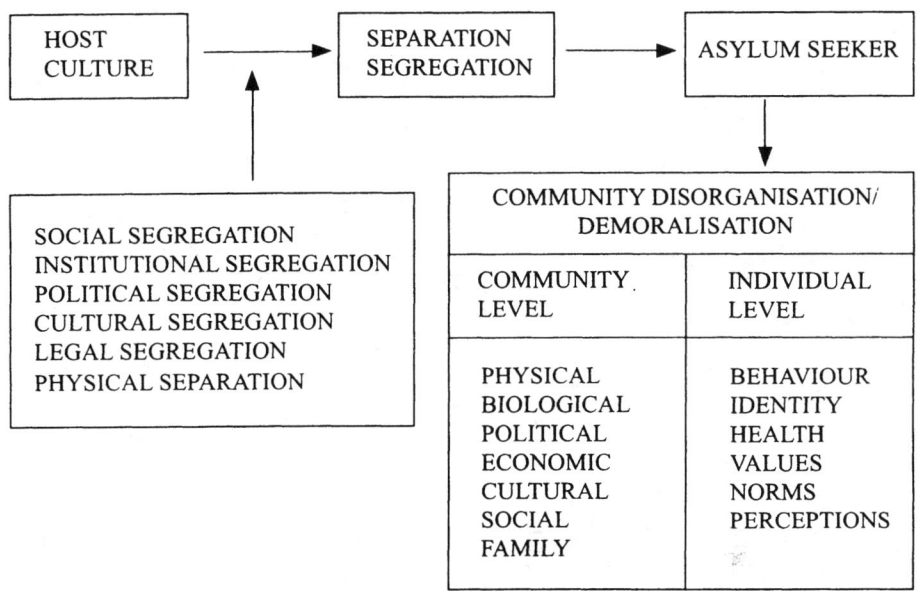

Figure 2.4   Community Disorganisation and Individual Demoralisation in Hong Kong (asylum seekers detention centres)

A detailed framework for analysing the social conditions in the refugee detention centers camps

The proposed framework for analysing determinants of the social world of asylum seeker detention centres (Fig. 2.5) looks at the 'presenting cultural factors' as distant determinants. The presenting cultural aspect of the asylees is the sum total of experience and values of the asylum seekers as presented on the day of his/her arrival in a detention context. International political context is another distant determinant which influences the social world of the asylees in detention centres. International political opinion is often the source of solace and hope for the detainees. There are international political compulsions such as the economic and political embargo on Vietnam that has had an influence on the refugee flow. The resources for the social services and other necessities are often derived out of the international political context. The service agencies are also affected by the 'totality of the institution' and experience a process of 'trained inability' an inability to deliver appropriate service. Asylum seekers often arrive in Hong Kong with a set of 'cultural baggage'. It is important to understand the presenting cultural factors of the

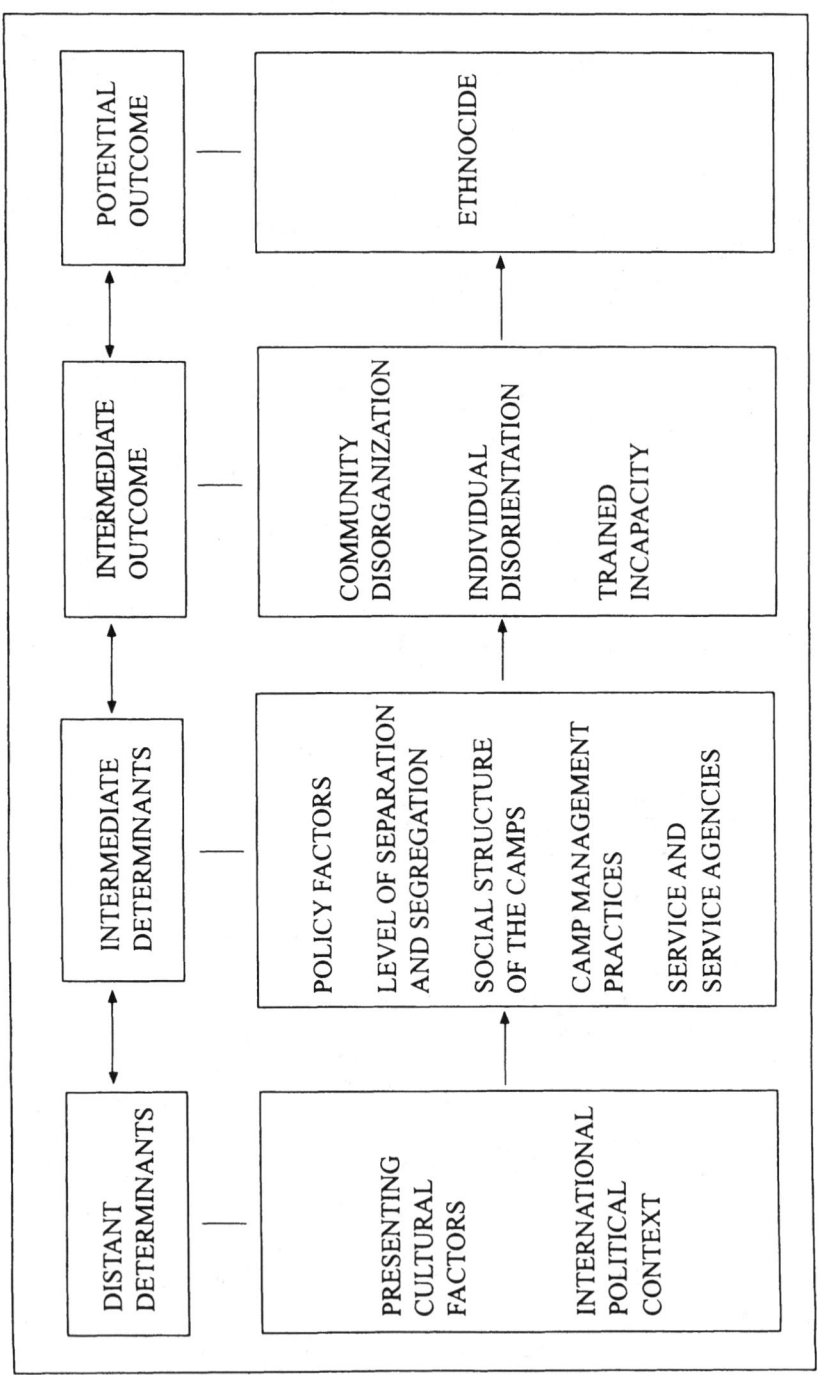

Figure 2.5   A Framework for Analyzing the Determinants of the Social World of Asylum Seeker Detention Centres

asylum seekers to understand the process taking place during the detention.

The framework for analysing the determinants of the social world of the asylum seeker detention centres has been proposed by arranging four major cluster of variables; distant variables, immediate variables, outcome variables and ethnocide as the potential outcome variable in a cause effect paradigm. The distant determinants are the presenting cultural factors and international political context. Factors that contribute towards intermediate determinants include refugee policy, level of separation and segregation, social and personal resources of the asylum seekers who are under detention, asylum seekers level of access to resources, social structure of the camps, camp management practices, and service agencies. Thus community disorganisation, individual disorientation, ethnocide and trained incapacity of the social service agencies are the outcome of this process.

The intermediate detrimental factors are a set of factors which are inter-linked with the local policy issues, initiatives of the UK-Hong Kong government, level of separation and segregation in each camp, personal and social resources - relatives abroad, remittance of money from abroad, ability to communicate with the outside world, friendship/relative network abroad, level of access to the camp resources, the pattern of community structures and participation profile of the camp residents, the differential management practices of the camp management, and the service delivery characteristics of the agencies. The outcome of the socio-cultural process in the detention centres on an individual level is that of disorientation. Hence, the Vietnamese community showed trends towards gradual social disorganisation. At a collective level 'ethnocide' is the potential outcome of the detention process.

Ethnocide and typology of refugees

Often the term 'refugee' is used to refer to a different set of social reality associated with forced migration. The nature of contact with the host society, the direction of socio-cultural changes among the refugees and the mode of change vary according to the typology of refugees (Figure 2.6).

The resettled refugees mostly experience a continuous contact with the host culture. Assimilation is the dominant mode of the change. The change is linear. Those waiting to be resettled into another country are in an 'anticipatory contact' with the host culture. An 'anticipatory assimilation' - an emotional preparation to subject oneself for assimilation to a host culture is the characteristic at this stage. The direction of change is linear.

'Asylum seekers' and 'temporary refugees' often share several characteristics in their refugee career. Both groups may be separated from the host culture. The separation leads to cultural stagnation, 'disculturation', and the mode of change is ethnocide.

Typology of refugees	Nature of contact	Direction of change	Mode of change
Refugees resettled	continued contact	Linear	Assimilation
Refugees to be resettled	Anticipatory contact	Linear	Anticipatory assimilation
Asylum seekers detained	Separation	Disintegration	Ethnocide
Temporary refugees/	Contact	Linear	Diffusion
Asylum seekers determined as non refugees	Separation	Return migration	Ethnocide

Figure 2.6   Typology of Refugees and Direction/Mode of Cultural Change

The asylum seekers determined as non-refugees in Hong Kong were detained under the conditions of complete separation and segregation from the general population. The mode of change for this group is also 'ethnocide' and the direction is an 'anticipatory cyclic change'. The linear model of refugee career alone can no longer be able to explain the refugee reality. In Hong Kong camps, several asylum seekers - temporary refugees will eventually have to go back to Vietnam.

The UK-Hong Kong government envisaged that with an 'orderly departure' program for all the non-refugees starting in June 1992, the repatriation program would be completed within three to four years. Till October 1992, the UNHCR voluntary repatriation scheme had returned 22, 693 persons back to Vietnam from Hong Kong.

If the detention camp conditions were in a continuous state of cultural limbo, conditions back in Vietnam was also not very rosy. The international economic embargo on Vietnam was still in force and unemployment was rampant (on February 3, 1994, President Bill Clinton lifted America's 19 year old embargo on Vietnam). The prospect of an immediate reintegration of a returnee was slow, especially, for one who had sold all their belongings for securing enough funds for their family to escape to Hong Kong. Many children of school going age had to drop out of school to escape to Hong Kong.

The returnees were now faced with a cyclic pattern of life experiences unlike the resettled refugees who experienced a linear mode of transition in their life (Figure 2.7). A large number of asylum seekers escaped from Vietnam due to real or perceived persecution and discrimination or due to the lure of the developed west, or to join family members, or out of sheer adventure spirit. Their life cycle, phase or events of their 'short refugee life' was; flight, first asylum, and detention in the camps, repatriation decision, repatriation and reintegration in the situation they left behind.

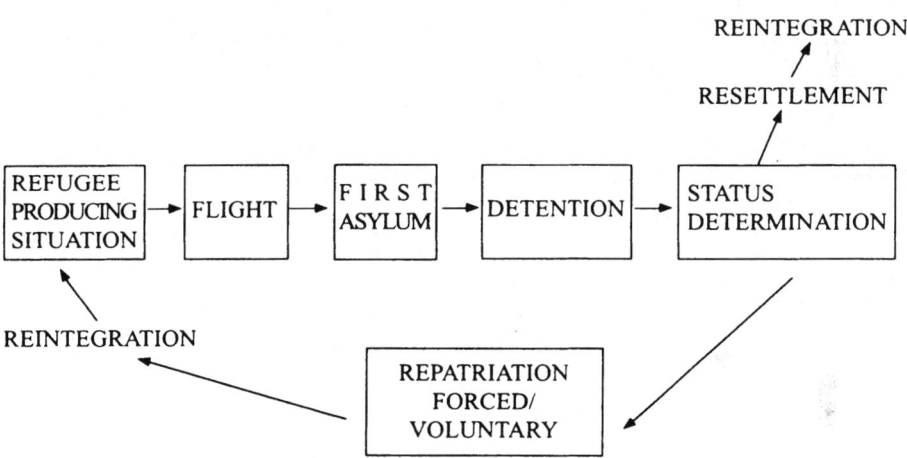

Figure 2.7   Events or Phases of Refugee Career. A Comprehensive Model

Conclusion

Developing an appropriate theoretical framework to explain the socio cultural consequence of refugee detention in Hong Kong is a daunting task as the issues are myriad and multidimensional. The Vietnamese asylum seekers view the issue of detention as unjust because they came to Hong Kong due to an explicit understanding that, they would be assured asylum considering they escaped the persecution of the communist Vietnamese government. However, the Hong Kong government regards them as economic migrants. The international community initially looked at them with sympathy as asylum seekers (this was in the context of the 'cold war'). Later, as the 'cold war' was over, the international community lost much of its interest in them. Many social service agencies looked at this situation as an international humanitarian issue, a case of large number of *clients* seeking various services. Some refugee administrators looked at the issue as one of logistics and a source of income.

There is a need to view the detention centres from an international political perspective and as an international human rights problem of an unprecedented nature. In essence, it is humanitarian issue operating in an international, regional, and local political context. This chapter presented a series of theoretical constructs to guide the inquiry into the socio-cultural conditions in the detention camps. It also identified gaps in the existing body of refugee literature. An attempt was also made to fill these gaps with the concepts of 'total institutions', 'community disorganisation', 'individual disorientation', and 'ethnocide'. This chapter also contributed a framework for analysing the social conditions of the detention centres and a typology of refugees. It conceptually argues that the socio-cultural process that took place in the detention centres was a process of ethnocide and this phenomenon is explained and substantiated with the conceptual framework and with the data presented in the following chapters.

3 Options and Choices

Introduction

Even though, ethnocide is the product of being detained for several years in refugee detention camps, several macro factors, not immediately related to the day to day living conditions of the camps also contribute toward this process. This includes the cultural history of Vietnam, general socio-political conditions in Vietnam, specific factors contributing to the asylum seekers' escape from the country, the process of escape. This chapter discusses and explains some of such factors . In addition, it also presents a brief overview of Vietnamese history and culture. Macro factors, which may have directly contributed to the decision of the asylum seekers to escape Vietnam, have been discussed along with the process of flight and the experience en route to the 'first asylum country'.

Vietnam, the physical, historical and cultural setting

Vietnam is situated on the eastern coast of Indo-Chinese peninsula, bordering China, Cambodia and Laos; to the east, lies the South China Sea. The culture of Vietnam has been deeply influenced by two major Asian cultures: The Chinese culture from the north and the Indian culture from the west. Vietnam has a recorded history of more than two thousand years that can be generally divided into five distant periods. They are:
1) Prehistoric period (until 111 BC).
2) Chinese domination (111 BC to 938 AD).
3) Era of independence (938 - 1883).
4) French domination (1858 - 1954) and;
5) Socialist-communist era (1954 - till present).

   The pre-historic era is reflected in the myths and legends of Vietnamese culture. According to such legends the first Vietnamese kingdom was established in the Red River delta. China sent troops to conquer the Kingdom of 'Nam Viet' in BC 111, and established a direct rule over the country and annexed it as a province of China. In 938 AD, the King Ngo Quen defeated the Chinese and established his kingdom. This era was known as the era of independence, which came to an end in 1858 when the French conquered the Vietnamese (Huynh Dinh Te, 1987).

When the Second World War broke out the Japanese troops occupied Indochina with the consent of the French. When the Japanese surrendered to the allies in August 1945, the Vietnamese people declared independence and formed a republican government. The French however, tried to re-establish their power over Vietnam and there arose a conflict between the French and the Vietnamese republic. In 1954 through the Geneva agreement the French rule came to an end and Vietnam was divided into two separate states along the 17th parallel with North Vietnam under communist control and South Vietnam under non-communist regime. Communist North Vietnam soon attempted to take over South Vietnam and a war broke out between the two, under the explicit support of the super powers, which ended after twenty years of destruction of several thousands of human life and property. On April 30 1975, the communist Vietnam finally took over the south. Hundreds and thousands of people fled Vietnam fearing persecution from North Vietnam. Thus began the exodus of asylum seekers from Vietnam.

Vietnamese culture encourages its individuals to forgo their own interest for the sake of their immediate and extended families. Most often, anything a Vietnamese does is for the consideration of his family. Even, the decision to leave their country in order to seek asylum in another country is based on the deliberation for the betterment of the family. Vietnamese culture teaches the virtue of harmony, moderation, modesty, moral courage and self control which makes a well-mannered person in society. To preserve a good name they may be willing to even run away from their own country than take the humiliation of loosing their good name among family and friends. Ability to provide food and shelter to one's own family is the minimum requirement to have a good name and standing among their peers, friends, and families.

The Vietnamese family may be the most severely battered socio-cultural institution due to the exodus of the asylum seekers from Vietnam. Often, families of the asylum seekers are dispersed over distant geographical and national boundaries. Respect is the underlying theme of man's relation to the wider social relationships and family. Language and non-verbal communication are the mode by which respect is demonstrated. Whilst, in detention camps even a well-respected Vietnamese elderly scholar will just be an asylum seeking old man in the eyes of the camp managers.

'*Tet*', the Vietnamese New Year gives a real insight into the Vietnamese culture. *Tet* is the day for demonstrating all the unique cultural traits of

Vietnamese, such as respect to elders, family bonds, day of family gathering, reciprocation of kindness and obligations. One of the most important complaints of the Vietnamese asylum seekers was their inability to practice the New Year (*Tet*) appropriately in the Hong Kong detention centres.

'Migration researchers' often describe the migration process as a product of 'push and pull factors'. To a certain extent this framework is useful in explaining the process of refugee displacement. This chapter discusses the individual, socio-cultural and political factors associated with the 'push factors' and the context of asylum seeker's motivation to leave their country. These factors contributed to various socio-cultural aspects of life in the detention camps.

The context and motivation to leave Vietnam

Ascribing economic motivation as an exclusive reason for the escape of the Vietnamese may be too simplistic an explanation. Even though future economic benefits may be a crucial factor, there are myriad social, cultural and political reasons behind the decision to escape from Vietnam and to undertake an extremely dangerous and often life-threatening voyage to an unknown destination.

The asylum seekers give different reasons for their escape from Vietnam. Some of them articulated their reason for leaving Vietnam was to seek a better life. This general answer is often interpreted as purely economic reason for leaving Vietnam. But Vietnamese often tend to begin a conversation in very general terms unless they are specifically asked for the details. Often this cultural trait is interpreted as a basis for not having a 'well found fear of persecution'. Some of the general reasons cited for their departure from Vietnam are:

- General political disagreement with the government;
- To rejoin family members abroad;
- Avoiding military draft;
- Deserted military draft;
- Unable to practice their profession;
- Unable to manage economically;
- Escape from re-education camp;
- Released from re-education camp;
- Escape the New Economic Zone;
- Did not wish to go to the New Economic Zone;
- Unable to pursue education;

- Unable to practice religion;
- For the ethnic Chinese to avoid racial discrimination;
- Having links with, or served the South Vietnamese government;
- Having links with the French colonial government;
- Being a member of a family with - 'bad elements' - such as child of a former official of South Vietnam;
- For being a 'capitalist';
- Being deprived of livelihood;
- Being deprived of education, and identity card;
- To avoid punishment for making illegal departure;
- Having committed criminal offences;
- General dissatisfaction with corruption, heavy taxation;
- Restriction of movement, and travel;
- General fear of persecution;
- Some others may have just followed their friends, parents, spouse or relatives;
- Some children were sent by their parents hoping for a better life for them;
- Children were sent because the parents could not manage enough money for the passage for all;
- Some physically disabled, or ill, escaped hoping for better medical care;
- Some came to Hong Kong only to receive UNHCR reintegration allowance.

Often the officer in-charge of refugee status determination expects a clear answer - a reason for being a refugee - among these myriad reasons which precipitated their decision to leave the country.

Ethnic factors

The ethnic composition of the Vietnamese asylum seekers has changed during the course of time. The first wave of refugees comprised mostly the South Vietnamese elite from Saigon City (Table no 3.1 ethnic origin of arrivals). Most of them were wealthy and had 'connections' to escape from Vietnam with their wealth. Earlier aid workers recounted stories of escorting Vietnamese refugees to the bank to deposit their money and valuables and offering security services to the refugees to protect their valuables.

During 1978 the refugee scenario began to change slowly. At that time all Vietnamese who came to Hong Kong were called refugees. However, this expression changed during the course of time to asylum seekers, Vietnamese migrants, and economic migrants. According to the Hong Kong government,

Table 3.1   Ethnic Origins of Asylum Seekers (1979 to September 1992)

Year	Chinese from		Vietnamese from		Total
	South Vietnam	North Vietnam	South Vietnam	North Vietnam	
1979	17 972	37 536	9 8253	3 341	68 748
1980	62	43	5 599	1 084	6 788
1981	87	61	6 050	2 272	8 470
1982	91	27	6 051	1 667	7 836
1983	47	11	1 904	1 689	3 651
1984	49	21	1 563	597	2 230
1985	13	10	687	402	1 112
1986	50	25	914	1 070	2 059
1987	13	23	999	2 360	3 395
1988	82	162	5 012	13 072	18 328
1989	1 717	486	3 032	28 877	34 112
1990	4 256	296	1 861	182	6 595
1991	2 319	222	8 586	9 079	20 206
1992	7	-	1	1	9
Total	26 765	38 923	52 084	65 693	74 other

Source: HK Government, 1992

the Vietnamese authorities were prepared to 'export' the politically and economically 'un-assimilable' Chinese population (Davis, 1991).

When the controversial vessel '*Huey Fong*' entered Hong Kong waters with 3,383 refugees in December 1978, it also had caches of gold valued at HK$6.5 million. The captain and 10 others were arrested and charged with conspiracy in human trafficking. However, the issue is, 'what is an asylum seeker expected to do with his/her personal belongings, including wealth?' Even some humanitarian aid workers appear to have a mental block against well to do asylum seekers. Even though, Hong Kong was reluctant to receive the shipload of refugees under pressure from the US Senator Edward Kennedy, Hong Kong nonetheless, accepted them.

It was a known fact that money, often gold, changed hands for arranging an escape from Vietnam (as a fee for fuel, food, to buy a suitable vessel and other arrangements for the travel). Nevertheless, the international community was generally sympathetic to the refugees during this phase of the refugee saga. Small boats continued to arrive in the territory mostly with ethnic Chinese refugees. During 1988, a sudden surge of asylum seekers changed the ethnic composition of the refugees. More North Vietnamese began seeking asylum in the territory.

The international community was alarmed by the sudden shift in the asylum seeking population. South Vietnamese and ethnic Chinese were considered allies of the US in their war against Communism. When the communist North Vietnamese asylum seekers began arriving in large numbers, Hong Kong government hastily introduced a refugee status determination procedure to identify 'genuine refugees' with the implication that North Vietnamese were fleeing from poverty and not necessarily due to political reasons.

The religious composition of the asylum seeker population reflected the national situation. Some Christians and Buddhist monks had special reason to fear religious persecution if they remained in Vietnam. Several Buddhist priests, and Catholic priests escaped from Vietnam because of religious persecution from the communist regime. Some of the Buddhist monks are still under detention in Hong Kong. Majority of the earlier asylum seekers had secondary school or higher education. Amongst the late arrivals, the percentage with primary or no education gradually increased.

The political factors

Consolidating political victory over South Vietnam was the primary agenda of the North Vietnamese communist government upon victory over the American troops and the South Vietnamese army in 1975. The communist Vietnamese government initiated several programs for 'nation building' and to bring citizens into the communist ideology. Many citizens resented this. Even though the overall aim of some of these programs was social development and self-subsistence, punishment and persecution was the sole purpose of some of the other programs initiated by the government.

Re-education camps

Although, several functionaries of the South Vietnamese army managed to escape the invading North Vietnamese army, several of them were taken as prisoners. As a punishment, most of them were sent to re-education camps, new economic zones and to forced labour camps. The intensity of punishment was decided based on ranks and level of involvement in the war. The party assumed that the prisoners acted against the party and the people because of their 'class background' so they had to be de-classed and re-educated into a socialist-communist orientation. High ranking officials and military officers of the pre 1975 South Vietnam government were routinely sent to re-education camps for political re-education and hard labour (Refer table 3.2 for location and details of some of the re-education camps).

The 'city people's committee' was the organ responsible for considering the records of persons to be sent for 'concentrated re-education camps' on recommendation from relevant precinct or district people's committees, and also by the director of the city public security service. The city people's committee was responsible for suggesting punitive measures to the ministry of interior for approval. Precinct and district public security officers were responsible for implementing the decisions for sending people to re-education camps. On July 4 1987, Ho Chi Minh City people's committee promulgated regulations governing the enforcement of measures on concentrated re-education and the system of concentrated education through forced labour in Ho Chi Minh City.

According to these regulations the following categories of persons were to be subjected to 'concentrated re-education'. Past or present counter-revolutionary elements: those charged with many crimes; stubborn elements that refused to be re-educated despite repeated re-education efforts by the relevant ward or village administration. Professional hoodlums and perpetuators of crime: those who disturbed public order and security, those who gathered for merry-making and brawling, those elements who were engaged in social vices such as professional prostitutes and drug addicts. In addition, those who escaped from re-education camps, those able bodied persons who refuse to earn a honest living, those who were involved in speculation and hoarding of goods which were banned, and those who dealt with counterfeit items (Saigon Giai Phong, July 4, 1987). Pregnant women and women with babies less than a year old; persons suffering from serious illness that needed medical treatment; persons from families of war invalids; and persons with families facing difficulties and who were the main bread winners of the family were differed from being sent to the 'concentrated re-education camps'. The persons taken as prisoners for political reasons were taken to 'political re-education camps' and detained for several months or years.

The re-education camps were run by the military until 1977 and thereafter they were handed over to the police. The main activity in these camps was to write 'self-criticism' for the mistakes done against the Vietnamese society and to read it to the authorities besides hard labour. Several re-education camps existed in Vietnam. Camp conditions varied according to the military and the political background of the inmates. The higher-ranking inmates had more difficult conditions in the camps. The camps in North Vietnam were harsher than the camps in South Vietnam. Those condemned for longer periods of re-education were transferred to the camps in the South towards the end of their detention.

Table 3.2   Location and Details of some of the Re-education Camps in Vietnam

S.no	Name of the camp	Province	duration	nature of detainees	approx no
1	Cui Lang	Chau duc	1975-1978	Former policemen	2,000
2	Ha Tay	Ha Son Binh (N)	1978-1983	Former naval commanders	1,000
3	Nam Ha	Ha Nam Nih	1983-	"	1,200
4	Xuan Loc	Dong Nai	1983-1987	"	700-1,200
5	Gia Tiung	Kon Tum	1976-1984	Escape organizers	4,000
6	Vuon Dao	Tien Giang	1978-1980	Former policeman	2,000
7	Long Giao	Long Khanh (S)	1975	Ex-SVN Naval staff	400
8	Tam Hiep	Bien Hoa	1975	Ex-SVN Naval staff	400
9	Yen Bai (1)	Hong Lien (S)	1976	Ex-SRV Military	350
10	Yen Bai (2)	"	1976-1977	Ex-SRV Naval staff	180
11	Yen Bai (3)	"	1977-1978	Ex-SRV Naval staff	180

Forced labour was imposed as a penalty on all inmates of the re-education camps. It was also imposed as a penalty for military draft evasion, escape attempts, suspected anti-Communist activities, and small businessmen without a license. Till 1982 the camps with military officers in detention were restricted. But from 1983 onwards inmates from ex-military, politicians, and civilian backgrounds were detained together. Housing and sanitation conditions varied according to the camps. They were minimal and overcrowded. Water was scarce, medical facilities were limited or non-existent in most of the camps. Visitors were strictly controlled along with the facility to send or receive mail.

Food conditions varied from camp to camp. Generally, meals were given twice a day, consisting of a bowl of rice and vegetables and some meat or fish depending on the availability of the items. The re-education camps were either in existing military barracks, or built by the prisoners themselves with dried grass and earth. The family registration of the inmates was cancelled or transferred to the camp authorities register.

Probationary release before the end of actual detention term was mandatory. During such probationary period the inmates were expected to report to the local authorities about their whereabouts and movements. Even after the detainees were released from the 're-education camps' it invariably took time to get their names included into the 'family registration card' (*Ho Khu*) which is essential for any job or public assistance.

The lower ranking functionaries were given re-education at the local level. They were given political lectures during the day and were sent home during the night. The duration of the local re-education varied from a few days to a few weeks. The local party functionaries gave political lectures either at the local schools or at the village communes.

National labour duty

All citizens of employable age (18-55 for men, 18-50 for women) were expected to contribute free labour for 15 days as their input in nation building. The free labour was used to build roads, clean wastelands, de-sludge community ponds, clearing former minefields for cultivation, repairing irrigation canals and bunts.

Local authorities would also request free labour for local projects, for a minimum of 15 days a year without any compensation. Clearing drainage, cleaning garbage, sweeping streets, and repairing local government buildings were some of the local projects. Even though offering free labour for the nation building was mandatory for all citizens, often, the most difficult task was reserved for the 'politically unacceptable' persons and their family members.

In schools both teachers and students.were expected to perform national labour duty on weekends and holidays. Children from 'bad families' were expected to do more menial jobs than children from 'patriotic families'.

In addition to 'normal national labour duty' there was another labour duty for all male citizens. Pioneer youth labour duty for three years was a compulsory voluntary labour duty without compensation for all male citizens between the age of 18 to 20 years. This duty came in effect from 1976 onwards. The labour duty was to be carried out locally in labour camps or in the New Economic Zones.

During the Vietnam - Chinese war in February 1979, the authorities ordered military draft for all male citizens between the ages of 18 to 24 years. According to the 1986 constitution, it is mandatory for all male citizens of 16 years of age to report for initial draft registration. Physical examinations were conducted at the age of 17 and the actual draft age was between 18 to 24 years.

Those with 'bad family background', draft evaders, or those arrested during escape attempts (of draft age) and otherwise not qualified were sent to perform forced labour or difficult military labour. The maximum duration of forced labour was two to three years. Names in 'Ho Khau' were reportedly ordered cancelled or transferred to the control of the military authorities for those enlisted in military services or to the authority in the labour camps or New Economic Zones for those required to work there. It was mandatory to complete military service or national defence and economic labour duty for the re-enrolment of names in 'Ho Khau'.

The New Economic Zones

The international community retaliated by imposing an economic embargo on Vietnamese communist authorities for defeating the United States and South Vietnam. The international economic embargo forced the Vietnamese authorities to strive for self-sufficiency in several areas of national economy. Agricultural produce was one of the priority sectors in achieving self-sufficiency. Many Vietnamese citizens were drafted to 'New Economic Zones' where intensive agricultural activities were expected to be carried out in very primitive conditions with rudimentary agricultural tools, virgin land was expected to be brought under the hoe by relatively inexperienced new farmers.

Communication, health care, and education facilities were non-existent or limited in these areas. The whole family or a few members were requested to go to the New Economic Zones. Those who went were usually required to clear the forest and plant crops. They worked for several hours daily, depending on the demands of the local authorities. The local authorities usually retained 40 to 60 per cent of the crops produced. In addition to the hard labour, the 'new farmers' were punished for trivial matters with fines, selective study of communist dogmas, and were given additional menial jobs such as cleaning the police station.

Considering the fact that the primary objective of the New Economic Zones was to increase agricultural production, the government would collect rice and other crops in large quantities to distribute to other areas of the country. The people who produced the crops were not allowed to sell the crops, and violation of this policy would result in confiscating the entire production and subsequent punishment. The New Economic Zones were usually organised under the leadership of a group leader. There were restrictions on the movements of the residents and visitors. Escaping or unauthorised absence from the New Economic Zones was usually penalised and the escapees were sent back. Cancelling the name from the family registration book was another consequence for escaping from the New Economic Zones. By the end of 1980, the Vietnamese government realised that the New Economic program had failed and citizens were excused from going to the New Economic Zones on valid grounds such as old age, or illness in the family. However, suspected anti communist activists were not allowed to escape from their requirement to go to the New Economic Zones.

Family registration and Bio-data

The family registration card commonly known as '*Ho Khau*' is the principal tool of social control. All details of the members of the household are included in the family registration card. It is an easy means by which to monitor its citizens. However, if one's name is listed in the family book it does not automatically mean that the registered person is staying with the family.

'*So Yeu Ly Lich*', bio-data or curriculum vitae, is a document required for every person applying for a job, for a license to engage in an occupation, or for a student applying for higher education. This document is written by the applicant and submitted to the local authority for certification. Once it is certified that the person belongs to a 'bad family background' he/she will probably have trouble in getting a job, or receiving a higher education.

Escape attempts

Escape attempts have been considered as an offence against the state. The 1986 criminal code of Vietnam incorporated several articles under crimes against national security. According to articles 85, 88, and 89, fleeing to a foreign country or remaining abroad in a foreign country with the intention of opposing the people's government, illegally organising or forcing others to flee to a foreign country or remaining abroad in a foreign country and illegal entry into or exit from Vietnam can attract a punishment ranging from warning, re-education, or three to 20 years punishment.

According to the informants of the study, often arrests were made by the village guerrillas, coast guards, local police, local guerrillas, border police, and naval force or by the regional force. The punishment was more severe for the organisers of the escape. However, children and women with very young children were usually released after a few days of investigation.

The preparation for the 'flight'

The experience of the flight and the context of departure from one's own country have direct implications on the pattern and the capability of the asylum seekers' coping capacity in the detention centres. Several asylum seekers succeeded in escaping from Vietnam only after many unsuccessful attempts. The preparation and organisation of an escape often took weeks or even months. A careful planning of the logistics of escape had to be worked out, a suitable vessel, adequate food and water, help of navigational tools had to be arranged very secretly. Often resources were pooled to arrange the logistics and supply.

The preparation of escape varied according to the destination. Those who chose to escape through the south western tip of Vietnam to the Southern coast of Thailand had to plan for three or four days provisions, fuel, water, and a boat which was not necessarily too sturdy. But pirates heavily infested this route.

The details of imminent departure were restricted to a few to avoid detection by the local authorities. The word was passed around about the exact date of departure to the 'passengers' to meet at a pre-arranged place. Most of the payment would have to be made at an earlier stage and the balance to be paid later at the country of first asylum or at resettlement in a 'third country'. Sometimes the payment was directly sent to Vietnam by relatives settled in a 'third country'. The average price to be paid for an escape was two *teals* of gold (1 teal = 37.42 grams approximately) or the equivalent.

Table 3.3 Comparative Arrivals of Vietnamese Asylum Seekers in SouthEast Asia Since ICIR II Conference July 1989-April 1994

Countries of Temporary Asylum:	1989 Jul To Dec	% of Total Arr.	1990 Jan To Dec	% of Total Arr.	1991 Jan To Dec	% of Total Arr.	1992 Jan To Dec	% of Total Arr.	1993 Jan To Dec	% of Total Arr.	1994 Jan	Feb	Mar	Apr	Total	% of Total Arr.	Cum. Total Arr.	%of Cum. Total Arr.
Hong Kong	11015	42.7%	6595	21.3%	20206	90.1%	12	20.7%	101	13.0%	106	4	7	13	130	68.1%	38059	47.5%
Indonesia	3551	13.8%	12328	39.9%	1397	6.2%	18	31.0%	23	3.0%	1	0	0	0	1	0.5%	17318	21.6%
Japan	1946	7.6%	374	1.2%	357	1.6%	17	29.0%	638	82.1	21	0	24	14	59	30.9%	3391	4.2%
Korea Rep.	79	0.3%	0	0.0%	0	0.0%	0	0.0%	0	0.0%	0	1	0	0	1	0.5%	80	0.1%
Macau	0	0.0%	0	0.0%	0	0.0%	0	0.0%	0	0.0%	0	0	0	0	0	0.0%	0	0.0%
Malaysia	4231	16.4%	1326	4.3%	0	0.0%	1	1.7%	0	0.0%	0	0	0	0	0	0.0%	5558	6.9%
Philippines	1756	6.8%	1108	3.6%	252	1.1%	0	0.0%	1	0.1%	0	0	0	0	0	0.0%	3117	3.9%
Singapore	831	3.2%	147	0.5%	6	0.0%	0	0.0%	0	0.0%	0	0	0	0	0	0.0%	984	1.2%
Thailand	2363	9.2%	9054	29.3%	202	0.9%	10	17.2%	14	1.8%	0	0	0	0	0	0.0%	11643	14.5%
Total Arrivals	25772	100%	30932	100%	22420	100%	58	100%	777	100%	128	5	31	27	191	100%	80150	100%

Information is based on statistics from Durable Solutions Unit, UNHCR Geneva 46.05.94

Often the boat master had to bribe the local security and barter with other ocean going vessels for essential provisions. Some asylum seekers were forced to procure new vessels from Chinese fishermen from the South China coast for a price. There are reports of Chinese fishermen demanding a male child in lieu of a boat. The other passengers in the boat would then force a mother to surrender her child. Women and children, single passengers, or those travelling with a group of people who were not their relatives or friends were especially in a vulnerable situation. (Refer to table 3.3, for the details of comparative arrivals of Vitnamese asylum seekers in Southeast Asia.)

Tragedy at sea

It is important to elaborate on the perils of escape to assess the motivation of the asylum seekers to escape from Vietnam. How genuine are the Vietnamese refugees in Hong Kong is a question often asked by refugee administrators, the media and the general public. Each one has their own criteria to measure the 'refugee worth' of an asylum seeker. A large majority of the asylum seekers made a long and hazardous voyage across the South China Sea to Hong Kong. It has also been reported that some of them travelled to China by land and crossed over to Hong Kong. The Vietnamese refugees arrived in Hong Kong not only in small boats; they arrived by any means available to them; some were also rescued at sea by ocean-going vessels. The breakdown of arrivals since 1980 is as follows (Table 3.4).

Table 3.4   Vietnamese Asylum Seekers: How They Came to Hong Kong

Year	small boat cases	ship-rescue cases	total arrivals
1980	5908 in 200 boats	880 in 20 ships	16,788
1981	6674 in 235 boats	1796 in 34 ships	8470
1982	7403 in 263 boats	433 in 7 ships	7836
1983	3301 in 142 boats	350 in 7 ships	3651
1984	1888 in 77 boats	342 in 7 ships	2230
1985	1069 in 49 boats	43 in 3 ships	1112
1986	1821 in 102 boats	238 in 5 ships	2059
1987	3291 in 165 boats	104 in 5 ships	3395
1988	18101 in 590 boats	348 in 7 ships	18449
1989	34116 in 824 boats	391 in 5 ships	34507
1990	6409 in 275 boats	186 in 4 ships	6595
1991	20179 in 580 boats	27 in 2 ships	20206

Source: HKG Oct., 1992

It is also important to note the distance involved in whichever escape route they have taken. It was to Hong Kong (500 nautical miles), east across the south China sea, to the Philippines (900 nautical miles), across the gulf of Thailand to go to Thailand (1500 nautical miles), across the South China sea to Malaysia (1500 nautical miles), further south to Singapore (1600 nautical miles), some of them travelled as far as Indonesia (2000 nautical miles).

Cravens and Bornemann (1990) recorded the perils of the voyage of the Vietnamese asylum seekers. According to them, the voyage to Thailand or Malaysia was particularly hazardous because of the ruthless Thai pirates who disguised themselves as fishermen. Their attack on refugees typically consisted of robbing the refugees of their valuables, sexually assaulting women, throwing people overboard, and kidnapping women and young girls. It has been reported that several refugee vessels were rammed and sunk to dispose the evidence of piracy.

In 1989, 18 people died and 734 people were reported missing due to pirate attacks in the South China Sea. On January 15 and 16, 1989, naked bodies of 11 Vietnamese women were washed ashore in the coastal province of Nakhon Si Thammarat in Southern Thailand. They were apparently victims of a brutal pirate attack (Refer table nos. 3.5 and 3.6 for details of the piracy encounters in the Gulf of Thailand and in the South China Sea off Malaysia).

Table 3.5   Piracy Encounters in the Gulf of Thailand

	1986	1987	1988	1989
Total persons arrived	4,392	12,841	5,448	2,652
Number of women raped	58	67	28	46
Number abducted	53	4	34	68
Number of deaths	18	0	21	6
Number of missing	111	36	77	313
Boats arrived	448	1,111	343	168
Boats attacked	58	91	37	21
Percentage of boats attacked	13	8	11	13
Number of attacks	87	117	56	25

Source: Richard B. Cravens and Thomas H. Bornemann; 1990

Table 3.6   Piracy Encounters in the South China Sea off Malaysia

	1986	1987	1988	1989
Total persons arrived	7,399	8,013	13,317	14,098
Number of women raped	84	13	39	64
Number abducted	31	11	59	70
Number of deaths	0	2	7	12
Number of missing	28	36	344	316
Boats arrived	215	215	331	286
Boats attacked	40	27	55	46
Percentage of boats attacked	18.6	12.6	16.6	16.1
Number of attacks	53	37	55	58

Source: Cravens and Bornemann, 1990

Conclusion

Available data points to the fact that the prevailing political and social environment was predominantly the main factor in the decision of the asylum seekers to leave Vietnam. Though an equally strong 'pull' factor was developed through the initiatives of the international agencies, the USA and their allies encouraging them to leave Vietnam. The peril at sea was a severe price one was forced to pay for a potentially better future than the continuing uncertainty of Vietnam. Moreover, an international norm had been evolved which encouraged the Vietnamese to leave Vietnam for greener pastures.

The Vietnamese who were late to take up this offer and left Vietnam after the 'cut off date' was generally unaware of the shift in the policy of automatic asylum for the Vietnamese refugees. Various factors, which might act as distant contributory factors to the process of ethnocide in the detention camps in Hong Kong, have been explained in this chapter.

4 Personal Agony: A Commodity in Humanitarian Politics

Introduction

This chapter presents an analysis of international initiatives on Vietnamese refugees in the personal context of the refugees. The Vietnamese asylum seekers in Hong Kong were prisoners of international politics (Knudsen, 1990), and their fate as refugees and asylum seekers in Hong Kong was intricately interwoven with several international political factors. Prior to 16 June 1988, all the Vietnamese asylum seekers arriving in Hong Kong were automatically given refugee status. However, gradually more North Vietnamese began seeking asylum in Hong Kong. Most Vietnamese refugees detained in the camps felt that they are punished or betrayed by the international community though the refugees from Vietnam attracted several international initiatives unprecedented in the global refugee history. This chapter is divided into two section. Section 1 presents two cases of refugee claim. The first case '-Mr Hung's story' which was typical of many of refugees detained in Hong Kong camps which was well presented. The second case was presented by a young brother and his sister. Like many other asylum seekers who are not well educated or well versed in English, the case is an example of poorly presented case. Section 2 is a detailed analysis of the international context of various initiatives to deal with the refugee issues in Hong Kong.

Section 1

The personal context: Case 1

Mr Hung, was a soldier in the South Vietnamese army. He spent more than four years under detention in Hong Kong before his claim for refugee status was accepted. His son was born in Hong Kong whilst he and his family was under detention. Mr Hung's story is typical of many refugees detained in Hong Kong camps. However, Mr Hung was lucky, unlike many other refugees detained in the camps. Mr Hung's case of 'refugee claim' was accepted at the first instance.

The following is the refugee claim he presented to the Immigration department. The same format was used by most of the refugees who presented their case in writing. However, a large number of refugees did not present a written application. During the initial part of the refugee saga in Hong Kong none of the refugees had access to independent legal council. Moreover, all refugees were denied access to the UNHCR handbook on 'refugee status determination procedure'. The camp authorities were of the opinion that the refugees would misuse, access to such a book in order to falsify their claim for refugee status. The refugees who did not have access to the 'handbook on refugee status determination procedure' and the 'questionnaire' used in determining the refugee claim were in a disadvantageous position. The 'assistance' they received was only the from a Hong Kong immigration officer taking their 'testimony' when they were called to present their case.

Before Mr Hung's re-settlement to USA, he and his family were shifted through different detention camps in Hong Kong. Upon his arrival in Hong Kong, they were detained in Green Island detention centre first, then they were moved to Whitehead detention centre. When they had settled down in Whitehead detention centre they were again uprooted and transferred to High Island. From High Island detention centre they were again shifted to Sek Kong detention centre. When Shek Kong camp closed down he and his family was moved to Tai Ah Chau detention centre. Finally, before their departure to USA, Mr Hung's family was moved to Kai Tak refugee departure centre.

Mr Hung was lucky to work with a camp agency as an interpreter, which provided access to basic stationary materials to write his refugee claim. He was also resourceful enough to get a copy of the 'questionnaire' used in processing refugee status claim. (To protect the privacy of the respondent the names and address has been changed.)

Name of the applicant: Mr. Hung - vrd 69/90, FN TAC 108/1 -c1/2/33c, Tai Ah Chau Detention centre, 07 december, 1992

To Hong Kong Immigration Department,
Claim for refugee status

Dear Sir,
I would like to take this opportunity to submit my statement for refugee status determination as follows:

GENERAL BACKGROUND

1.Full Name: Mr P. L. HUNG
Place of Birth: Ha Noi
Date of Birth: 19 April 1951
Nationality: Vietnamese
Present Address:
FN TAC 108/1 - C1/2/33C - Tai Ah Chau Detention Centre, Hong Kong
Last Address in VN:
XXX/1xx, DIEN BIEN PHU Street - Ward 3 District 3, Ho Chi Minh City
Ethnic Origin: Vietnamese
Profession before leaving Vietnam: Hawker, selling lottery tickets
Religion: Ancestor Worship

2. Spouse: 1st Marriage
Full Name: D. T. XUAN
Place of Birth: Cho Lon
Date of Birth: 07 May 1952
Nationality: Vietnamese
Present Address: Unknown, in Vietnam.
Ethnic Origin: Vietnamese Profession: Tradeswoman
Religion: Ancestor Worship
Date of Marriage: February 1974
Date of Divorce: January 1985

3. Daughter:
Full Name: P. N. QUYEN
Place of Birth: Ho Chi Minh City
Date of Birth: 11 May 1975
Nationality: Vietnamese
Present Address: Unknown, in Vietnam.
Ethnic Origin: Vietnamese
Profession: Student
Religion: Ancestor Worship

4. Son:
Full Name: P. N. CHAU
Place of Birth: Ho Chi Minh City
Date of Birth: 07 February 1982
Nationality: Vietnamese
Present Address: XXX/XX, DIEN BIEN PHU Street, Ho Chi Minh City, Vietnam
Profession: Student
Religion: Ancestor Worship

5. Spouse: 2nd Marriage:
Full Name (2nd Wife): T. T. M. LINH
Place of Birth: Quy Nhon Province
Date of Birth: 20 January 1965
Nationality: Vietnamese
Present Address:
FN TAC 108/2 - C1/2/33C - Tai Ah Chau Detention Centre, Hong Kong
Last Address in VN:
XXX/X, DANG VAN NGU Street, Ward 14, Phu Nhuan District, Ho Chi Minh City
Ethnic Origin: Vietnamese
Profession: Coffee Shop Waitress
Religion: Ancestor Worship

6. Son:
Full Name: P. L. HOANG
Place of Birth: Queen Elizabeth Hospital, Hong Kong
Present Address: FN TAC 108/3 - C1/2/33C - Tai Ah Chau Detention Centre, Hong Kong

Details of the applicant

7. 1951 - 1954: Babyhood, living with parents in Ha Noi, North Vietnam
8. 1954: Migrating to South Vietnam along with parents. Residing in District 3, Saigon
9. 1957 - 1962: Attending Primary School
10. 1962 - 1969: Attending High School
11. 1969 - 1972: Attending University
12. 04 July 1972: Joined the ARVN when I was just finishing the first year of the Faculty of Education, VAN HANH University. Attending Session 3/72 for Reserve Officers of the Army at DONG DE Military Training Centre, NHA TRANG. Service Number: XX/142.800
13. 1972 - 1975: Served in the ARVN till the fall of Saigon. (30 April 1975 the fall of South Vietnam).
Last Rank: Artillery Second Lieutenant (ARVN)
Last Position: Artillery DLO
Last Unit: Artillery Sector of DINH TUONG. Military Section

14. 28 June 1975 - 28 May 1981: PERIOD OF IMPRISONMENT IN RE-EDUCATION CAMPS
28 June 75: Date of Arrest
28 May 81: Date of Release

I was in the following camps:
TRANG LON: June 1975 to July 1976

AN DUONG: July 1976 to August 1977
TAN HIEP: August 1977 to June 1979
CHI HOA: June 1979 to August 1979
XUAN PHUOC: August 1979 to May 1981.

15. June 1981 - October 1985: PERIOD OF HOUSE ARREST UNDER SURVEILLANCE OF LOCAL AUTHORITIES AND PEOPLE.

On release, I had to report to the local public security office (Ward 3, District 3, HCM City) where my mother was living instead of in Ward 1, Tan Binh District, HCM City, where my wife from first marriage and daughter were living as written in the "Release Order". My wife's parents did not want to be associated with a "bad" element like me. They were afraid of getting into trouble. So they refused to let me live with them. Under surveillance of the local public security officers of Ward 3, District 3, I firstly underwent a probation period of 12 months as written in my "Release Order". But, it was later extended twice, (12 months for each time) by the local public security for I "had not really washed out my old thoughts yet". On 23 October 1984, I was given back "citizenship rights". I was issued with an Identity Card on 23 October 1985.

16. January 1985: Receiving "DECREE ABSOLUTE", by the order of which, my daughter QUYEN was to live with her mother, and my son CHAU with me.

REMARKS:

i) In my period of probation, we (my wife and I) lived separately in our parents' respective houses. Once a week, I visited her and my daughter. But my local authorities and her parents never allowed me to stay overnight at her premises.

ii) On 07 February 1982, she gave birth to my son.

iii) June 1984: our family conflict became more and more serious. It led to a big quarrel in which I slapped her. This happened after the fact that no one in her family, even she and our daughter, had not participated in the funeral of my father who had died in (27/4 Lunar Calendar) 1984. As a result of which, few days later, she sent a request for divorce.

iv) My wife has a paternal uncle who was a lieutenant colonel of the communist government. After 1975, her parents leaned on him to become 'a revolutionary family' and became rich since then. That is why they no longer wanted to be associated with such a 'bad family' as ours.

17. December 1985: My name was finally entered in my mother's household registration records.

18. January 1986: I started working at CO SO SAN XUAT BANG KEO HOA BINH (HOA BINH Masking Tape Manufacturing Enterprise) run by Mr. N. KHAI, one of my old classmates. November: I was prevented from continuing work when the CO SO was upgraded to become TO HOP (State-run Joint Enterprise) whose workers would become 'government employees' with monthly supplies of food subsidies and ration cards. The number of the TO HOP's workers would be increased twice as many as the old CO SO. The denial was made by the District's Handicraft and Commerce Office and resulted because of my background of being a 're-educated puppet officer'. I was quite sure about this as I was given a gentle hint by the CO SO's owner that I could not continue working because of my background once CO SO was upgraded to TO HOP which would be run by the Governmental District Handicraft and Commerce Office.

19. 1987: Unemployed.

In December: Applying for a job at XI NGHIEP CHE BIEN THUC PHAM QUAN I (Foods Processing Factory, District 1). About a month later, my application was sent back with the word 'NEGATIVE'. I am quite sure that it was because of the endorsement by the public security officer, which I had to attach to my application as required procedurally. The endorsement revealed that I was a re-educated officer. The factory management would know at once that I used to be a serviceman of the old regime.

20. February 1988: (After the Lunar New Year) I failed once more in finding a job. I persuaded my mother to submit a request of 'Letter of Introduction' to the People's Committee, Ward 3, District 3. This was in order to exercise a profession of lottery tickets agent for the CONG TY XO SO KIEN THIET THANH PHO HO CHI MINH (Lottery Company - for the Construction of Ho Chi Minh City). The President of the People's Committee shortly refused the request saying that: 'The Letter of Introduction is only issued to revolutionary families or war-invalid families, or those whose families have contributed some merits to the revolution. But never for such a puppet officer family' as ours.

April: At home, arranging lottery tickets into series of same numbers for earning some money.

November: I started working as a hawker, selling lottery tickets without licence. At this time, I became acquainted with my present wife, LINH, who was a waitress in the coffee shop PHUONG which I used to drop in for selling lottery tickets around 2:00 or 3:00 p.m. everyday.

21. 1989: Continued selling lottery tickets as a hawker without licence. December: I was summoned by the public security officers to attend a meeting of re-educated

oifficers at the police station in the first week of December. The purpose of the meeting was so called political education. But in actual fact it was for propaganda and for us to make self-criticism reports. I reported my recent movements and activities, i.e. I had to report where I went hawking, to whom, and the duration of my hawking; I was also asked whom I had often contacted, what I had discussed, who was my best friend. A few days later I was assigned by the local officer LOAN to sell lottery tickets for Ward 3 at a fixed place on the curb where I displayed my tickets on a folding table. I was to buy lottery tickets from THANH (the lottery ticket-selling agent of the Ward) at a higher price than what I used to pay my previous agent. Moreover, I did not have the right to return to him those tickets that I could not sell. Afterwards, although I was there for a few days, I had no customers. I would have made a big loss if I kept on selling at the assigned place. All these reasons made me leave the place and go hawking illegally again, and reduce the amount of lottery tickets I bought from THANH to 10,000 dong instead of 50,000 dong as before. Consequently, THANH and LOAN hated me.

22. Jan. 17 1990: Got married to LINH. After our marriage, I made a request for temporary absence at the locality for 3 months, so I could live with my wife at our rented house located at XXX/2 Xo Viet Nghe Tinh, Ward 17, Binh Thanh District, HCM City. But, LOAN, my local public security officer allowed me to be temporarily absent for one week only for 'security reason' as he said. This meant that I had to make a request again and again every week.

Mar 28 1990: Escaping from the local authorities. Reason will be hereafter presented.

Mar 30 1990: Leaving Ho Chi Minh City for Hai Phong intending to escape to Hong Kong.

Apr. 28 1990: Arrived in Hong Kong.

REASONS FOR FLEEING FROM VIETNAM:

1. COMING FROM REACTIONARY FAMILY - MIGRATING NORTHERNER:

My father was a member of VIET QUOC (The Nation of Vietnam) party prior to 1954. In 1954, he took his wife and his children away from North Vietnam to South Vietnam. Five of our eight siblings served either in the Administration or in the Army of the former South Vietnamese Government. After 1975, three of us were sent to re-education camps for years. Because of these above points, the Vietnamese communist government always classifies my family as a BAD, REACTIONARY one.

2. BEING A MEMBER OF A PARTICULAR SOCIAL GROUP:

As stated earlier, I was an Artillery Second Lieutenant of the ARVN. As a result, I had 6 years of re-education and 4 years of home arrest, afterwards, under the communist government.

DETAILED PERSECUTIONS AND THEIR REASONS, CHRONOLOGICALLY I SUFFERED AND EXPERIENCED UNDER THE VIETNAMESE COMMUNIST REGIME

I. June 28 1975 - May 28 1981: PERIOD OF BEING DETAINED IN RE-EDUCATION CAMPS.

Core Reason: Before April 30 1975, I served in the ARVN with the rank of Second Lieutenant, Artillery branch, since 4 July 1972. After April 30 1975, Ho Chi Minh City Military Management Committee issued an announcement to summon all those who were involved in the army of the former regime, ranking from second lieutenant to captain within 3 days, i.e. 26, 27, and 28 June 1975, promising just 10 day long re-education. I was tricked into reporting and detained for re-education, not for only 10 days but for 6 long years.

1. Persecution: As mentioned above, I went through various re-education camps as: TRANG LON, AN DUONG, TAN HIEP, TRANG BOM (a sub-camp of TAN HIEP), CHI HOA, and XUAN PHUOC. Persecutions which I suffered and experienced during this period differed slightly from camp to camp as summarised hereafter: Political re-education and Brain Washing: The communist authorities forced me to 'study' six political lessons (in three months' period at TRANG LON Camp) the contents of which could be summarised as follows:

'The US empire is the invader - The Republic of Vietnam Government is a puppet government - They both have been against the People and Revolution, and harmful to the Fatherland - You (they meant us), NGUY QUAN (servicemen serving the puppet government), and NGUY QUYEN (administrative officials serving the puppet government), and those who are guilty owe a blood-debt to the People and Revolution - The communist party and people's government are very humane and generous for having spared your lives and created opportunities for you to be re-educated and brain washed'. In order to 're-educate' us, they applied measures as terrorising, torturing, shackling, starving, to force us 'to think' and to repeat those above mentioned lessons in every political sessions, in every evening discussion after hard labour as well as in our then daily activities. Those who acted or behaved differently from what we had been taught during re-education for one reason or another would be punished. Being detained and shackled in the 'connex' (small-size container) was reserved for minor violations and that of being shot dead for severe violation like NGUYEN NGOC TRU (1977) or TA VAN HOA (1979).

2. Hard Labour: Most of the time I was in re-education camps, I had to perform hard-labour from 08 to 10 hours a day, under the observation and guard of security officials armed with rifles. We were allowed to rest on Sundays and big holidays and New Year days, as well. But, at TRANG LON and XUAN PHUOC, we were only allowed to rest on Sunday afternoon only. And always, after working time, from 7:00 p.m. to 09:30 p.m., we had to sit down in groups or teams to discuss. But, actually to criticise and denounce each other. The hard labours that I had to do could be summarised as follows:

TRANG LON: Building houses, common meeting hall,...

AN DUONG: Ploughing to plant rice,...

TAN HIEP: Clearing mine fields, planting vegetables,...

TRANG BOM: Clearing waste land for farming.

XUAN PHUOC: Digging fish breeding pond and making bricks.

Those who appeared lazy or not able to accomplish the task assigned would be criticised and punished. With minor mistakes, part of our daily ration would be cut; for severe mistakes we would be detained in the 'connex'.

3. Diet in Re-education Camps: At most camps I went through, diet was categorised into 4 grades in accordance with the classification of re-educatees': the active ones, the fairly active ones, the passable ones, and the positive ones. The right of diet classification was completely in the hands of the officer-in-charge dependent on his bias and partly on the 'education behaviour' of the prisoner. But in reality, the active grade was often reserved for 'denouncer' or 'informant'. Personally, I used to obtain the passable grade, comprising of 2 meals per day, one bowl of rice plus one bowl of dried cassava plus one 'ocean soup' for each. The diet classification was made weekly. When I was disciplined, my diet was decreased to one bowl of rice at each meal. More specifically, during one month when I was disciplined at XUAN PHUOC, I was only given half a bowl of rice at each meal and the rice was deliberately mixed with an excessive amount of fish sauce, combined with fish worms. It was extremely salty such that I always felt so thirsty I had to drink my urine for I was only given 2 spoons of water for each meal.

4. Disciplinary Punishment: I was disciplined several times as follows: At TRANG LON, two weeks detained in 'connex' for 'singing yellow music that expressed my fondness of the old regime'. At TRANG LON, one month detained in 'connex' for 'obstinately not accepting guilt of having killed people and revolutionary soldiers'.

Explanation: In the course of studying 6 political lessons, I was forced to answer the question: 'How many people and revolutionary soldiers did you kill during the time you served in the puppet army'? First of all, my reply was 'None'. The officer-in-charge disagreed; he tore my self-criticism and forced me to write another. Like the first one, he kept on tearing my criticism several times for my answers were either 'None' or 'I do not know exactly'. As a consequence, I was detained in the 'connex' till I became so frail and terrified that I had to make a final self-criticism in which I accepted that I had killed hundreds of people and revolutionary soldiers. Then, I was released. At CHI HOA, I was detained for two months, shackled, and beaten up in a solitary cell for leading a movement of struggle for the human rights of re-educated officers at TAN HIEP on Christmas Eve 1978.

Explanation: The TAN HIEP camp included 6 areas, namely K1, K2, K3, K4, K5, and K30. Each could hold some 1,000 prisoners, with the exception of K30, which was used as a clinic. Barbed wire fences separated these areas from each other. At the end of 1978, I together with some of my close friends unanimously started leading K4 where I was imprisoned to co-operate with other areas to raise up a movement of struggle for the dignity and human rights of re-educated ARVN officers. The actual day to make the first move was Christmas Eve, 24 December 1978.
Some months later, the movement was slowly extinguished by the camp authorities through arrests of more than 300 persons including me. Afterwards, we were brought to CHI HOA Prison for investigation with shackling and beating and torturing in isolated cells. Two of us were tortured and beaten to death. At XUAN PHUOC, one month detained, tortured, beaten up, and starved in an isolated cell for the 'guilt' of blaspheming 'Uncle Ho'.

Explanation: In my collective detention room at XUAN PHUOC, there was a slogan which said 'BAC HO SONG MAI TRONG SU NGHIEP CUA CHUNG TA' (Uncle Ho lives forever in our works) and was painted on the wall. Personally, I was irritated, angered by it. Then, one day after work, I added one more letter in the last word TA to transform it into TAO. TA or TAO has the same meaning as 'I' and 'ME'. CHUNG TA or CHUNG TAO likewise, means 'WE' and 'US'. But, in Vietnamese, CHUNG TA and CHUNG TAO are extremely different. The former indicates respect when addressing to elderly people, superiors, parents, leaders, while the latter indicates impoliteness, disrespect, rudeness, when addressing to inferiors, children, or when cursing, in this case 'Uncle Ho'. For this, I was detained, tortured, beaten up, and starved.

II. June 1981 - Dec. 1985: PERIOD OF HOUSE ARREST AND SURVEILLANCE by local AUTHORITIES AND PEOPLE. The following are the persecutions I had to suffer and experience in this period.

1. I was ordered to report at the police office every Monday morning with a self-criticism notebook in which I had to write down my movements and daily activities. I could only leave after I had met my local security officer and presented him with my self-criticism notebook and answered his annoying questions of what I had jotted down in the notebook. If things were OK, then he signed the notebook and I could leave. If not, I had to make another self-criticism. At times, I had to spend the whole Monday at the police station without drinking or eating.

2. I was not allowed to be absent at night in the local area without the local authorities' permission. This rule partly contributed to the conflict between my wife and I gradually. She did not want to live with my family and me. On the other hand, I was not allowed to stay at her parents' house.

3. My family and I had to submit a request for permission whenever we want to have 5 or more persons at our place. We had to clearly state the purpose of the gathering, date, time, names and number of guests as well as their relationship with us.

4. I had to perform unpaid labour every year under the order of local authorities. If I wanted to be exempted from labour, I had to pay twice the amount of money the others had to pay. The payment was based on the price of rice at that time. While other people paid 15 kilos of rice, I had to pay 30 kilos of rice per year. I also had to perform other kinds of labour in the local area under the order of the local authorities, like dredging mud from the TRUONG MINH KY canal (10 days in summer of 1982), cleaning BAN CO market and more often, cleaning ditches in my neighbourhood every year in the rainy season. Others were not asked to do so.

5. I used to be detained one or two days depending on the security situation, during the big holidays of the Communists on 30/04, 19/05, 02/09. At the police office I had to write reports of my activities of the past, or do some cleaning, washing for them.

6. The local authorities used to check the census record of my family and to ransack our house, approximately once a month while other families were not.

7. Having no citizenship rights meant that I had neither ration-card nor food subsidies. I could do nothing legally to earn a livelihood. I had to completely depend on my mother who received money from my brother in Norway for the whole family. In fact, in 1982 and 1983, I did odd jobs such as: riding three-wheel car for carrying

corrugated steel only when hired, selling sulphuric acid (H2SO4) to battery-charging shops, working as street-trader, buying and selling medicine, chemical substances. But I had to work illegally, if arrested, it meant imprisonment, and most important of all was the interrogation by the local public security officer in charge. I had to tell the truth and beg for his compassion and sympathy. But he would not be moved. So I was punished by writing self-criticism, reporting every day for weeks, or doing any kind of work for the locality under his order. In 1983, I gave up illegal odd jobs on my mother's advice.

8. I was not allowed to sing or listen to or play guitar to the kind of 'yellow music' which I love the most. The local public security officer forbade me to play such music only, but not other kinds of music. One time, I played 'yellow music' with my guitar in the hope that nobody could hear. But, the reality was not to be. Someone reported to the security officer and I was punished in a similar manner for a month. Besides, my guitar was confiscated and 'SHE' never came back to me. These persecutions led me, according to the local authorities' viewpoint, to the way of breaking local rules and regulations. This resulted in a long period of home arrest for me till 23/10/84 when I was given back citizenship rights but those persecutions remained unchanged until December 1985 when I got my household registration record. Altogether, the home arrest period lasted four and a half years instead of one year as was written in my 'release order'.

III. 1986 - 1990:
1. Durable persecutions: The above mentioned persecutions remained unchanged in this period with the exception of minor changes. I had to continually report to the police office, not weekly as before, but monthly on the first day of the month, bringing with me my self-criticism notebook in which I had to jot down my daily movements and activities.

2. Other persecutions: Nov. 1986: Being prevented from continuing to work at CO SO HOA BINH as it was upgraded as the state run TO HOP as stated previously. December 1987: Job application at 'FOODS PROCESSING FACTORY' , the first district, rejected as stated above. February 1988: Being denied legal job as a lottery ticket agent. Details stated supra. December 1989: Being forced to sell lottery tickets for the locality and assigned to sell at fixed place. Details stated above. January 1990: After my marriage, I made a request for temporary residence at my rented house for 3 months. But, the local security officer merely allowed me to temporarily reside there for a week. This meant that I had to make the same request again and again every week while the other citizens did not need to do so. March 1990: I was intercepted, harassed and all of my lottery tickets were confiscated, money and two cassette tapes were also taken away when I was hawking those tickets, by the local public security officer.

Afterwards, I was accused of 'STORING AND CIRCULATING REACTIONARY DOCUMENTS - ESCAPE - DETRIMENTAL TO THE STATE SECURITY' for just storing two cassette tapes whose contents refer to the call for struggle for genuine democracy and freedom in Vietnam. Meanwhile, there were many other citizens who had joined in the 'renovation movement' by publicly criticising the government policy. But none of them had been arrested because they were Vietnamese Communist party members. Their background was apparently different from mine.

FATHER

Full Name: P. V. Y
Y.O.B: 1923
P.O.B: Ha Dong (North Vietnam)
Education: French Baccalaureate Diploma
Pre 1975 occupation: Teacher

1954: Fleeing from North Vietnam for fear of communist persecution due to his involvement in the VIET QUOC (The Nation of Vietnam) Party led by Mr. DINH BUOI.
1964 - 1975: My father was one of the owners of the private high school PHAN SAO NAM which was a financial source for the DAI VIET DUY DAN party, headed by Mr. THANH GIANG. During this period, his position in the party was UY VIEN XU BO MIEN DONG (Member of the Eastern Area Party Committee) and he was particularly responsible for culture and education.
June 1975: After the fall of South Vietnam, he was summoned to attend at PHAN SAO NAM high school for a political re-education session together with many other ex-teachers of the school for a month. During this session, he was denounced by Mr. DO VAN NHIEU, one of the teachers, to be one of leaders of DAI VIET DUY DAN party and completely against communism.
September 1975: He was arrested at home and sent to re-education camp for the above-mentioned reason.
September 1978: He was released from LONG GIAO camp and put under surveillance of local authority and people for six months.
1984: He died of 'bi tieu tien' (obstructed urination) for not being treated at the hospital due to having no census record, after he had lost his mind since 1980 and paralysed since 1982.

MOTHER

Full Name: L. T. THUAN
Y.O.B: 1922
P.O.B: Ha Dong (North Vietnam)
Current address: XXX/14 Dien Bien Phu Street
Ward 3, District 3, HCM City

BROTHER 1

Full Name: PHI NGOC HAI
Y.O.B: 1943
P.O.B: Ha Noi (North VN)
Education: Graduated BAN DOC SU (Bachelor of Art in Administration), The National
Institute of Administration.

Pre 1975 occupation: ARVN Lieutenant.
Administrative Service Chief of MY THO Town.
Post 1975 occupation: Teacher of Vietnamese in Norway

16/12/1968: Date of his joining in the ARVN

Reserve Army Officer Training, 9/68 session. Serial number: XX/143.248

30/04/75: He was arrested and sent to a re-education camp, namely BEN GIA (CUU
LONG Province). Meanwhile, his private house located at TRUONG TAN BUU
Street, Saigon, was confiscated. In 1977: He escaped from the camp and secretly
returned to Saigon. The following year, he made a clandestine departure to Philippines,
and has since resettled in Norway. Now he is living at Ammerudhellinga-Oslo 9 -
0959 Norway.

BROTHER 2

Full Name: P. L. SON
Y.O.B: 1944
P.O.B: Ha Noi (North Vietnam)
Education: Master of Science, University of Texas, USA.

Pre 1975 occupation:
- Director of Project Service (Petroleum and Minerals Directorate).
- Dean of Faculty of Petroleum (MINH DUC University).
- ARVN Second Lieutenant (Joined in 1972).

Post 1975 occupation:
Unemployed: Current Address: Hung Vuong St. Vinh Long Town, Cuu Long Province.
2 May 1975: He was arrested at home and sent to re-education camps, namely TAN
HIEP, VINH PHU (North Vietnam), and Z30A XUAN LOC, DONG NAI, for his
involvement in the South Vietnamese Government with a high ranking position. 1978:
His private house was confiscated and his wife and son were sent to Le Minh Xuan
NEZ in the anti-capitalist campaign. June 1984: He was released from Z30A Camp
and was under house arrest for 12 months.

BROTHER 3

Full Name: H. L CHUNG
Y.O.B: 1948
P.O.B: Ha Noi (North VN)
Education: 1/12.

Pre 1975 occupation: ARVN Air Force Sergeant.
Post 1975 occupation: Farmer.
Current Address: 30/4 Street, Ward 15, Go Vap District, HCM City.

June 1975: He was ordered to attend a re-education session at his locality for seven days.

YOUNGER BROTHER 1

Full Name: P. L. DUNG
Y.O.B: 1953
P.O.B: Ha Noi (North Vietnam)
Education: 2nd Year of Law School, Saigon University.

Pre 1975 occupation: B-Grade Governmental Official at the Customs and Taxes General Office. Post 1975 occupation: Bread Vendor. Current Address: Nguyen XXX Street, Ward 8, District 3, HCM City. June 1975: He was summoned to attend a one-month political re-education session at his general office. Afterwards, he was dismissed from his old office for his family background. 1976 - 1980: He was forced to join the THANH NIEN XUNG PHONG (Pioneer Youth) and did hard labour at the NEZ. 1980 - 1987: Being unemployed because of family background. 1988: Working as a bread vendor.

YOUNGER BROTHER 2

Full Name: P. L. ANH
Y.O.B: 1956
P.O.B: Saigon (South Vietnam)
Education: 12/12.
Pre 1975 occupation: Student.
Post 1975 occupation: Lottery Ticket Hawker.
Current Address: Thich XXX XXX Street, Phu Nhuan District, HCM City.

Post 30 April 1975: He was expelled from his university because of family background. 1976 onwards: Prohibited from doing his military service for many years. On the other hand, he was ordered to join the hard labour team of the locality. This team's duty was to do any kind of work assigned by the locality without payment. This happened due to his family background. 1980 - 1982: Being imprisoned in Tan An Prison, Long An Province, for engaging in clandestine departure. 1983 - 1986: Joining in the Youth Pioneer to avoid the threat and persecution by the locality. 1987: Selling lottery tickets after finding it impossible to find any job in the state run factories or companies.

YOUNGER BROTHER 3

Full Name: PHI LE MINH
Y.O.B: 1958
P.O.B: Saigon (South Vietnam)
Education: 11/12.

Pre 1975 occupation: Student.
Post 1975 occupation: Unemployed.

Current Address: XXX/14, Dien Bien Phu Street, Ward 3, District 3, HCM City.
1976 - 1980: Prohibited from doing military service but ordered to join in the hard labour team of Ward 3. 1980 - 1982: He made a clandestine departure with his brother ANH and was arrested and imprisoned at Tan An Prison, Long An Province, for two years. 1985 - 1988: He was arrested and forced to perform the CUONG BUC LAO DONG QUOC PHONG (The National Defence Forcible Labour) after being classified by the local authorities as 'bad element'.

YOUNGER SISTER

Full Name: PHI THI LE NGUYET
Y.O.B: 1964
P.O.B: Saigon (South Vietnam)
Education: 12/12.

Post 1975 occupation: Unemployed.
Current Address: XXX/14, Dien Bien Phu Street, Ward 3, District 3, HCM City.
1982 - 1983: She could not get through the university entrance examinations due to the classification of student's family background in which she was classified as 'Category 12'.

CLANDESTINE DEPARTURES:

1. June 1982: I joined a clandestine departure at PHUOC HOA Village, BARIA Town, organised by my friend, LOI, who had been an ex-naval lieutenant of ARVN, who had been in the same re-education camps with me. Unfortunately, the attempt failed.

I was arrested and escaped shortly afterwards by bribing the 'DU KICH XA' (village militiamen). When I returned home, I was detained at the local police office for my absence from the locality for three days and two nights (In fact, I had been absent four days and three nights but they did not know about that). I had prepared a false statement, so when he questioned me, I replied that I had gone to visit my brother CHUNG at XOM MOI and drink wine with him. After the drink, I caught such a severe cold that I was delirium. The local public security officer did not believe me at first. But finally, my brother CHUNG brought him a letter of clarification over my case, stamped by my brother's local authority and signed by his local security officer who had been bribed by him for this letter. When released, I was ordered to report every day at the police office from 7 am - 11 p.m. for a month, where I had to serve like a servant for all officials and clean furniture, sweep floor, wash dishes.

2. March 30 1990: Fleeing from Vietnam for the second time, and it was successful after a one month long trip to Hong Kong.

FEAR OF PERSECUTION IF BEING SENT BACK TO VIETNAM:

I would like to present hereafter my fear of being persecuted by the Vietnamese authorities if I am sent back to Vietnam which will be based on the definition of the 1951 Convention relating to the refugee status.

1. COMING FROM AN ANTI-COMMUNIST THREE-GENERATION FAMILY:

Based on the above mentioned facts, the Vietnamese authorities have classified my family as a BAD and REACTIONARY one which has been against communism for three generations, since the time of my grandfather, father, and my siblings. During long years under the Vietnamese communist prisons, most of my family members somehow had to partly pay the 'BLOOD DEBT' which the Vietnamese Authorities have placed on us because of our involvement in the former regimes and of our political opinions which are different from communism. We have been offered no social rights like other people. The Laws of Vietnam did not and do not protect us as impartially as others. We have to always bend our heads and swallow our bitterness to survive in a society where people are constantly educated and brainwashed by the authorities to discriminate against such families as ours. Besides, we had to and have to struggle one hundred times more than ordinary people to survive.

2. BEING A MEMBER OF A PARTICULAR SOCIAL GROUP:

As stated above, I was an Artillery Second Lieutenant of the ARVN. After the fall of South Vietnam, I was sent to re-education camps for six years and afterwards four years of house arrest. During the following years, I had citizenship rights, ID card, and census records. I though that I might have a normal life, but the reality was that it was not to be. For example, an ordinary citizen could sing or listen to 'yellow' music, and nothing happened consequently, even though 'yellow music' has been banned in the communist regime. But, from the political viewpoint of communists, I would certainly be accused of 'still being fond of the old regime'. Any cadre could say 'US goods are better than Vietnamese' with no problems, but if I did it, I would certainly be accused of 'still venerating the US Empire'.

Often, when I had to report to the local security officers at the police office, I was commanded by the chief security officer to take off my glasses and squat in the corner. I was not allowed to stand. However, the other people in the office were not ordered to do so. Fifteen years under the yoke of the communist regime were 15 years I had always to bend my head down in front of the local public security officers. The image of the Vietnamese communist security officers and years of re-education have haunted my frequent nightmares. All because 'I am a re-educated puppet Second Lieutenant'.

3. HAVING POLITICAL OPINIONS WHICH DIFFER FROM COMMUNISM:

On March 13 1990, as stated supra, I escaped before the local public security officers discovered the contents of the two cassette tapes. This consequently resulted in a 'Warrant of Arrest' which accused me of 'STORING AND CIRCULATING REACTIONARY DOCUMENTS - ESCAPE - DETRIMENTAL TO THE STATE SECURITY'. The two cassette tapes originally came from the 'Forum of Freedom' Group, headed by a group of South Vietnamese intellectuals, comprising of Mr. DOAN VIET HOAT. Mr. HOAT had been an old friend of my brother SON when the two were studying in the USA and had come back to Vietnam in 1971. Mr. HOAT was the very person who supplied to my brother those above mentioned political pamphlets and the cassette tape of 'Letter from the Heart sent to Strugglers'. The content of the tape does not call for a military struggle or the overthrow of the Vietnamese communist government. The tape directly expresses the certain and obvious collapse of the socialist bloc in front of the wave of democracy in the world. The omissions, mistakes of the Vietnamese communist government in every field, like the economy, politics, during the past years, the call for the awakening of Vietnamese communist leaders to political changes of the world were in the tape. It also expressed not to ignore or throw away the only chance so as to follow the Eastern European countries' examples to develop the country and bring welfare and happiness to the Vietnamese people. It called for all sectors in the population to grab this only chance for peaceful struggle to force the Vietnamese authorities to actually implement the genuine democracy and freedom. It called for the Vietnamese communist party to end its monopolistic role and give back real freedom to every branch such as education, communication, press, culture.

The intention of the 'Forum of Freedom' group does not aim at forming a political party other than calling for the awakening of all sectors in society to organise self-help groups to ask for democracy and freedom. Personally, formerly as well as presently, I have always agreed with the view points of struggle of this group for it shares my main concern for the welfare and happiness of my people. In February 1991, the First Day of the Year of the Horse (Lunar Calendar), my brother HAI phoned me from Norway, at the Sek Kong CFSI office, to send New Year greetings to me. He informed me that the Vietnamese authorities had arrested several members of the 'Forum of Freedom', Mr. DOAN VIET HOAT included. As for my brother SON, he had moved to his wife's home village at Vinh Long Town after my escape in order to avoid the impending harassment by the local authorities.

I firmly believe that after the arrest of the 'Forum of Freedom' members, the Vietnamese security officers probably know that the two cassette tapes seized from me was the product of this group. For this main reason, I really have a great fear of being arrested and imprisoned by the Vietnamese authorities if I was to be sent back to Vietnam.

DOCUMENTS AND PHOTOGRAPHS WHICH CAN SUPPORT OR PROVE MY CLAIMS

1. MY DOCUMENTS AND PHOTOGRAPHS:

Pre-1975:
- Baccalaureate diploma I, stamped on 26/8/1968.
- Baccalaureate diploma II, stamped on 5/8/1969.
- Certificate of the first year, faculty of education, VAN HANH University, stamped on 15/8/1972.
- 'In-service certificate' issued by the DONG DE Military Training Centre on 11/8/1972.
- 'Marriage certificate' issued by the General Staff Office of the ARVN on 7/2/1974.
- 4 photographs of me, showing that I am wearing military uniform.
All these document and photograph support my claim of being a serviceman of the ARVN.

Post 1975:
- 'Release order', issued and stamped by the XUAN PHUOC camp management on 28/05/81.
This supports my statement of being re-educated by the Vietnamese communist authorities for six years.

- 'The Citizenship Right Restoration Determination', issued on 23 October 1984.
- 'Identity Card', issued by the HCM City Public Security on 23 October 1985.

These support my statements of being under house arrest for over four years.

- 'Decree Absolute' issued and stamped by the Tan Binh District People's Court on 24 November 1989.
This supports my statements of being divorced and of being a lottery ticket hawker.
- Some pages (Pages 770-777) of the novel 'DAI HOC MAU' (Blood University) written by HA THUC SINH, one of my fellow campmates.
This supports my statements of being at TAN HIEP Re-education Camp and leading the human rights movement against the camp authorities at K4.

2. FAMILY MEMBERS' DOCUMENTS AND PHOTOGRAPHS:

FATHER
- 'Letter of Certification', issued and stamped by the PHAN DINH PHUNG High School on 12 July 1954.
This supports my statement that my father was a teacher in Hanoi, North Vietnam, prior to 1954.

- 'Teaching Permit', issued and stamped by the Director of Private School and Mass Education Directorate of the then Republic of Vietnam (RVN) on 1 October 1963.
This supports my statement about the fact that my father kept on teaching after fleeing from North Vietnam to South Vietnam at PHAN SAO NAM High School.

BROTHER 1: P. N. HAI
- 'Graduation Diploma of BAN THAM SU', issued and signed by the Dean of the National Institute of Administration on 10 December 1968.
- 'Graduation Diploma of BAN DOC SU' (Bachelor of Art in Administration), issued by the Dean of the National Institute of Administration on 30 December 1974.
- One photograph of him, showing that he is wearing military uniform.
These support my statements regarding my brother's background that he was a high-ranking government official of the former regime.

BROTHER 2: P. L. SON
- 'Diploma of Master of Science in Petroleum Engineering', issued by the University of Texas, USA, Austin on 15 May 1971.
- 'Marriage Certificate' issued in the State of Texas on 28 May 1970.
These support my statements that my second brother graduated from USA with the degree of MS in 1971.
- 'Duty Card', issued by the Petroleum and Minerals Department of the RVN on 14 March 1975.
These support my statements that my second brother worked for the RVN as Director Assistant of Project Service.

- Photographs of him, showing that his marriage in the USA, and the time (1972) when he was participating in the military basic infantry training at the DONG DE Military Training Centre, NHA TRANG with me.

BROTHER 3: P. L. CHUNG
- 'In-service Certificate', issued on 21 August 1972 by Colonel NGUYEN DINH GIAO.
This supports my statement that he was an ARVN Air Force serviceman.

All of these above-mentioned details are respectfully submitted with the hope that they will be helpful in the examination of my claims for refugee status. Thank you very much for your generosity.

Very respectfully yours,

P. L. HUNG

The personal context: Case 2

This is a case of the refugee claim by a young brother and his sister. The immigration department considered the younger brother as the principal applicant on the basis of gender. Even though, the sister is older and can speak better English than her brother. The immigration authorities decided to reject refugee status to both of them without interviewing or considering the experiences of the elder sister.

(The case of Mr NGUYEN VAN)

Mr. Buu and his sister Ms. Van's claim for refugee status were rejected. Their mother was Chinese and father was Vietnamese. Hence Mr Buu and his sister wrote their case initially in Chinese on which they had very little grasp, as they did not study Chinese formally. The final format was translated into English by one of their co-asylum seeker. Their elder brother was already settled in USA and had acquired US citizenship. He was willing to sponsor them to US for re-settlement. However, this didn't help them much. On the contrary, apparently, their case was weakened by this fact, as their motivation to leave was doubted. They came to Hong Kong in 1989 immediately after Hong Kong changed its asylum policy, and started screening asylum seekers for refugee status determination. They did not know about the changes in Hong Kong immigration policy and the detention procedure till they arrived in Hong Kong.

Mr Buu's refugee claim:

I am N. T. BUU, born in 1970 at Bienttoa City, Buddhist in religious belief, educated up to 8th grade (8/12). I left Vietnam on April 18, 1989 and arrived in Hong Kong on June 17, 1989, with my older sister. My father N. C. BANG was born in 1926 at Haiphong. He is also a Buddhist by religious belief. He was a Vice-Director of Bienttoa Sugar factory and a correspondent for two publications. My mother is T. T. LAN HUONG born in 1925 at Thuan Hai Province, she is Chinese in origin and also a practising Buddhist. She was a Chinese medicinal herb seller and the owner of a husked rice factory. Now she renounced all her worldly belongings and is residing at An Quang Pagoda in Ho Chi Min City. I have three brothers, N. T AUC, N. T. TAI and N. T. MAN. Mr. Auc was born in 1962 at Saigon, completed his education in Vietnam up to 7th grade, and is currently living and working at Santa Ana, California. Mr. Tai was born in 1963. He is also currently living and working in California. My younger brother Mr. Man was born in 1965 in Saigon, his address and details of his whereabouts are unknown to the family. My sister N. T. H. VAN was born in 1967 in Saigon, and is currently living with me in the camp.

My father was formerly a vice-director of the Sugar Factory BIENHOA, and he was also correspondent of two newspapers, White and Black and The Great National. When the communist took over South Vietnam he genuinely feared about his freedom and dignity. He anticipated persecution and revenge because of his writings in the newspaper. He wrote several articles supporting the republic of Vietnam government against the Northern Communist before the communist take-over. Fearing persecution, my father went underground to evade re-education and he did not present himself before the communists' when they began confiscating our property, land, farm, and our house. Our house located in 'Bten Hoa' was confiscated. The Republic government of Vietnam granted this house to us. My father was the owner of the house because he was the vice-director of the sugar factory. So my family had to move to THUAN Hai province.

Our second house was located at XX Galong Street Phan Thiet. My mother owned this house along with two other buildings, namely the husked rice factory called 'Hiephoa' and the Chinese medicine herb shop called 'Dai An Hoa'. My father evaded communist detection for nearly two years, hiding in Phan Thiet. He tried to escape from Vietnam for the first time in March 1977, but was arrested and sent to jail. He was released in November 1977. My parents arranged our escape again. We tried to escape again in March of 1978. This attempt was also unsuccessful. This time the authorities confiscated our belongings and properties. They forced our family to go to the new economic zone at Nghi Auc. In June 1978, my father was arrested and he was sent to re-education camp.

Since our first unsuccessful attempt to escape from Vietnam, my family was under close observation (spied) by the local authorities. In June 1978, our house at XX

Galong Street Phan Thiet was confiscated, and my mother and we were again sent to new economic zone at Nehi Duc, at Phan Han Thiet province while my father was still in re-education camp. The house was confiscated because my mother was an ethnic Chinese and as the wife of the vice-director, our family was rich according to the local standards.

While we were living in NEZ, my mother had a very difficult time to bring us up. She had never done any manual job earlier in her life. She got malaria and was taken to the hospital in Phan Thiet. After a few months we escaped from the NEZ to Saigon with the help of our aunt. We began living at her house in XXX HUNG Vaong Street at Saigon. After a month of our stay at my aunt's place the local authorities were suspicious about her house and kept a vigil at her house. My aunt was forced to bribe the police, for not creating any problems for us.

During 1978 - 1980 after two years residing temporally in Saigon, I was refused permission to go to public school but we were allowed to attend only the night school. While we were temporarily residing in Saigon with my aunt we had to support ourselves to avoid the heavy burden on my aunt in running the household. My mother sold glutinous rice at the hamlets and at schools in the afternoon and helped to augment my aunt's meagre income. My two brothers had to repair bicycles at the roadside and the third brother sold ice cream in the market. My sister supported the family by doing odd things at home. Life was a miserable struggle to meet both ends. We led a hand to mouth existence. My mother and my brothers were forced to do free labour for the local government. They were asked to clean the dust, and clear the garbage.

From 1980 to 1985, I continued to attend the additional night school and helped my mother and my aunt during daytime. My brothers continued to repair bicycle for a living. They used to work till late at night hoping to get a few more customers. Staying late for customers also was not easy. They had to explain to the police the reason they were working late away from home. On March 10, 1982, when working as cycle repairmen, my brothers were arrested for not paying tax and repairing cycles without a license. They were arrested and their tools were confiscated. While they were loading the confiscated goods in the trucks, taking advantage of the crowded street, my eldest brother ran away and disappeared in the street. But the second brother along with their tools and some of his friends were arrested and taken into custody.

My brother's friends were released after initial interrogation. My brother was detained after the preliminary interrogation citing that his father was a vice-director of a company and also the correspondent of a defunct newspaper and belongs to a reactionary family. The other complaints were that his elder brother ran away with **his support and he must know where he is hiding, and they did not pay tax for their** trade. The police began making trouble by coming daily to my family looking for my elder brother. They arrested the whole family and took us to the local police station to investigate my elder brother's whereabouts.

After interrogating nearly all through the day, they told my mother to pay tax immediately. They freed my mother, aunt, the third brother, and my sister. But they kept my younger brother in custody. After 10 days, they could not locate our elder brother. They suspected that our family was aware of the whereabouts of my elder brother. They again arrested my second brother and put him in prison. He was transferred to Tonglechan camp on March 20, 1982 for re-education. They alleged that my brother showed disrespect to the party cadres. When he was at Tonglechan camp, my family received news that my eldest brother managed to escape from Vietnam and was living in Thailand. He was at the Thailand refugee camp from 1985 to 1987 till he was resettled in the USA. In 1985, my mother was already 60 years old. She often talked about how she missed her children, and her wish to see all of them grow up and gather together in the family. Everybody enjoys living in happiness but after the fall of Saigon our family was shattered into pieces. Our family was scattered and has never been able to gather together. She was a faithful Buddhist. She could not do anything to help improve the situation, but became a heavy burden on her sister. Now she spends her time doing religious duties at An Quanc pagoda, and has denounced all worldly affairs.

On April 30, 1975, my second brother was set free after three years in prison. Often, the local authorities followed us, we never had opportunity to get a job or learn a trade in our society. We were allowed to work as a porter at the rice market for a living. Our miserable condition continued. On August 28, 1987, my father was set free. But he could not live in the house. He had to present himself and sleep in the local police post till September 2, 1987. During this time the local authorities closely monitored the movements of my father. Since he had to present himself before the local authorities, he hardly went anywhere. Sometimes, he discreetly visited some of his friends, the other correspondents of Black-White newspaper. I was told, later on that his friends and collages did not present themselves before the government and they were evading their re-education order. One day, when my father was talking with his friends, suddenly the police came in and caught three persons, two of them ran out, my father was arrested. He was set free after a month but his colleague were kept under detention.

My father was told that if he continued with his anti-party activities, he would receive the same fates of his friends'. During this time I was dismissed from the additional night school at the beginning of the eighth grade. My father was depressed and sad about the education of his children and the family was being affected by his activities. He began making plans for our escape for the third time during October 1987. As part of our escape plan, we moved to Bocong province. We were divided into several small groups to avoid detection. My sister and I were in one group. When the appointed time came, we used a small boat to reach the escape vessel. My second brother was waiting on board for us. Only he was lucky enough to escape this time. The guards along with the other group consisting of my third brother and my father spotted the boat, in which my sister and I were. The guards began shooting at our boat in which my sister and I was.

All our boats were widely separated in an attempt to escape from the coast guards. The escape vessel speeded away to avoid being caught. We were in the sea for a day and our engine failed. One fishing boat towed us to the shore at 'Lono Hai'. All the women and children were on board of the fishing boat and the men had to stay in the towed boat. When we approached the shore, the fishing boat let our boat go. Still the engine was not working, and the boat floated to Vungtan after several hours of trying to repair the engine. The coastal guards arrested all of us. We were taken to the Judge at Tien Gang Province and we were detained at Tien Biang prison for attempted illegal escape. After one month in Tien Gang prison they sent me to the re-education camp at My Phuoc.

I was kept in prison from 26/10/1987 to 1/9/1988 at the re-education camp at MyPhuoc at Tien Gang province. At this time, my family was in a miserable situation. At the time of escaping my second brother (Mr. Tai) luckily went out of Vietnam. My father, my third brother, the fourth sister did not manage to go out. I was in the prison; my father and my third brother had to hide themselves as animals. They did not return to the locality. My sister, VAN, as she was a girl, the police put her in prison only for a short time. My family had been torn to pieces, and we never could get-together again.

On 1/9/1988, I was temporarily set free. After spending a long time in MyPhuoc Prison when I came home, the police again arrested me and kept me in the police post until 3/9/1991. But, every week I had to present myself to the local government on Sundays and had to do cover in the locality. I lived at my aunt's house until 10/4/1998, then the police reported me and my sister out of the city. They forcibly made my aunt to write a letter that promised not to keep my sister and me in her house anymore. Therefore, my sister and I had to go to the NET NGFM DVIC. We would be hopeless and desperate if we didn't obey the decision of the local government. The police constantly made trouble for my aunt. We couldn't live in NET, we had no place to live and were afraid of falling down the same situation as before. We decided to leave Vietnam. I felt that we had no basic human rights, my family was persecuted and discriminated. Our family was divided into pieces so we decided to escape from Vietnam. That is why I escaped from Vietnam.

Ms Van, Mr Duc's sister was never called to present her claim or to corroborate her brother's claim. Duc was 18 and his sister was 21 years old when they arrived in Hong Kong. They were assigned separate bunks in different locations in the camp. Their elder brother from the US came all the way to Hong Kong to meet his younger siblings and to rescue them from the camp. He managed to meet them for a few hours in the visitor's room, behind barbed wires, under the gaze of the police officers. He was not allowed to present their case to any of the local authorities.

Section 2

The international political context

The framework presented in the second chapter of this book presents the international political context as a distant determinant of such process. In this Section the international political context of Vietnamese asylum seeking process and their subsequent segregation by the host culture is elaborated by analysing various political factors associated with the international political initiatives which has direct bearing on the social conditions of the asylum seeker detention camps.

In order to understand the phenomenon of Vietnamese seeking asylum in a neighbouring country, there is a need to explore the role of different international forces and interests involved in influencing the refugee movement. It is important to understand, how these interests changed over a period time. Various factors contributed to this shift. USA's foreign policy in Indo-China region and it's political designs in the Asia region, the role of United Nations especially United Nations High Commission for Refugees (UNHCR), the policies of British government in dealing with the refugees, are some of the important factors which are discussed in this Section.

International initiatives can often influence various factors directly related to the process of ethnocide. These factors are
a) duration of detention
b) flow of return migration
c) detention policy
d) monitoring the quality of living conditions in the camps
e) resource allocation for social services and the over all direction of the asylum seekers future life.

Most importantly, the refugee issue in Hong Kong should also be understood in the context of 'cold war' strategies to contain the spread of communism, and efforts to ridicule and undermine the legitimacy of communist regimes, particularly under the leadership of the **United** States of

America. The human consequences of such a policy continue to linger even after the cold war strategy was retracted.

During the first seven months of 1979, 66,000 asylum seekers came to Hong Kong, prompting the then British Prime Minister, Margaret Thatcher, to initiate an international conference to discuss the problem. The Hong Kong governor at that time, Sir Murray Maclehose, visited London, New York, Washington and Geneva to warn the international community, that if nothing effective was done internationally, patience in the recipient territories could snap, with disastrous results.

The 1979 Geneva conference on Indo Chinese refugees had a double-edged success. It resulted in pledges for a world-wide resettlement program and an undertaking by the Vietnamese government that it would take steps to control 'illegal' departures of refugees. Pledges made by the participating countries at the Geneva conference rose to about 260,000 resettlement places for the Vietnamese refugees in South East Asian camps. Before the conference only 130,000 places were available. Adequate funds were also allocated for the UNHCR to administer the resettlement program.

As part of other global initiatives by the UNHCR, the government of Socialist Republic of Vietnam and UNHCR signed an agreement to provide legal provision for the departure of persons from Vietnam with close family links abroad. This agreement became known as the 'Orderly Departure Program (ODP). The initial response of international community was to provide a 'humanitarian' shelter for thousands of asylum seekers who were seeking refuge in other South East Asian Countries. By the end of 1988, the rate of arrivals in South East Asian countries exceeded the offers of resettlement. The first asylum countries shared the feeling that they would be left with a large number of asylum seekers, once the resettlement quota was over. In this context the Malaysian government requested the UNHCR to work towards evolving more durable solutions for the asylum seekers.

According to Knudsen (1990) the Vietnamese asylum seekers in Hong Kong were prisoners of international politics, and their fate as refugees and asylum seekers in Hong Kong are intricately interwoven with several international political factors. The local, regional and international politics play an important role in shaping their adaptation capabilities with the host society.

The United Nations as the inter-governmental organisation provided the essential framework for durable solutions of the refugee situation. United

Nations hosted two major international conferences to deal with the issues related to the Indo-Chinese refugees. The United Nations High Commission for Refugees (UNHCR) is the United Nation's body instrumental in offering protection, assistance and durable solutions for the Vietnamese asylees in South East Asia.

The complexity of the refugee issue in South East Asia was made more complicated due to several 'political interests', involved. The decisions influencing the daily life of asylum seekers in the camps was often taken by people who were far away from the actual life experiences of the asylees. As a large number of political factors was operating in shaping the 'Hong Kong refugee scene', analysing the role of each force would be an important contribution towards understanding the situation. Some of these dominant factors are:

a) Foreign policy and public opinion of the United States of America on South East Asia;

b) Refugee policy of countries accepting Vietnamese refugees, commonly known as 'third countries' or 'resettlement countries';

c) Refugee policy of first asylum countries like the Philippines; Indonesia; Malaysia; and Hong Kong in offering temporary asylum for the Vietnamese.

d) Special role of the British government in relation to Vietnamese asylum seekers in Hong Kong.

e) Local UK-Hong Kong government policies,

f) Local public opinion,

g) The role of United Nations and the UNHCR,

h) The interpretation of the Comprehensive Plan of Action (CPA) to deal with the South East Asian asylum seekers,

i) Non-Governmental Organisations (NGO) and inter-governmental agencies like International Organisation for Migration (IOM); Search and Rescue Organisation;

j) Local regional and International agencies involved in a variety of functions,

k) Vietnamese governments' decision regarding the treatment of the asylees,

l) Re-reintegration structures in Vietnam,

m) Function and role of resettlement agencies in Vietnam,

n) Chinese government's political initiatives on refugees in the context of transfer of sovereignty of Hong Kong to the Chinese government,

o) Other regional refugee assistance institutions.

p) The capacity of asylum seekers who were determined as non refugees,

q) The political leverage of refugee groups resettled in a third country.

The comprehensive plan of action (CPA)

The second major initiative of the international community resulted in the second Geneva conference on Indo Chinese refugees. It was held on 13 and 14 June 1989, at Geneva. The participating countries adopted a Comprehensive Plan of Action (CPA) to deal with the Vietnamese refugee situation. CPA offered an administrative framework to deal with the Vietnamese refugee issue. However, the real basis of CPA was to present a humanitarian face to a haphazardly planned and clumsily executed 'cold war' strategy. CPA was presented as an international humanitarian response towards the massive exodus of refugees from Vietnam. Seventy-six Countries met in Geneva to identify solutions for the problem that was fourteen-year-old at that time. The 'Comprehensive Plan of Action' proposed that all the Vietnamese asylum seekers who arrived in a 'first asylum country' had to go through a refugee status determination procedure.

During the Conference, the British Secretary of State for Foreign and Commonwealth affairs claimed that the burden on Hong Kong had become intolerable. He warned that without an early action on all the aspects of CPA, Hong Kong would 'simply be unable any longer to maintain the policy of first Asylum' indicating that it was the British government's decision on Hong Kong policy towards the Vietnamese refugees. Also perhaps it was an indication that the patience of British government's support for the ill-planned cold war strategy was wearing thin.

The main points of CPA included:
1) Strategies to discourage clandestine departures from Vietnam, with the help of mass media, at both local and international level.
2) It proposed to open regular channels of immigration from Vietnam as an alternative to clandestine departures. Orderly Departure Program was encouraged as opposed to clandestine departure.
3) Temporary refuge was to be offered to all asylum seekers from Vietnam.
4) A region-wide refugee status determination process was determined on the basis of the 1951 convention on the status of refugees, and its 1967 protocol was to be applied in the humanitarian spirit.
5) An international program for resettlement of Vietnamese refugees was proposed. This program was aimed at all refugees who reached the first

asylum countries of South East Asia before the CPA was implemented and 'the newly recognised refugees' were determined through the new 'Refugee Determination Process'.

6) Non refugees were requested to go back and efforts were to be made to facilitate their voluntary return.

7) A special trilateral arrangement between the UNHCR, Thailand and Laos was proposed to deal with the asylum seekers from Laos.

8) A steering committee was appointed by the conference to undertake the necessary follow up for the Plan of Action.

One of the major drawbacks of CPA was it failed to take into consideration of the social and cultural consequence of detention of asylum seekers. However, when looking at the merit of CPA from the point of view of an administrative response to contain a backfired 'cold war' strategy, one cannot expect much of a genuine human concern. In the global refugee history perhaps, Vietnamese refugees are (and small number of Cambodians and Laotian) the only group of refugees who received such unique initiatives such as a 'comprehensive plan of action'.

The role of United States of America, its foreign policy and public opinion

This part of the study briefly analyses the political role of the United States Foreign Policy in South East Asia and the role of public opinion in shaping the pattern, nature, and direction, of asylum seekers adaptation to the Hong Kong society. Due to various geo-political factors, USA was forced to re-evaluate it's political interest in South East Asia at the fag end of cold war era. This had a direct impact on the future of refugees stranded in the South East Asian region.

In order to understand the role played by the US foreign policy and public opinion in shaping the current situation, it is necessary to understand the historical context of this process. The Americans were already in Vietnam even before the French forces captured Saigon in 1861. The first American Captain John White of Salem, Massachusetts, set foot in Vietnam in 1820. According to Karnow (1983), the involvement of the United States in its longest - and undeclared- war- didn't start when the first American combat battalions splashed ashore at Danang in March 1965. As early as 1950, France, supported by the United States, was fighting to regain its hold in Indochina against the communist led nationalist movement. On July 26, 1950, Truman signed a legislation granting $15 million in military aid to the French for the war in Indochina.

The 1954 'Geneva agreement' provided a settlement to the first Indo China war. According to this agreement Vietnam was to be divided at the 17th parallel until the general elections were held in 1956 for the whole of Vietnam. However, the elections were never held. The Northern part of Vietnam controlled by the 'Vietminh' - the Vietnamese resistance movement who fought against the French forces from 1946 to 1954 - formed the Democratic Republic of Vietnam. (DRV). The southern part under the leadership of Ngo Dinh Diem formed the Republic of Vietnam (RV), with the support of United States. Eisenhower's special envoy, General Collins, arrived in Saigon to affirm American support to South Vietnam, including a $100 million aid.

As a prelude to the massive refugee outflow from Vietnam, hundreds of thousands of refugees fled from North Vietnam to South Vietnam with the help of US Navy. By 1955, United States began to funnel aid directly to the Saigon government and also agreed to train the South Vietnam Army in their assault against communist North Vietnam. The 'Vietnam era' began with the ambush of American Major Dale and Sergeant Chester by the Communist guerrillas on July 8, 1959. Thus began the 16-year-old (direct and indirect) American intervention.

The late 1960s' massive domestic upheaval in the USA against it's involvement in Vietnam - popularly known as 'Vietnam era' provided a venue for political socialisation of an entire generation of American youth. By 1968, the American troops in Vietnam increased to 540,000. During 1970, the public protest against American involvement in Vietnam reached its peak. The infamous 'Kent University incident' took place on May 4, 1970, when the National guardsmen killed four anti-war students at the University campus in Ohio. The largest ever helicopter evacuation on record occurred on April 29, 1975, when the Americans were evacuated from Vietnam. The very next day guerrillas took over South Vietnam. Thus beginning the mass exodus of Vietnamese in search of asylum.

The Americans lost about the 55, 000 soldiers in a futile war in Vietnam. Some 2,200 servicemen are still officially listed as missing. This emotional and political factor contributed toward USA decision to humiliate the Communist Vietnam by whatever means, including encouraging a large number of Vietnamese dissidents to leave the country.

The first 'visible' Vietnamese refugees who entered into the US were 'orphaned children', evacuated by the American 'humanitarian operation' known as 'operation baby lift'. It was a political drama rather than a humanitarian venture. The arrival of the 'war orphans' generated massive public support in the USA. Dignitaries received the children at the airport, and the media gave wide coverage that attracted public sympathy and contributions from individuals and corporations. Many volunteered to give assistance to these children. The public mood was culminated into a necessary legislation, the Indo-Chinese Migration and Refugee Assistance Act of 1975 (PL 94-23) (Eisenhart, and Wayne, 1984). Not much is written about what happened to these children, the process of their adaptation to the host society and their personal life histories.

When the United States military evacuated Saigon on April 29, 1975, tens of thousands of Vietnamese people in small boats followed the retreating Sixth Fleet into the South China Sea. They were taken to processing centres in the Pacific and then moved to one of the four reception centres in the United States - Arkansas, California, Florida and Pennsylvania. It is estimated that from April 1975, until December 31, 1975, about 138,000 Indo-Chinese refugees entered the United States. Since 1975, until December 1991, 69,338 Vietnamese were resettled in the United States from Hong Kong alone. The initial wave of refugees from Vietnam were South Vietnamese government functionaries and dignitaries who believed that the US government owed them refuge, since they helped them fight Communist North Vietnam.

The Voice of America (VOA), and the British Broadcasting Corporation (BBC) radio transmissions to Vietnam were the main source of external information for the asylum seekers. According to many of the asylum seekers, the VOA actively encouraged its listeners to leave Vietnam in order to seek freedom.

The 'Amerasian Refugee Children' was another touchy issue for American public. Amerasian refugees were children of American fathers (usually servicemen) and Southeast Asian mothers. Most of these children have been raised in single parent households with little or no education. The US government responded to this population by framing legislation for their migration and subsequent integration into the American life by introducin the 'home coming act'.

Impact of the economic embargo

South Vietnam received US $1.6 billion annually during the war that was about 70 per cent of the national budget. During the same period the Soviet Union's grants and aid to the then North Vietnam ranged from US $ 270 million to US $ 1 billion. This was the major source of economic sustenance for Vietnam. After the victory of North Vietnam, American aid and support dwindled and finally completely vanished. Because of the withdrawal of economic assistance by the international community under the leadership of the US, the economic crisis in Vietnam aggravated. The economic situation worsened during Vietnam's war with Cambodia. The Chinese government alone cancelled a US $ 300 million aid to Vietnam. The continuing economic embargo by the international community at the insistence of US was a major block for the reintegration of Vietnam into the world economy. Vietnam remained chronically poor under the burden of an economic embargo. Vietnam remained chronically poor under the burden of an economic embargo.

A change in the US policy to lift the economic embargo imposed would accelerate reintegration and enable the return of Vietnamese asylum seekers determined as non-refugees, who are reluctant to return from Hong Kong refugee camps. This would enhance the process of voluntary repatriation of Vietnamese asylum seekers from the South East Asian camps. If it is assumed that several asylum seekers specially from the fishing villages of North Vietnam were merely 'economic migrants' rather than 'political refugees', then the US lead economic embargo on Vietnam had direct bearing upon the economic distress which led to population displacement.

Several lobbies within the country actively resisted any move by the US to lift the economic embargo on Vietnam. The dominant groups among them were the relatives of the American military personnel 'Missing In Action', or Prisoners Of War (MIA-POW) allegedly unaccounted by the Vietnam government. South Vietnamese communities resettled abroad also strongly opposed any move to normalise American relations with Vietnam and to resume Economic Aid. They argued that economic aid would only strengthen the hold of 'communist dictators' within Vietnam. It appears that this policy also might have contributed to the prolongation of detention centre camp life of several asylum seekers.

The US opposition to forced repatriation

The British-Hong Kong government used forced deportation of Vietnamese from Hong Kong camps as an alternative to the voluntary repatriation program for 'screened out' non-refugees. The US was consistently opposed to any forced repatriation of Vietnamese asylum seekers who were determined as non-refugees. Several prominent US public figures consistently took interest in Vietnamese refugees in different ways. In December 1988, a bipartisan group of 40 experts on Indochina called for talks between the new Bush administration and first asylum countries aimed at pressurising

Vietnam into dealing with the refugee exodus. This group also urged the newly elected president to obtain immediate promises from other industrialised democracies to accept a larger share of refugees from South East Asian camps.

Hong Kong detention camps came under severe criticism by the former US president Jimmy Carter. On July 12, 1987, he denounced the camps as prisons for several thousand Vietnamese. Connie Mack, the US senator on a visit to Hong Kong on August 22, 1989, opposed the Hong Kong policy of forced repatriation. On September 16 1989 the second most senior official of the US State department, Mr. Lawrence Eagleburger, rejected the British demands for forced repatriation of the Vietnamese asylees. On December 6 1989 another US congressman Mr. John Porter went on record to express his opposition for forced repatriation. He warned that mandatory repatriation of Vietnamese asylum seekers could damage Hong Kong's chance for a safety net of foreign passports in the wake of transfer of Hong Kong sovereignty to China in 1997.

On February 10, 1990, the US State department Deputy Secretary Lawrence Eagleburger, told US congressmen that Hong Kong's policy of forced repatriation of Vietnamese boat people was viewed with total abhorrence within the top levels of the Bush administration. Soon after the 'Gulf War', US congressman, Mr. Robert Dornan presented a proposal to Mr. Bush, President of USA and the Emir of Kuwait, Sheikh Jabir al Ahamad al-Sabah, urging them to send Vietnamese from the South East Asian camps to rebuild Kuwait. He described the Vietnamese as hard workers, who would make model citizens. He urged the Emir to begin a feasibility study to allow the 'boat people' as guest workers. In his letter to Mr. Baker, the Secretary for State, he stated that even if Kuwait could be convinced to take just 10,000 of the 110,000 boat people from the South East Asian camps, it would have a tremendous practical and political benefit for all involved, especially USA. Moreover, The US would be recognised as the driving force behind the proposal. It is alleged that this proposal encouraged several Vietnamese to leave their country for Southeast Asian refugee camps. This also raised false hopes for many asylum seekers living in detention centres and strengthened their decision to remain in the camps. Even though, the US government vehemently protested against forced repatriation, it became a routine affair in mid 1990, so much so that, even interest in this issue in the US dissipated.

The role of US media

The United States media played a crucial role in directing favourable public opinion towards asylees in South East Asia. On June 21, 1989, 'The Washington Times', criticised Hong Kong's decision to repatriate Vietnamese asylees. The newspaper warned that Hong Kong people themselves might become refugees in need of a safe haven after the 1997 Chinese take-over of the territory.

The role of US NGOs

Several US NGOs were actively involved in advocating for better protection of human rights of the asylum seekers detained in Hong Kong. Their international diplomatic initiatives and lobbying had direct impact on the living conditions of the asylees in Hong Kong. 'Asia Watch', a US NGO, founded in 1985, to promote human rights, criticised the UK-Hong Kong government in failing to protect vulnerable groups of Vietnamese who were forced to return to Vietnam. In a report entitled 'Refugees at risk' (1992), Asia Watch criticised UK-Hong Kong government's failure to protect the 'Nung minorities' and persons who are liable to be punished as 'counter revolutionaries' by Vietnam because of their statements or associations during their long stay in Hong Kong.

Lawyers' committee for Human rights and the Women's Commission for Refugee Women and Children (1993), requested United Nations Human Rights Commission to send a working group to review UK-Hong Kong's arbitrary detention of asylum seekers, which was against the international principles. The lawyers' committee for human rights and the women's commission submitted a statement to the UN human rights commission that the Hong Kong policy of prolonged detention of Vietnamese asylum seekers violated international law. The immigration ordinance which was the basis of detention violated international law, which prohibited the actions prescribed by the immigration ordinance and also Hong Kong's actions were illegal under the international covenant on civil and political rights. These NGOs suggested that the U.K.-Hong Kong government should allow all Vietnamese to be at liberty and to be allowed to work until a comprehensive political resolution was arranged. As an alternative they suggested that the government should open the detention centres allowing free movement during daytime and all asylum seekers should be provided with an individual hearing by a judicial officer.

However, the callous handling of the Haitian refugee crisis by the Americans invited criticism and weakened the American position against forced repatriation of Vietnamese asylees in Hong Kong. The US policies and public opinion had a detrimental effect on the process of refugee adaptation, direction and the nature of adaptation. The international community under the leadership of the United Nations had worked out several solutions for the asylum seeker problem. All these initiatives were summed up as durable solutions.

'Durable solutions'

The internationally accepted durable solutions of refugee problems were resettlement, local integration, and voluntary repatriation. In the Hong Kong context it was decided, to encourage only resettlement and voluntary repatriation. Citing acute population density, local integration of Vietnamese was ruled out by the authorities, even temporary permission to freely stay in the territory was denied. One had to prove his/her claim for refugee status to immigration as a prerequisite to avail the resettlement option. The refugee status determination procedure was a long and cumbersome administrative process.

Refugee status determination procedure in Hong Kong

Prior to 16 June 1988, Vietnamese asylum seekers arriving in Hong Kong were automatically given refugee status and resettled. According to Hong Kong government, during the mid 1990's, it became increasingly clear that the great majority of asylum seekers did not possess a 'well found fear of persecution' in Vietnam and therefore were not entitled to refugee status (HK government, October 1992).

It is not clear how Hong Kong government reached this conclusion. The only significant change was that more North Vietnamese began seeking asylum in Hong Kong. Resettlement countries were reluctant to resettle North Vietnamese asylum seekers in large numbers. In the first five months of 1988, of the 5,000 refugees who arrived in Hong Kong only 1,000 were resettled. From 16 June 1988, all asylum seekers were subjected to 'hastily prepared refugee status determination procedures'. These were amended following an agreement between the Hong Kong government and UNHCR. It is not clear what remedial measures were taken towards asylum seekers who were caught in the middle.

It came as a rude shock for them to know that they would be detained as illegal immigrants in Hong Kong and would have to go through a refugee status determination procedure. Prior to their departure many asylum seekers did not know the new procedure. Several respondents claimed that if they had known about the detention they would not have attempted to come to Hong Kong. Unlike other South East Asian first Asylum countries it was unique of British-Hong Kong to detain all asylum seekers and imprison them for several years before they could even face a status determination procedure wherein a majority of them were screened out and deemed as non-refugees.

The Procedure

The Vietnamese asylum seekers after being intercepted in Hong Kong waters were placed in orderly lines and made to wait in the sun/rain placed in locked trucks escorted by the police to 'Green Island Reception Centre' where they are detained. This was the beginning of a series of moves through various camps. An immigration officer interviewed them first and collected basic personal data. The refugees who spent years in Vietnam not reacting to authority figures such as police and prison officials are now interviewed by similar figures, where a wrong answer in Vietnam would make them receive many years in New Economic Zones or some form of punishment.

The asylum seekers often gave information, which was not necessarily accurate or specific. This could be because of neglect or fear, or simply exhaustion. They were rescued after a tedious and perilous voyage in a fragile boat, and exposed to the vagaries of nature. However, in most cases the information given at the first interview invariably acted as a detrimental factor in their refugee status determination at a much later stage.

The information given in the first interview was cross-checked only at the formal refugee status determination interview after three or four years. Any discrepancy in the information is interpreted as 'doubtful credibility'. This information is then noted in the file in code for the information of immigration officers and UNHCR appeals lawyers. The refugee status determination interview varies from a few hours to several days. Usually only the principal refugee claimant, that is, the male member of the family is called for the interview. If other members of the family are called they are expected to know details of matters or events related to their spouse and members' of the family. Vietnamese families tend to be very large and knowing every detail of all the family members in the right chronological order is not easy.

Often, chronological events take more precedence than details. For example, the immigration officer might ask the wife of the principal applicant; 'tell us what your husband's elder brother was doing in 1978'. Often the objective of the cross-examination is to prove that the applicant is unreliable and does not merit refugee status. The asylum seekers were asked to present their 'life-story', rather than to file an application to claim refugee status.

The immigration officers conducted the interviews in Cantonese, through an interpreter who translated the questions and the answers between Cantonese and Vietnamese. The answers were recorded in English. Though the immigration officer was expected to ask questions based on an interview guide. Very few asylum seekers have seen a copy of this interview guide. At the earlier stages of the refugee saga, UNHCR deliberately withheld information on the existence of such interview guide from the asylum seekers, stating that they may create false stories to claim refugee status. This standardised interview guide itself was riddled with loopholes as it did not take into consideration gender and age variations of the respondents.

According to many of the respondents of this study such interviews took place in an intimidating and hostile environment. The interviewing officer was in uniform and no attempts were made to reduce the anxiety of the respondents. Swearing, calling names, ridiculing, shouting and banging on the table was often part of the interview process. The immigration officer often took only notes at the interview, the formal record was written after a few days. At the initial stages of the implementation of refugee status determination procedure, the asylum seeker had no opportunity to know what the immigration officer had written in the file till his/her case was rejected.

On the basis of the information given by an asylum seeker, immigration officers can take a decision to refuse refugee status with the endorsement of a Senior Immigration Officer. The immigration officers are also responsible in identifying cases for 'family reunification'. If an immediate relative of an asylum seeker have already been accepted as a refugee, the asylum seeker could join them through this procedure. After four to five weeks, the decision of the immigration office is communicated to the asylum seeker in writing. The individuals 'screened in' are then transferred to an open camp waiting to be sent to the regional transit Centre in the Philippines. Those screened out have the right to have their case reviewed through another administrative procedure, independent of the Immigration Department, known as the Refugee Status Review Board (RSRB). Being screened out in camp lingo is called 'first chicken wing'. This is because asylum seekers are served chicken wings every Wednesday the day this decision is made known to them also a chicken wing is not a 'flying wing' (implied that it will not help you to fly to a resettlement country).

Even though the British-Hong Kong Government claimed that UNHCR was monitoring several cases of refugee determination procedure, this argument was debatable. In any given week UNHCR-Hong Kong was capable of offering individual monitoring for less than 15 people, whereas immigration department claimed to be screening about 400 people in a week.

In essence, if an asylum seeker is well educated and receives a little help in preparing his refugee claim, he has a better chance than a poorly educated asylum seeker who is not able to grasp the legality of the refugee determination process.

Pre-screening legal counselling

UNHCR legal consultants offered pre-screening counselling on an ad hoc basis for asylum seekers. Mostly, the presentations were made to a group. Anybody could theoretically request for a pre-screening counselling. However, the asylum seekers were reluctant to use this facility. They were reluctant to disclose their case to the lawyers, because UNHCR also played the role of a judge. At the end of the arduous task of proving their refugee claim when all avenues had been exhausted the UNHCR could use their 'mandate' to give an asylum seeker refugee status. Even lawyers from Hong Kong Bar association were not allowed to represent the refugee claimants during the initial period of the refugee status determination process, as no clear guidelines were present. After an uphill battle by some socially conscious lawyers from the Hong Kong Bar, a precedent was set. Hong Kong lawyers were allowed to represent asylum seekers, but this was mostly after the first screening was completed by the Hong Kong immigration. By then a majority of them were already determined as 'non-refugees'.

The Jesuit Refugee Service (JRS) set up a small pre-screening counselling service in High Island Detention Centre (HIDC) in November 1990. They were soon asked to leave the camp, ironically, by the asylum seekers themselves. JRS was forced to close down their office in the HIDC as all the cases counselled by their staff lost their claim for refugee status. However, they soon opened an office in another detention camp. When the Hong Kong government established a Refugee Status Review Board (RSRB) to review cases of refugee claims rejected by the immigration department some of the lawyers left JRS to become part of the much more lucrative RSRB. Several asylum seekers who sought assistance of legal counselling from JRS staff genuinely panicked about their cases due to the potential conflict of interest. However, no effort was made by any agencies or authorities to reduce the anxiety of the asylum seekers. Often such issues were brushed aside as trivial.

At no stage of the refugee status determination procedure, did UNHCR or any other agencies, took any special efforts to offer copies of refugee status determination procedure to the refugees. A booklet was instead produced by the UNHCR, commonly known as the 'Blue Book' which provided general information for asylum seekers. This booklet was provided to all the 'head of the family' 'prior to screening', free of charge. This book was not a legal document and it did not give any clue regarding the finer aspects of refugee determination process in Hong Kong.

The Review procedure

A screened out asylum seeker could give a 'notice of application for review', within a period of 28 days. The copies of the immigration officer's file on those cases would then be passed on to the RSRB and the Agency for Voluntary Service (AVS, was a UNHCR administrated body), for appeal counselling. AVS took up cases that according to them were 'strong', and the AVS counsellor prepared a written submission to the RSRB. If the cases were not taken up by the AVS, there was an option to submit their case directly to the RSRB by the asylum seekers if they wished to do so, however, without any legal assistance.

The RSRB was an administrative body consisting of three Boards. Each Board consists of a Deputy chairman (A civil servant), and a member (a lay member of the public employed by RSRB. The Board would sit in closed sessions, neither the applicant nor the legal counsellor was allowed to be present). On rare occasions the board visited the asylum seekers in detention centres for reviewing the case. A UNHCR legal consultant would inevitable be present during such visits.

The Board's decision was made based on the information contained in the immigration officers file, written submission of the asylum seeker or the counsellor and further information if any. The immigration department's decision could be reversed with the vote of only one member of the Board, and the asylum seeker could be screened-in as a refugee. The immigration department informed the asylum seeker in writing the decision of the RSRB.

The UNHCR had also developed a system to review certain cases. The UNHCR mandate review board was working under the Assistant Chief of Mission in charge of the Legal Section. An AVS counsellor, any private lawyer representing a client, relatives of the asylum seekers, and the asylum seeker themselves could make a submission to the UNHCR mandate review board. UNHCR have mandated less than 1, 000 people in Hong Kong. It was estimated that an average of 12.7 per cent of the cases were screened-in as refugees at the first instance and 9.2 per cent were screened-in by the review procedure. Overall, about 20 per cent cases were decided positively.

Several authors and lawyers (AI 1990, Clark et al., 1990, Weil et al., 1993) have raised several drawbacks of the screening process. These drawbacks includes:

- The interviews were cursory.
- The interpreters were unqualified.
- The objective of screening was to 'exclude' and not to include the applicants as refugees.
- The applicants were ill informed about the screening process.
- UNHCR did not monitor all the cases.
- The details of the process was not an internationally accepted process even though it was claimed to be so.
- The refugee case review was not done by a judicial body but by an administrative body.
- Screening was considered as 'a matter of luck'.
- Most of the immigration officers were inexperienced and had no grasp of international refugee laws related to the refugees and asylum seekers, or the social and political conditions of Vietnam. Benefit of doubt in favour of the accused is an accepted legal principle. But in Hong Kong, if the immigration officer somehow doubted the statement of asylum seeker his/ her claim was rejected immediately.
- The process of accepting refugees was not based on humanitarian concern alone. Political concerns played a dominant role in this process. From an international political context, some group of asylum seekers were more 'desirable refugees' than others. The special desirability of refugees was determined by the historical, political, economic and diplomatic desirability of that group for 'international interests'. Internationally accepted 'durable solutions' of refugee problems were resettlement, local integration and repatriation. Most of the 'durable solutions' for a particular group of refugees was often dictated by the international political context. The political context

rather than altruistic tendencies of some Nations also dictated the degree, nature, intensity, and direction of adaptation or the process of Ethnocide of refugees.

Repatriation

The most suitable and durable solution for the refugee problem is considered to be voluntary repatriation to their home country. The repatriation practised in Hong Kong can be described as a process of change from limbo to the certainty of uncertainty. Local integration has not been considered as a possible solution for the Vietnamese in South East Asia. The emphasis was on resettling the refugees in a developed country until the screening policy was established. The CPA changed this process, emphasising the need to repatriate large numbers of asylum seekers back to Vietnam.

UNHCR and the Vietnamese Government signed a Memorandum of Understanding (MOU), regarding the voluntary repatriation of asylum seekers to Vietnam on December 13, 1988, in the spirit of Article 12 of the Comprehensive Plan of Action (CPA) adopted in June 1988. It stated that:

> Persons determined not to be refugees should return to their country of origin in accordance with international practice reflecting the responsibilities of states towards their own citizens. In the first instance, every effort will be made to encourage the voluntary return of such persons.

The Memorandum of Understanding signed by UNHCR and Vietnam government contained the following provisions to protect the interest of returnees.
a) The returnees would not be prosecuted or submitted to discriminatory treatment for their illegal departure.
b) UNHCR would have full access to the returnees and
c) The returnees would be assisted materially upon arrival in Vietnam.

The first Voluntary repatriation program was implemented in Hong Kong on March 2, 1989. Around 75 Vietnamese non-refugees were repatriated that day. UNHCR chartered special flights to repatriate them from Hong Kong. The expenditure of this exercise was equally divided between the Hong Kong government and the UNHCR. Since September 1990, according to an agreement between the Governments of Vietnam, United Kingdom, Hong

Kong and UNHCR, they extended the program to Vietnamese asylum seekers who 'did not object' to repatriation to Vietnam.

On December 12, 1989, eight men, 17 women, and 26 children who were 'screened out' were forcefully taken out of a detention centre by riot police around 4 am, under heavy security and flown to Hanoi in a specially chartered 'Cathay Pacific' flight, paving a new road in refugee repatriation from Hong Kong. The composition of the first batch that was forcefully repatriated was carefully selected. They were mainly women and children, only few were men.

Many screened-out asylum seekers clutched to the slim hope of further policy changes. They feared possible persecution, punishment or discrimination, once they went back to Vietnam. Given a proper environment and tangible economic and political changes in Vietnam, and subsequent information about such changes, voluntary repatriation might have emerged as a viable alternative for some of them. Many asylum seekers did not have any material incentive to go back to Vietnam. During the 1989-1992 period, 34 per cent of the returnees were unemployed (Fig 4.1 details of the occupations of the returnees).

An asylum seeker, both screened-out and not yet screened would decide

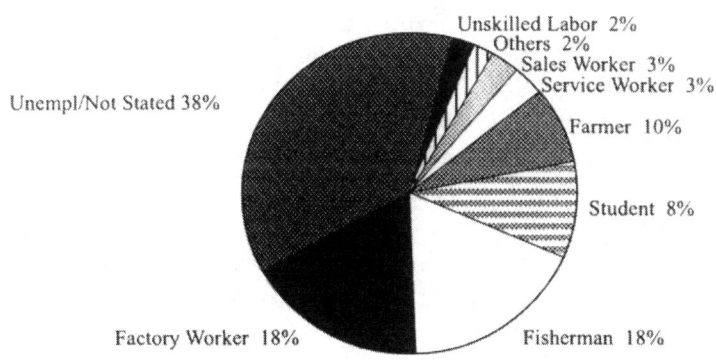

Respondents: 5,749 (Excludes Age <15)
Situation as of 29.02.92

Figure 4.1   Voluntary Repatriation to Vietnam. Occupations of 1989-1992 Returnees Hai Phong Province

to go back to Vietnam due to several reasons. There were also cases of refugees in the process of resettlement to another country, deciding to go back to Vietnam. Nostalgia, disillusionment, peer group pressure, family commitments, intolerable living conditions in the camp, advice from the agencies, UNHCR encouragement, overall camp conditions, feelings of hopelessness were some of the reasons that attributed to their decision to return to Vietnam voluntarily.

The UNHCR field staff offered regular briefing sessions for the camp population on voluntary repatriation procedures. Once the asylum seeker decides to return he/she would have to fill the voluntary declaration form regarding their whereabouts in Vietnam. This is then forwarded to the Vietnamese government through the UNHCR Branch office in Hanoi. The Vietnamese officials then contact the given address to verify their identity. A Vietnamese government delegation consisting of immigration department officials interviewed the asylum seekers who opted to go back to Vietnam. In Hong Kong, the Vietnamese delegation regularly carried out interviews in Lo Wu and White Head Voluntary Departure Centres.

The Vietnamese delegation questions the person intending to return to Vietnam to ascertain their identity. They also quizzed them about their activities in the camp, affiliation to the camp agencies, and other activities the applicant was involved in, while they were in Hong Kong. The time from the formal request for repatriation to the actual repatriation takes about four to six weeks. Asylum seekers are transferred to Lo Wu or White Head Departure Centres upon the formal submission of their application for repatriation.

When the returnees arrive at the airports either at Hanoi or Ho Chi Minh City, both UNHCR and the Vietnamese officials receive them, along with the Local TV crew. Often, the returns of the Vietnamese asylum seekers are shown on the local TV news. Relatives confirm their arrival through the media. The returnees are then transferred from the airport to a transit centre administered by the Vietnam government, for two to three days. The returnees are then subjected to a medical examination and briefed on the reintegration program in Vietnam. The department of immigration arranges transportation for the 'returnees' back to their homes.

The returnees are expected to go back to their original place of residence in principle. If somebody is interested in moving to another place they are urged to make a request while being interviewed by the Vietnamese delegation in Hong Kong. Exceptions are made because of a recent marriage or absence of close family members. However, it is not clear what happens to the escapees from the New Economic Zone (NEZ), whether they are asked to go back to the NEZs for their family registration cards (*Ho Khau*). There are several such inarticulated concerns for the prospective returnees.

The family registration card, *Ho Khau* - is ready within two to three weeks for the returnees. It is assumed that it would take a little longer for those who settle in a new place and for those who did not possess a card prior to their departure. Reports were circulating in the camp that some of the returnees had been asked to pay large amounts as registration fee for a new '*Ho Khau*'. The returnees and their spouses were questioned separately by the local functionaries.

The material incentive for voluntary repatriation was the financial assistance given by the UNHCR and European Economic Community (EEC) to those who returned. The existing assistance from UNHCR is US $50 at the time of departure for the principal applicant and US $30 per month for one year after their return to Vietnam (Table 4.1 for the details of UNHCR and EEC Assistance to returnees to Vietnam from Kong Hong). The local assistance was distributed in co-operation with the Ministry of Labour, War Invalids and Social Affairs of the Vietnam government.

In the Hong Kong context, voluntary repatriation was the most favourable durable solution suggested to the asylum seekers by UNHCR and Hong Kong government. Those who opted for voluntary repatriation received a re-integration allowance and a free passage to Vietnam from Hong Kong in a specially chartered flight. The UK-Hong Kong government hoped that the repatriation program would be completed within three or four years with an 'orderly departure' program for all the non-refugees starting June 1992. But, if did not.

The UNHCR voluntary repatriation scheme managed to return 22, 693 persons to Vietnam from Hong Kong by 1992 (UNHCR 1993) Besides, 42,383 asylum seekers opted to go back to Vietnam 'voluntarily' by May 1994. Since the beginning of the voluntary repatriation scheme a high percentage of asylum seekers returned from Hong Kong than other countries in the region (Refer Table 4.2 Regional voluntary repatriation departures of Vietnamese). During 1989-1992, 56 per cent of the returnees were from Hai Phong province (See Fig 4.2 for details of province of origin of the Vietnam returnees).

Conclusion

Unlike many refugee issues, the Vietnamese refugee situation operated in unique personal as well as international context. Several significant international interests were involved in the cause and consequence of massive

Table 4.1   UNHCR and EEC Assistance to Returnees to Vietnam from Hong Kong

A] Returnees under UNHCR Auspices

CATEGORY OF RETURNEES	UNHCR ASSISTANCE x(In US$)			EC AISSTANCE		
	Principal Applicants	Family members		Possible Loan	Possible Training	Possible Indirect Community Assistance
		Adults	Children under 16 at date of Departure			
1. Pre-September 27 1991 Arrivals						
a. At Time of Departure Hong Kong (one time assistance)	$50/$25(UNAM)	$50	$25	N.A.	N.A.	N.A.
b. After Return to Vietnam	$30/month up to one year	$30/month up to one year	$30/month up to one year	Yes	Yes	Yes
2. Post-September 26 1991 Arrival						
a. At Time of Departure Hong Kong (one time assistance)	$50/$25 (UNAM)	$50	$25	N.A.	N.A.	N.A.
b. After Return to Vietnam	Up to $50 (base on VN assessment)	None in Principle*	None in Principle*	No	No	No
3. Double Backers Pre-September 27 1991 Arrivals						
a. At Time of Departure Hong Kong (one time assistance)	No	(1st time only) $50	(1st time only) $25	N.A.	N.A.	N.A.
b. After Return to Vietnam	No	(1st time only) $10/month up to one year	(1st time only) $10/month up to one year	Yes	Yes	Yes
4. Double Backers Post-September 26 1991 Arrivals						
a. At Time of Departure Hong Kong (one time assistance)	No	(1st time only) $50	(1st time only) $25	N.A.	N.A.	N.A.
b. After Return in vietnam	No	No	No	Yes	Yes	Yes

Table 4.1   Continued

B] Non-UNHCR Repatriation Programme**

5. Double Backers Pre-September 27 1991 Arrivals						
a. At Time of Departure Hong Kong (one time assistance)	No	(1st time only) $50	(1st time only) $25	Yes	N.A.	N.A.
b. After Return to Vietnam	No	(1st time only) $10/month up to one year	(1st time only) $10/month up to one year	No	Yes	Yes
6. Double backers Post-September 26 1991 Arrival						
a. At Time of Departure Hong Kong (one time assistance)	No	(1st time only) $50	(1st time only) $25	No	N.A.	N.A.
b. After Return to Vietnam	No	No	No	No	No	No
7. All Other Returnees Pre-September 27 1991 Arrivals						
a. At Time of Departure Hong Kong (one time assistance)	$50/$25 (UNAM)	$50	$25	Yes	N.A.	N.A.
b. After Return to Vietnam	$30/month up to one year	$30/month up to one year	$30/month up to one year	Yes	Yes	Yes
8. All Other Returnees Post-September 26 1991 Arrivals						
a. At Time of Departure Hong Kong (one time assistatnce)	$50/$25 (UNAM)	$50	$25	Yes	N.A.	N.A.
b. After Return in vietnam	up to $50 (base on VN assessment)	None in Principle *	None in Principle *	Yes	Yes	Yes

Notes: *   Up to $50 may be provided to needy cases based on assessment by Vietnamese authorities.

**   Pending final decision to be taken by Steering Committee V persons falling in corresponding catedgories in A and B above will receive the same assistance.

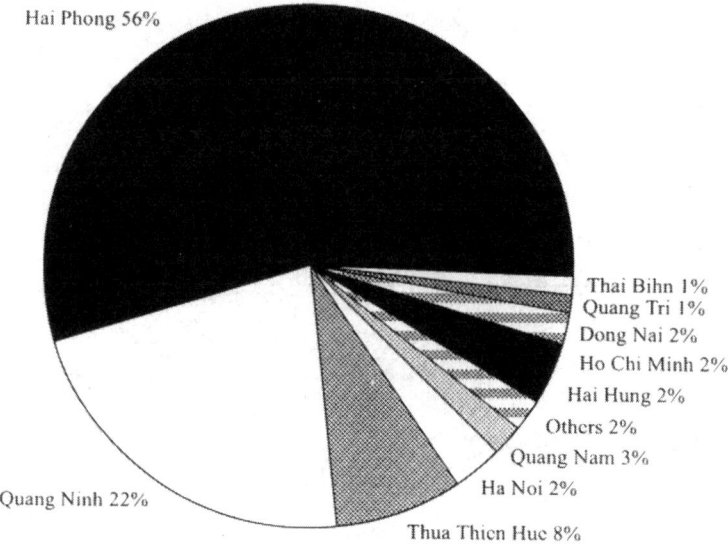

Hai Phong 56%

Thai Bihn 1%
Quang Tri 1%
Dong Nai 2%
Ho Chi Minh 2%
Hai Hung 2%
Others 2%
Quang Nam 3%
Ha Noi 2%
Thua Thien Hue 8%

Quang Ninh 22%

Total Respondents: 16, 087
Situation as of 29.02.92

Figure 4.2   Voluntary Repatriation to Vietnam. Province of Origin of Returnees (1989-1992)

refugee flow from Vietnam. The political interests of the international community and the pathways, which sustained the refugee flow, has not yet been clearly understood. Students of international politics may perhaps explore this issue further in future. It may also be a worthwhile exercise to contrast the plight of more than 100,000 refugees who fled to India from Tibet to seek asylum and still remain there as refugees. Tibetan refugees escaped from circumstances similar to Vietnamese refugees. However, there have been no great international initiative or a comprehensive plan to address the concerns of these refugees. The UNHCR did not show any inclination to set up an elaborate refugee assistance programme for the Tibetan refugees citing a lame excuse that India is not a signatory to the international refugee protocols. None of the members of the international community lined up to offer quotas for re-settlement to Tibetan refugees in the developed countries. It appears that in the global refugee scenario certain refugees are more 'desirable' than some other refugees. The desirability of refugees are mostly based on the potential value of them in 'international power games'.

Even though, the refugees from Vietnam attracted several internationaly unprecedented initiatives in the global refugee history, most Vietnamese detained in the camps' felt that they were punished or betrayed by the international community. The refugees detained in Hong Kong camps remember the power of the international agencies to punish them rather than their altruism. The initial international attention lavished on them was just a reflection of the political value attached to the Vietnamese refugees by the international community.

The United Nations hosted two international conferences to deal with this situation. A comprehensive program was agreed to at an inter-governmental forum. The role of United States, the foreign policy of global super power's and public opinion played a crucial role in influencing the outcome of social and cultural changes among the study population. Most importantly, when the edifice of cold-war came tumbling down, the political value of Vietnamese refugees also minimised, pushing the refugees issue into the peripheral political agenda by many international governments. This contributed to the misery of several refugee, rather than solving their problems. Refugee detention in Hong Kong should be understood in the context of a phenomenon of using human misery as a commodity in international politics.

Photo 4.1   White Head detention center. A view from outside

Photo 4.2   Three tier sleeping arrangements inside the Nissan hut. Each family is allotted one bunk

Photo 4.3   A 'Normal' day's activity

**Photo 4.4   The Shek Kong Camp residents dispersing immediately
after a police 'head count'**

Photo 4.5   A peaceful protest by the asylum seekers against the detention policy (According to some authors this is considered as a violent act.)

Photo 4.6   Children's Scout Group in Ta Ah Chau Camp (According to the camp management organizing this group was an act of subversion and against the implementation of CPA.)

Photo 4.7   The youth group meeting. The police observation tower
is in the background

Photo 4.8   Freedom or death: A protest march in progress at the
camp

5 The Power of the Host

This chapter deals with the local context of refugee detention and the nature of human right violations of asylum seekers in Hong Kong. The process of ethnocide took place in the asylum seeker detention camps was significantly influenced by the Hong Kong refugee policy. In order to understand the role of Hong Kong refugee policy, it is necessary to situate Hong Kong in its social and political context. The Hong Kong refugee policy was not essentially a reflection of the political or public opinion of the Hong Kong population. But was essentially a colonial appendage of the refugee policy of the British government.

Hong Kong was a British colony, administered according to a pattern developed in the nineteenth century for all parts of the British Empire till June 30, 1997. In formal terms, power was concentrated in the hands of a Governor chosen by the British government. He directed the activities of Hong Kong civil service and all acts of government were done in his name. According to the constitutional documents of Hong Kong, the Letters Patent and Royal Instructions, he was completely subjected to the British government control. The Secretary of State for Foreign and Commonwealth Affairs was empowered to issue directives, instructing him what should be done, and if he refused to obey he could be removed from office and a successor appointed (Miners, 1990).

It was the British government as part of its foreign policy detained 40,000 asylum seekers in Hong Kong. Hong Kong's special status as an appendage to the west provided an easy passage for earlier asylum seekers to the West. The late comers were detained when the policy was changed to suit the interest of the British government.

Human Rights Violation of asylum seekers in Hong Kong will be discussed in the following paragraphs. Universal Declaration of Human Rights (negotiated and agreed upon by the international community as basis of law of each country). The British government is not an exception in their obligation to implement basic human rights in its colony. Systematic human right violation is the source of individual disorientation, a first step towards community disorganisation and subsequent ethnocide of the asylum seeking population.

Asylum in Hong Kong: only for the Vietnamese

Offering political asylum was not exclusively an expression of humanitarian concern of British - Hong Kong government. Vietnamese asylum seekers were the only people who could request for asylum seeker status in Hong Kong based on their nationality. They were then subjected to a prolonged detention in specially constructed detention camps. Asylum seekers from many hard core communist countries were treated as illegal immigrants and jailed pending deportation to the county of their origin.

Granting asylum to any other nationality other than the Vietnamese was the exclusive domain of the Security Branch and the Political Advisors Office. There were no stated laws to determine the status of an asylum seeker from other countries. This was left to the lingering privilege of a colonial administration lacking in public accountability. There are several well-documented cases of such nature. Ms. Liu and Ms. Lin, two human right activists, escaped from Mainland China is one such case. Ms. Liu became a human right activist while working as a journalist for a Hainan Island newspaper. She went to Beijing with two of her colleagues to cover the Tianannmen Square protest. She reportedly wrote 54 poems describing the events collectively called 'The Blood and Tears in the Red Capital'. When she returned to her native place she was arrested and charged with waging malicious attack against the party, it's leaders and leaking state secrets. She was asked to sign a confession accepting re-education with labour for 10 years and to be subjected to treatment for an alleged mental illness. She managed to escape along with Ms. Lin to Hong Kong. Ms. Lin sought to flee fearing retaliation for helping Ms. Liu escape and providing shelter for her.

The Secretary for Security rejected her original request for Hong Kong residency. No official reason was given. It seems that the immigration department believed that their dissident activities were not severe enough to deserve asylum status. Followed by nine months of detention in Victoria Prison the two dissidents faced a deportation threat. Just few hours before the actual deportation the Canadian government accepted both of them as refugees. Later, Liu Yijun wrote from Canada about the brutal treatment at the hands of the Hong Kong authorities to which she appealed for help. She wrote why she weeps for Hong Kong.

> I would first like to make myself clear: what I am relating is only a few simple events among the many I have experienced in Hong Kong. I am not attempting to damage the reputation of Hong Kong as a free and democratic society. But we have reason to be saddened by the fact that such events are still happening - in a

city where the flag championing democracy and freedom flies high.

When I arrived in Hong Kong I was kidnapped and locked in a flat by a 'snakehead'. My identity was exposed when the criminals took my luggage. They instructed me to make contacts with certain organisations under the false pretext that I was an important political figure. They demanded a high ransom for my release and the return of my luggage. Armed police came to my rescue. When they broke open the iron grill, I quickly told them what had happened. I told them my luggage contained my important belongings.

It should have been obvious to the Hong Kong police how they - as experienced and professional officers - should deal with the case. It was a case of blackmail and unlawful detention. Had they considered carefully the fact that I - a victim - was in a desperate situation, could I have easily got my luggage back? My application for political asylum would also have been smoother.

Strangely enough, the team of officers (about 10 of them) in charge of the case did not pay any attention to our luggage (my friend Lin Lin was with me). They also took no note of the fact that as victims we had been surviving without food and little water for two days and two nights. The officers treated us like criminals. We were locked up and questioned throughout the night and into the next morning.

About noon, the officers broke us up in two groups. They beat us, tragically and inhumanely, despite the fact that we were helping them with their investigation. Imagine it. Those who were victims and were brought to the police station to help with an investigation were being beaten up. Those who were criminals were being bailed out in no time at all. How caring the Hong Kong police were when it came to the human rights of criminals And how cruel and violent they were when it came to handling the victims.

But there are even stranger things. The police beat us but did not pursue the accomplice. They even came to an agreement with the snakehead. We were told that he would be charged but the main charges against him were dropped. This should have meant that we would not be required to give evidence in court. But we were told differently. We were put in jail and were told that we were required as witnesses. We were imprisoned for four months. We never got to see the judge. We were not even told specifically of his ruling. Ironically, even when the snakehead was conscientious enough to offer our luggage, Hong Kong officials refused the offer.

The police did take our statement and pledged to find our luggage although they laughed when they made the promise. Meanwhile, the Hong Kong government told us that our luggage would help prove our case. I shudder when I think of the Hong Kong government officials who deigned to descend from their lofty perch to meet us. Our first meeting was conducted when officials were about to leave work for the day. At the second meeting, we were only asked a few questions. Other meetings followed, but the government had no interest in finding out anything more from us.

The Hong Kong government concluded that since we did not have any criminal record in China, we left China because of 'personal' reasons. Moreover, because we had been leading a quiet life, it was ridiculous for us to leave China. This they did not tell us directly. They told our lawyers. I, who was desperate and without hope, was finally, put into a psychiatric hospital. I was told it was very nice place and I would be there for only three days. I was put into solitary confinement for several days. I was made to work with those who were mentally ill, made to follow humiliating orders, and made to live in fear for a horrific 15 days. It was a life so awful I can hardly bear to recall it.

I have led a difficult life but I know I am not a mental patient. Psychologists in Hong Kong confirmed this. I have lost hope in the Hong Kong government. But I still love my country and my home village - and Hong Kong. Generation after generation of Chinese have suffered. For thousands of years, the fate of millions has been in the hands of one or a few. Many Chinese have sacrificed in their attempt to force change. How I wish I could be in my own country and with my own people. I did not hurt anybody. I do not want to hurt anybody. But why under the vast sky is there no place for me? Can Hong Kong - a city that champions' democracy and freedom - be so brutal?

In this Pearl of the Orient more respect should be paid to people. Their rights should not be stepped on. I felt so ashamed when the police seemed so enthusiastic while beating us up. Their skin was yellow and their hair was black. I wanted to cry, but I could shed no tears. It was thus surprising to find the Canadian immigration officers to be so friendly. They had time for me. They listened. With the materials my friends so untiringly obtained for me, I became a new immigrant.

I can see the bright heaven and the earth. I can walk freely on this piece of land, sometimes joined by pigeons and squirrels. I no longer live in fear. Now that I can breathe the air of freedom I do not mind having no money. I wish my countrymen could feel such freedom. I hope what I experienced will not happen again in Hong Kong. Freedom and democracy are something that cannot be accomplished easily. Do not lose too much by being complacent (SCMP, 27.09.1992).

The CPA and Hong Kong

Many Vietnamese are still confined in the detention centres or refugee camps across South East Asia, even after the CPA proposal, waiting for the refugee determination process or resettlement in a third country. Those who are determined as non - refugees are also waited in the hope that one day there may be changes in the international policy which would help them to resettle in a third country or at the first asylum country. They may be just buying time and hoping for tangible changes in Vietnam before they go back to their country of origin.

In dealing with the Vietnamese refugees across South East Asian countries, Hong Kong has taken lead in many aspects. Detaining Vietnamese refugees is one example. Since July 2, 1982, all Vietnamese seeking asylum in Hong Kong were detained in various Detention Centres in the territory.

The CPA did not specifically propose detaining Vietnamese asylum seekers, yet all the Vietnamese asylum seekers in Hong Kong were detained under the U.K. - Hong Kong immigration law. The asylum seekers who were 'screened-in' (accepted his/her refugee claim) were initially transferred to an open centre (Pillar Point refugee camp) subjected to their resettlement into another country. When it became difficult to resettle refugees directly from Hong Kong this policy was changed and those 'screened in' were, transferred to Kai Tak transit centre pending their transfer to a regional holding centre in the Philippines. Those determined as non-refugees (screened out) were also detained along with asylum seekers who were yet to be screened for their refugee status. Although, the British - Hong Kong Government and the United Nations High Commissioner for Refugees, hoped that all asylum seekers determined as non - refugees would voluntarily go back to their country of origin, a large number of the 'screened out' population were not keen to go back to Vietnam immediately.

The cost of (Ethnocide) caring asylum seekers in Hong Kong

It is estimated that for the past 14 years Hong Kong government spent about HKD 4, 899 million, to look after the Vietnamese asylum seekers. It was only possible to spend such a huge amount of the tax payers money because Hong Kong was a crown colony of the United Kingdom. Any democratically elected government would face nightmares about the cost of caring for asylum seekers. The public accountability for such an amount could cost many votes for any political party.

The British government during the same period paid HKD 650 million, and the international community through the UNHCR spent about HKD 919 million (Refer table 5.1 for details of the expenditure on Vietnamese asylum seekers by the Hong Kong government). The tremendous increase of expenditure by Hong Kong was attributed to the construction of barracks and payments for administration and staff. The asylum seekers in effect were not benefiting from the increased expenditure by the Hong Kong government.

Apart from this, during 1992 UNHCR spent about HKD 402.36 million for various programs (Refer table 5.2 for the details of UNHCR assistance programme for Vietnamese in Hong Kong during 1992).

Table 5.1   Expenditure on Vietnamese Asylum Seekers (In HK $ millions)

Year	HK Government	UK government	UNHCR
1978/89	1,316	——	146
1989/90	819	215	128
1990/91	919	131	182
1991/92	879	202	238
1992/93 (estimated)	966	102	225

Source: HK government 1992

Table 5.2   UNHCR Assistance Programme for Vietnamese in Hong Kong 1992

		HK$ (million)	US$ (million)
Food, relief items utilities and medicines	Hong Kong Government	273.55	35.34
Education, Social Services and Health	Non-Governmental Agencies*/ UNHCR	84.09	10.85
Resettlement Processing	Caritas / UNHCR	2.21	0.29
Status determination (not including Legal Consultants)	UNHCR / AVS	23.70	3.05
Voluntary Repatriation (not including costs of flights and reintegration)	UNHCR / AVS	18.81	2.43
	Total:	402.36	51.93

* Hong Kong Housing Services for Refugees
  Agency for Volunteer Service
  Hong Kong Christian Aid to Refugees
  Medecins Sans Frontieres - Belgium
  Save the Children Fund
  Community and Family Services International Caritas
  British Red Cross Society
  International Social Service - Hong Kong Branch

UNHCR Hong Kong
January 1992

Human Rights Violation of asylum seekers in Hong Kong

Even though the main theoretical frame of reference of this thesis is 'ethnocide', developing a human right perspective is equally important to expand the scope of the concept of ethnocide itself. The need and importance of human right perspective as an important tool to explain and understand the refugee - asylum seeker dilemmas is becoming increasingly clear to refugee researchers and for those involved in humanitarian intervention. The individual disorganisation of the asylum seekers is the main consequence of human rights violation. Individual disorganisation is subsequently a contributory factor in ethnocide. The analysis of the human right violations of the asylum seekers was carried out based on the framework of the universal declaration of human rights (UDHR) accepted and proclaimed by the United Nations general assembly. The legality of detention of Vietnamese asylum seekers was based on the British Prison Laws with certain amendments. Prolonged detention without a judicial process in itself is against the principles of English Law. Detention and inhuman treatment of Vietnamese asylum seekers was a violation of several universal instruments for the protection of human dignity and freedom. Specifically, UK-Hong Kong was violating the following instruments and specific articles:

1. Universal Declaration of Human Rights adopted and proclaimed by the United Nations General Assembly Resolution 217 A (III) of 10 December 1948.

Articles violated by UK - Hong Kong were, article 1, 2, 5, 8, 9, 10, 13, 16 (3), 18, 19 and article 20.

2. Convention relating to the status of refugees of 28 July 1951.

Articles Violated by UK - Hong Kong are article 12, 15, 16, 17, 18, 19, 20, 22, 24, 26, 28, 32, and article 33.

3. International Covenant on Civil and Political Rights adopted by the United Nations General Assembly on 16 December 1966.

Articles violated were 7, 9, 10, 11, 12, 14, 16, 17, 18, 19, 22, and article 24.

4. International Covenant on Economic, Social, and Cultural rights adopted by the United Nations General Assembly on 16 December 1966.

Articles violated by UK-Hong Kong were articles 10, 13, and article 15.

5. UN Convention on the Rights of the Child adopted by the UN General Assembly on November 20, 1989.

Articles violated by UK-Hong Kong were article 1, 2, 3, 4, 12, 13, 16, 19, 20, 21, 22, 23, 28, 29, 31, 37, and article 40.

6. Principles concerning treatment of refugees as adopted by the Asian - African legal Consultative Committee at its Eighth Session at Bangkok, 1966.

Articles violated by UK-Hong Kong government was article iii, vi, and article viii.

7. International convention on the elimination of All forms of Racial Discrimination adopted by the United Nations General Assembly on 21 December 1965.
   Articles violated by UK-Hong Kong were articles 1, 2, and article 5.

Violation of Universal Declaration of Human Rights (UDHR) in Hong Kong camps

United Nations General Assembly, on 10 December 1948 adopted and proclaimed the recognition of the inherent dignity and of the equal and inalienable rights of all members of the human family as the foundation of freedom, justice and peace in the world. The General Assembly proclaimed Universal Declaration of Human Rights as a common standard of achievement for all peoples and all nations, to the end that every individual and every organ of society, shall strive to promote the right and freedom to progressive measures, national and international, to secure their universal and effective recognition and observance, both among the peoples of Member states themselves and among the peoples of territories under their jurisdiction. (International instruments concerning Human Rights, refer Collection of International Instruments concerning Refugees, UNHCR, 1990, Geneva).

This declaration bound the Government of the United Kingdom and her colony Hong Kong to strive for the human rights of all people who were in Hong Kong territory including the Vietnamese refugees. For the past 11 years

United Kingdom and Hong Kong governments systematically violated the Human Rights Charter of the Vietnamese refugees in Hong Kong detention centres with impunity. The year 1993 was the 10th year of detention policy of Vietnamese asylum seekers in Hong Kong. The UK - Hong Kong government was violating articles 1, 2, 5, 8, 9, 10, 13, 16 (3), 18, 19 and article 20 in the case of Vietnamese asylum seekers. There are no legal or moral excuses for the UK-Hong Kong government to exclude the asylum seekers from the purview of the Universal Declaration of Human Rights.

Article 1 of UDHR proclaims that 'All human beings are born free and equal in dignity and rights. They are endowed with reason and conscience and should act towards one another in a spirit of brotherhood' (UDHR, 1948) The Vietnamese refugees were mere unwanted 'numbers' in Hong Kong territory and also for the Hong Kong asylum seeker managers. Asylum seekers were referred to by numbers in the detention centres. The physical appearance of the detention centres was often intimidating with high security fences, closed circuit surveillance cameras, barbed wires, primary and secondary fences, high power security lights, guard post and complete security inspection of visitors and the service agency staff. Prolonging the administrative detention under such cruel and inhuman conditions robbed all human dignity of the asylum seekers.

Article 2 of UDHR states that every one is entitled to all the rights and freedom set forth in this declaration, without distinction of any kind, such as race, colour, sex, language, religion, political or other opinion, national or social origin, property, birth or other status. Article 2 furthermore recommends that, 'no distinction shall be made on the basis of political, jurisdictional or international status of the country, or territory, to which a person belongs, whether it be independent, trust, non-self-governing or under any other limitation of sovereignty'.

Article 5 of UDHR suggests that 'no one shall be subjected to torture or cruel, inhumane or degrading treatment or punishment'. Detaining women and children in high security prisons for more than 5 years was indeed a degrading treatment. In detention centres a ritual of 'head counts' was frequently conducted. Women, children, elderly, sick and infants were forced to sit in the open ground for head counts and hut searches in the name of security measures. This type of treatment was cruel, inhumane and degrading.

There were several other forms of cruel, inhumane and degrading treatment by the refugee administrators in Hong Kong. Without justification or reasonable warning the asylum seekers, including children and women were tear-gassed several times. Forced repatriation was another form of cruel and inhuman punishment. It was highly deplorable to go ahead with such inhumane and cruel forced repatriation of the asylees at a time when voluntary repatriation requests from the asylum seekers were beyond the coping capacity of the UNHCR.

Article 8 assures the rights to remedy for human rights violation. Everyone has the right to an effective remedy by the competent national tribunals for acts violating the fundamental rights granted to him by the constitution or by law. Avenues for remedial action by the asylum seekers for the effective implementation of Human Rights were limited or non-existent. Several complaints were made to the Complaints Against the Police Office (CAPO), about the alleged excessive use of force by them. No action was ever taken in any of these cases of complaints. I, myself was an official witness to a few of these CAPO enquires. The enquiry duty was often assigned to women police officers. Quite often they themselves were vulnerable within the Hong Kong police force. According to my viewpoint they were keen on using the opportunity for enquiry to justify the actions of their fellow officers than finding the truth.

Twenty-four persons died in a senseless violent conflict during the 1992 Vietnamese New Year celebrations at Sek Kong Detention Centre (SKDC). This conflict could have been avoided if the camp management were not negligent in protecting the life of the asylum seekers. An enquiry commission was instituted and the report was never implemented or published for reference to the public or to the refugee assistance agencies.

I was present in the court when the alleged culprits of the SKDC violence were brought for the court proceedings. One asylum seeker who worked with me as a paraprofessional in the camp was also among the accused. One more reason to visit the court procedure was that one of the asylum seekers had taken photographs of the incident and had photographic evidence of the persons involved in the violence. He trusted me to develop the negatives of the photos. According to him all the real culprits were never booked. When I compared the photos with the persons who were presented in the court, I realised the true picture of the legal process.

Each accused was numbered and the number was written on their wrist. In the court, the number of each of the alleged culprits was called and they had to raise their hands to show the number on their wrists. Most of the asylees appeared confused and baffled by what was going on in the court. To make matters worse, the court proceedings were interpreted through three languages, English to Cantonese to Vietnamese and vice versa.

In 1991, an off-duty police officer entered a refugee centre and shot dead a refugee in the Pillar Point camp. According to the Vietnamese, the off-duty police officer shot the refugee in the back while he was fleeing from the scene. I was working in that camp when this incident took place. According to my research informants the police officer was in the camp to have cheap alcohol and to solicit sexual services from a refugee girl. The police officer was let off the hook, after the primary investigation found that the use of weapon was for 'self-protection'.

Article 9 declares that 'no one shall be subjected to arbitrary arrest, detention, or exile'. A prolonged administrative detention of asylum seekers under the immigration ordinance was a clear violation of article 9. Their arrest and detention was arbitrary. Detaining a person without the benefit of a legal trial is even against the basic principles of the English Law.

Article 10 underlines the procedural justice. Everyone is entitled in full equality to a fair and public hearing by an independent and impartial tribunal, in the determination of his rights and obligations and any criminal charges against him. The Vietnamese asylum seekers upon arrival in Hong Kong were arrested and detained without any time frame. Often they had to wait for two or three years for an administrative hearing. An officer of the immigration department who was not an independent and impartial authority heard the case. Even the Review Board was an administrative body rather than a judicial body with questionable partiality against the asylum seekers in general.

Article 13 of UDHR suggests that

1. Everyone has the right to freedom of movement and residence within the borders of each state.
2. Everyone has the right to leave any country, including his own, and to return to his country.

Asylum seekers were deprived of the freedom of movement. They were allowed to stay in the detention centres and specifically only in the bunks they were assigned. Even though asylum seekers wanted to leave Hong Kong they were allowed to leave only if they went back to Vietnam. The Hong Kong government passed necessary regulation to bring migrant workers from other overseas countries to ease the acute labour shortage. But any suggestion to employ the Vietnamese as a means to their freedom was met with instant rejection.

Article 16 (3), suggests that the family is the natural and fundamental group unit of a society and is entitled to protection by the society and State. Family reunion requests within the detention centres and outside Hong Kong moved at a slow pace. The local authorities arbitrarily send most of the male asylum seekers of Chinese origin who were married to Vietnamese girls back to China. Often leaving the wife and children in the camps. Considering the political and economic situation they are in many of them will not never see their spouses or their children ever in their life. The local UNHCR officials did not see this as a violation of fundamental rights of refugees and did not took any decisive steps to stop such deportations and to protect the integrety of the family of refugees.

Article 18 offers 'everyone has the right to freedom of thought, conscience and religion. This right includes freedom to change his religion, or belief, and freedom, either alone or in a community with others and in public or private, to manifest his religion or belief in teaching, practice, worship and observance'. According to the detention administrators even organising a poetry reading in the camp was considered as a political act against CPA. I was instrumental in organising such a poetry club in Tai Ah Chau and at Sek Kong Detention Centres. When some asylum seekers began writing poetry and independent articles in the camp-based magazines, those magazines were confiscated and those instrumental in the production of the magazines were severely reprimanded.

Religious practices were actively discouraged. Religious teachers and monks were often denied permission to enter the camps. Even when they were allowed to enter the camps it was under strict regulations. Strangely, some evangelical groups were permitted to enter the camps relatively freely. Apparently, these groups managed to obtain sanction directly from the security branch.

Article 19 declares that everyone has the right to freedom of opinion and expression; this right includes freedom to hold opinions without interference and to seek, receive, and impart information and ideas through any media, and regardless of frontiers. Media's access to the detention centres was under strict control. Free media was imperative in getting justice for the asylees. Access to the information from outside sources, newspapers, magazines and other reports were actively discouraged. Some camp management often confiscated any magazines circulated without their approval. Asylum seekers had very few avenues to express their opinions freely and without fear.

All the agency staffs were muzzled by the UNHCR guided media policy. They were not allowed to disclose information to the media, in the 'best interest of the asylum seekers'. The question faced by the agency staff here was whose interest should get priority, the interest of the client or the interest of the donor. This professional dilemma is yet to be sorted out. Often outspoken and articulate asylum seekers were labelled as 'trouble makers', 'predators' 'gangsters' and 'Big Brothers', thus undermining their efforts to become community spokesperson. Most of these articulate community representatives soon discovered that keeping a low profile was the best survival strategy in Hong Kong detention centres.

Article 20 of UDHR, suggest that everyone has the right to freedom of peaceful assembly and association. In Hong Kong detention camps the freedom of peaceful assembly was limited to the line-up outside the huts for occasional head counts when they had to sit outside the huts. All forms of 'independent and unsupervised' assembly of asylum seekers were banned under the guise of security.

Even organising children's scout group for the child detainees was considered as an attempt at 'subversion' according to the camp administration. As a community worker in Tai Ah Chau Camp, I was instrumental in organising a 'scout group for children'. I managed to get cloth for the scout uniform. Some of the women community leaders offered their help in stitching them. However, a request for taking another lot of scout uniforms into the camps, given as donation, was interpreted as an act against CPA and I was summoned by the camp manager to be warned in clear terms that I may face dire consequences.

The detention of Asylum seekers itself was against the letter and spirit of several other international treaties and traditions such as:
1. CPA,
2. Convention on the status of refugees,
3. International Covenant on Civil and Political Rights (ICCPR),
4. Universal Declaration of Human Rights,
5. International Covenant on Economic, Social, and Cultural rights,
6. UN Convention on the Rights of the Children,
7. Principles concerning treatment of refugees as adopted by the Asian - African Legal Consultative and
8. International convention on the elimination of All Forms of Racial Discrimination adopted by the United Nations General Assembly on 21 December 1965.

Conclusion

The UK-Hong Kong government wanted to deport all the Vietnamese at the earliest and as soon as the political value of the refugees' was diminished. The British government had promised to the Chinese authorities that they would solve the problem of the asylum seekers before 1997. The Chinese government also insisted that British government should find solutions for the refugee problem before they hand over the territory to them. There would be no legal or other rights for the Vietnamese after the 1997 hand over. The bill of rights of Hong Kong residents promulgated by the British government in Hong Kong excluded the Vietnamese refugees from its purview. By early 1994 all the refugee status determination procedures were completed. Reviewing the cases again took another year. Like many other colonial withdrawals, unfinished ethnic and political agenda such as Vietnamese refugees was left to the new masters to solve.

The process of ethnocide took place in the asylum seeker detention camps was significantly influenced by the peculiar social and political context of Hong Kong. In order to understand the role of Hong Kong refugee policy, it is necessary to situate Hong Kong in its social and political context. The Hong Kong refugee policy was not essentially a reflection of the political or public opinion of the Hong Kong population. But was essentially a colonial refugee policy of the British government. However, the asylum seekers experienced the local context as one of the power of the host culture to inculcate pain and humiliation on the refugees through systematic violations of their rights.

This chapter also presents a detailed account of the human rights violation of the asylum seekers in Hong Kong. International instruments for the protection of Human Rights are used as the yardstick for assessing the extent of violation of the asylum seekers detained in Hong Kong. This chapter contributes towards the growing area of knowledge in anthropology of the rights of individuals, especially, when they are facing difficult conditions. 'Individual disorientation' which is a contributory factor in ethnocide is directly related to the level and extent of human rights violation of the asylum seekers in the camps.

6 The Structure of Powerlessness

Pain and suffering are not simply individual experience, which arise out of the contingency of life. These may also be experiences, which are actively created and distributed by the social order itself (Das, 1994). This chapter narrates the linkages between the social order and the basis of individual misery and pain, and the chapter is divided into two parts. The first part of this chapter deals with the case study of a woman who was caught in the refugee saga. Gender specific life experiences of the refugees' gives a detailed insight into the social process of refugee production and the pathways through which pain and misery are contrived as an extension of the social structure itself. The 2nd section of this chapter deals with the physical structure, organisation of the camps and the process of legitimising the detention of refugees.

Asylum seekers often reach detention centre with their own emotional, cultural and social baggage. In addition, constant movement involved in the refugee experience diminishes the chances of developing delicate coping mechanisms by the individuals, families and communities. The personal concern of a woman is presented here to understand some of the 'oft described' mundane concerns of the ordinary people in the camps. Deeper understanding of such cases is important to understand the human dimension of the refugee issue in Hong Kong.

Ms. Ho Thi Xiem, (all real names in this case study have been changed) was born on July 2, 1959. She came to Hong Kong in 1989 hoping to reunite with her son and husband, Mr. Mai Tan Nhut, born in 1955, who came to Hong Kong an year earlier, in 1988. He escaped to Hong Kong after their brief estrangement. When her sorrow on separation from her child and husband became unbearable she decided to join with her husband in Hong Kong.

Even before his escape from Vietnam, Ms Xiem had doubts about her husband's sanity. She was hoping that the changed environment in Hong Kong might have improved the emotional stability of her husband. The Hong Kong camp condition did not do well for the sanity of her husband or to her marriage. Her husband became more aggressive and abusive. She was forced to seek protection and help from the camp authorities several times. She finally requested for a divorce from her husband. The following is her story. It was originally written in Vietnamese and was translated by a camp translator (another asylum seeker) into English.

Ms Xiem's Story

Life in Vietnam

I was persuaded to marry by my mother as at that time I was not at all willing to get married. But I did not have much of a choice because of my family's poor economic situation. I had no 'Ho Khau' (Household Registration Card) and my parents were receiving support from my husband's family for a long time. So finally, I had to give-in for the sake of my parents and other siblings.

Although my neighbours warned me about my future husband, I did not care what they said. When my parents visited his family, they were told that he is in robust health, except he had some minor infection in his left ear and it will be cured soon. They also told that even though he had a bad temper, they would support me once I became their daughter-in-law, which might also help him to overcome his 'short temper'. My would-be-in-laws said that I would be happy and they were willing to provide me with everything I wanted. They also told me that since I could sew, if I wanted a sewing machine I would be given one or if I wanted to do some other trade his mother would teach me the basics. I was also told that the income I would generate from my industry could be spent according to my wish.

My parents believed them and encouraged me to agree with their suggestion. I thought his family was rich and my husband was the youngest in the family, and I would also be helping my family, so I agreed to marry him. We were married on October 15, 1986 and I moved into to my husband's house. His parents gave me a teal gold (37.4 grams) and a sewing machine. A few days later his parents took back half of the gold and said, 'you are already married to this house. You have to take care and advise your husband to control his spending. You can keep the income you generate from sewing and can spend on whatever you want'. My mother in-law reminded me that she was spending money on food for the whole family.

Both my husband and I sewed clothes for customers, but I realised that he was not very good at it. Out of my income from sewing I gave some money to my younger sister and brother. My husband spent the remaining money. My in-laws again told me to advise my husband to control his extravagant habits. I obeyed his parent's advice. When one day he came home late, I told him about his parents' advice. He scolded me and used abusive language and told me that there is no need to give him advice. I was scared to see him in such anger.

Coping with a marriage

I was hoping that was he would change his behaviour one-day and I refrained from antagonising him. His mother blamed me for his anger. She advised me that I should talk to him only when he is happy. I should not advice him when he is sad or depressed. On several occasions, when I was sewing, he would come over and demand to sew. The customers would urge me to get their work done fast. When I told him that unless he speeds up his work we would lose our customers he got angry and scolded me. He asked me to give back the clothes to the customers, if not, he would damage everything.

His parents came into the room, hearing the commotion. They told me, if he wants you to give back all the clothes to the customers, then obey him. I was so scared that I rushed to return the clothes to the customers. When I came back he scolded and cursed me again. He told me that I would not be allowed to sew anymore clothes. I realised that when he was angry he was very different. I was scared when he was angry. Therefore I did not talk to him when he was angry. I went inside the bedroom and cried. When he saw me crying, he came into the room and tried to beat me up. His parents saved me. He scolded, screamed and shouted and insisted that I should stop crying immediately. His parents accused me that I was crying to irritate their son so I should stop crying. But I was unable to control my tears. I did not realise that he was just throwing tantrums. When his mother gave him some money to go out for playing cards, he took the money, just looked at me and walked away.

I was expected to behave as if everything was normal. Whenever I was sad he would chide me. Sometimes even though I wanted to cry I controlled myself. I wished to have a happy family life, a life where there is happiness and good communication between husband and wife, but I never had that luck. Many a times I wanted to talk to him but I was so scared to do so. He did not try to understand me and scolded me for petty reasons. I began suspecting that he was mentally ill. But I never told my parents about my doubts or about my sufferings. My parents knew that I was not very happy and they were sad about it. I cried when he was away. My mother-in-law advised me that he might change his behaviour when we had a child. I also sincerely believed the same and hoped to have a child.

When I was pregnant, he often complained that he had a headache and he could not sew anymore. Yet, he took all the money I earned from the sewing. When he was normal, he was nice and gentle. But when he was sad and depressed he would scold me and would not allow me to sew. Whenever he ran out of money he was grumpy as well. He scolded me whenever I was late to do the household chores. Several times when he came home and if his meals were not ready he would become angry. He would accuse me that I was lazy and I did not prepare meals for him to irritate him. One day he created a big fuss because I was delayed in preparing his food. As usual he came home and demanded food. I was afraid and I went inside the kitchen to bring his food into the dining room. He got very wild and hit me with the food tray. I was so scared that I began to cry. My tears made him more aggressive, he came over and tried to strangle me. When I screamed for help his mother came into the room to dissuade him. She gave him some money to go out and eat.

If I had to go out to my parents' house or anywhere else I had to take his permission. He forbade me from telling my parents anything about him. Once, he and I went to visit my parents and when we came back from the visit he began shouting at me and accusing me that I had told my parents something about him. That is why my parents were unhappy with him. He ridiculed my parents and he wanted to go back to my house to confront them. But his parents discouraged him in doing so.

When I was due for my delivery, I stopped sewing, so we had no money. He asked his mother for money but she also did not have any money then. He became angry and banged the table, threw chairs and damaged the furniture in the room. His sister came over and saw what was going on. Both she and my mother-in-law scolded me. They accused me of instigating him to ask money from his mother. His nephew was visiting our family. He was also scolded and beaten up by my husband. His nephew complained to his mother and she accused me that the aggression was under my influence. Physical aggression, abusive language and scolding became a daily routine for my husband. I was heart broken and felt too weak to do anything. Since my family was so poor I had no alternative other than to put up with all this abuse. I cried in silence to ease my pain.

Immediately after the delivery of my baby I was sick, yet he continued to nag me for no apparent reason. Even though he liked his child, he was not willing to take care of him. Once I was too busy, with household chores, and I asked him to take care of baby when the baby began to cry. He got so annoyed with the child and shouted at the child in rage. 'If you continue crying, I will throw you to the ground, and let you die'. Since then, I have never asked him to take care of my child. Once my child was sick and did not recover soon. My husband began accusing me saying that I did not know how to take care of the child, which is why the child got sick. I was in the kitchen preparing food for him. He came into the kitchen in a rage and I was so scared. I thought he was going to kill me. His parents advised me to hide. I wanted to run to my parents' house but I was scared to do so. I hid myself in one of our neighbour's houses. I was there only for a couple of hours and I was I intending to go back to his house. But my neighbours discouraged me in doing so. They told me, my husband was furious and he was looking for me.

Then, I went to my parents' house. When my mother saw me she began crying. My younger brother informed me that my husband brought all of my clothes and threw them on my mother's face. My parents scolded me when I tried to explain to them what had happened. There was nobody to listen to me. I cried, I could not say anything to anybody. That night, I slept in my mother's house. I was feeling so miserable about my parents' behaviour and I was missing my child. I could not sleep at night. At 3 AM my mother-in-law brought my son to me to breast feed him. My child was crying till then, because of hunger. My mother-in-law came back in the morning at 7, to take my son back to their house. Next morning my sister-in-law came to my parents' house to tell me that my husband was looking for me with a knife, so I should hide from him. My parents were so scared that they stayed at home all day to guard me. When my husband came looking for me later in the day I was hiding inside the house. The same evening he made an application for divorce. But my parents did not allow me to sign the document. They suggested that I should send a letter of apology to my husband instead. I knew my parents' predicament. They did not have enough food to eat. They have to take care of my brothers and sisters. If I joined as well, then it will be an additional burden for them. Since I don't have my 'Ho Khau', I may not be able to work and support my family. My options were limited. It was better to live in silence and in humiliation at my husband's house than live in the poverty of my parents' house. I wrote him a letter of apology.

In the evening, he came over to my parent's house to tell them that since I apologised he was willing to forgive me and to take me back. My parents were relived, at least temporarily. But my trouble was far from over. My husbands behaviour did not change, he was waiting for excuses to pounce on me. One day I left my child with my brothers and sisters at my parents' house. They loved the child very much. When my husband realised that our child was at my parents' house he became angry. He shouted at my younger brother and began strangling him. Fortunately, the neighbours intervened. Since then the neighbours began suspecting that my husband was mentally ill.

Sometimes, at night while I was sleeping he would wake me up to scold and curse me. Whenever I tried to wake up his parents on such occasions he would prevent me from doing so. He would strangle and threaten me with dire consequences if I woke up his parents. He began saying he did not need me, he had money, so he could have everything he wanted. He began complaining about frequent headaches. He requested money from his parents for medication. They took him to the General Hospital for medical examination. My parents did all the arrangements for his medical treatments. I did not know anything about his medical condition or his other plans. To my complete surprise, in August 1988, my husband fled to Hong Kong.

I was asked to do all the household chores of my husband's house and when my sister-in-law moved to her in-laws house, I had to take care of that household too. My sister-in-law took my sewing machine saying that since I was not using it she wanted to use it. I was too busy with household chores in two houses to sew anything. In my husbands absence my sister-in-law took over the role of abusing me. One day I was late in preparing meals for my sister-in-law's child. She began shouting at me, she screamed and threw the rice bowl at me, accusing me that I was a bad omen in the house, because of my bad influence she felt sick. The rice bowl hurt me and my clothes were soaked with blood, and her mother called the local nurse to bandage my wounds.

My sister-in-law continued her accusations against me. She attributed my bad influence as the reason for her illness and my husband's illness. My mother-in-law asked me to leave my baby with her and to go back to my parents' house. She gave me some money and my wedding rings back. She suggested that I do some business from my parents' house. When I went to my parents' house, they were angry with me. They accused me for all the trouble. They told me that once married I am expected to follow the husband whatever happens and they are not responsible for me anymore. Yet reluctantly they allowed me to stay with them. I was feeling miserable. I could not do anything because I missed my child. During nights I cried silently thinking about my fate. My parents were sad and their health was getting worse. My only way out from this drudgery would be to escape from Vietnam. I wanted freedom and a better future for my child and myself. I secretly wished to reunite with my husband and hoped that he would understand and accept me when I joined him.

Escaping from Vietnam

One of my sister's friends was aware of my situation. She promised to assist me to escape from Vietnam. We left Vietnam in the same boat. Just before we left I went to my husbands family. I told my mother-in-law that I missed my child and asked to see the baby and keep him with me for a short time. She was reluctant but when my son began crying she allowed me take the child and told me to bring him back in the afternoon. I hid at my neighbour's house and we escaped the same night, April 30, 1989. We left the shore on May 1, 1989 and we reached Hong Kong on June 7, 1989.

When we were all aboard the ship I realised that my sister-in-law was also escaping in the same boat. But she ignored me. On our voyage our boat capsized at Hsi Nom Island in China. We had to stay there for a month to arrange for a new boat. Who ever had gold was asked to sell it for food. I had my wedding ring with me. My sister in law suggested that her husband would help me to sell it. I handed over the ring to her. She sold it to the local farmers for 35 Yuan (Chinese currency). She gave me a packet of noodle saying that it was enough for my child. She took the rest of the money. I complained and she said that the gold was from her family so she had a right to it. Her husband threatened to beat me up if I complained again. When the boat mates recognised that she was my sister-in-law they dissuaded the quarrel, and asked her to give me 10 Yuan more.

Living in Hong Kong detention camps

When we arrived in Hong Kong, I felt resuscitated, happy and delighted. We were transferred to the Sek Kong camp after the initial formalities. My son, my neighbour, and some other boat mates, my sister-in-law and I were assigned to the same tent along with two other Northerners. I was anxiously looking for my husband. Somebody informed me that my husband was also in the same camp in another section, and I immediately requested for family reunion. My sister-in-law kept on harassing me for unknown reasons. Her main complaint was that I did not know how to take care of my child that is why he was often sick. She also accused me that I did not take care of my child therefore he was speaking in a northern accent. Since two northern Vietnamese families were sharing our tent naturally my son picked up the northern accent.

Some of the people from my tent helped me to get free ration cigarette from the camp management. I sold the cigarette in the camp to buy some fruit and noodles for my son. Whenever my sister-in-law saw me she would shout at me. One day she began beating me up for no apparent reason. Some of the people advised me to complain to the camp social worker, and I did likewise. With the help of the social worker I was moved to the hut at C 25. Eventually my husband joined me at C 25. My son was happy to hang around with him. He seemed normal when we met but I was very worried about his gestures and attitudes it was exactly the same as he had in Vietnam. He began mistreating us again. My son and I were not allowed to move from the bunk without his permission.

He would go to his sister's bunk and spend most of his time there. Whenever he came back it was just to check whether I was in my bunk or not. He advised me to cover the bunk carefully so that other people in the hut would not see when he beat me up. One day he strangled me accusing that I do not know how to bring up my child. He threatened saying that if I tell anybody about this, he would kill me. During night I was unable to sleep because of fear. My child and I were living in fear.

One day my husband requested me to get a paper and a pen to prepare the application for the refugee status determination process. Even though I was nervous to meet my sister-in-law, I ran to her hut to get paper and a pen. It took some time for me to arrange pen and paper. My husband got angry at this delay. He accused me that I was irritating him and he threatened to kill me. This time I went to the camp social worker's office. While I was sitting in the office, I saw he was searching for me. The social worker immediately called the police and asked me think about the options I had at that time. I decided to request for a transfer to another camp.

I was transferred to the Whitehead camp at the very same day. When I went to the Whitehead camp I felt better. I began to sleep and eat well. But I was disturbed by nightmares, I dreamed of living with his family and he became terribly ill and trying to strangle me. While I was at the new camp I decided to apply to get a divorce from my husband. A few months later, I got a letter from him. He accused me that I was cruel to him and if I did not want to live with him I have to return my son to him. In March 1991, he came to the Whitehead camp to visit us and gave my son HK $100 and some clothes and we talked for a while.

Even though, I had applied for a divorce I was in dilemma. I was reluctant and scared to go ahead with the divorce proceedings. Whenever my son was bullied by other children, he would cry and ask me 'why do the other children have father, but I do not have'. I felt so lonely and sad whenever my child got sick and I had to take care of him alone. I cried out my anguish in private.

Finally I came to terms with the fact that my husband was a chronically mentally ill person. Whenever I stayed with him my son and I were living in perpetual fear. When I came to Hong Kong I thought he might have changed, but in vain. On March 26, 1992, I managed to talk to him over the phone. He threatened me that he would take my son away from me if I went ahead with the divorce proceedings. Even if I manage to resettle in another country, or go back to Vietnam, he said; he would arrange to snatch my son away from me. I requested the camp management, social workers and lawyers to help me. My circumstances are poor I have no relatives in a third country, or in Hong Kong camps to help or to support me. My husband's family is rich, powerful and they have authority in Vietnam and overseas. So when he is threatening me, I am really afraid of my life. Please help me I can't live in fear all in my life.

Legitimising the detention of refugees

Some of the major refugee settlements in the world are continuing for more than 10 years. Tigranyans and Eritrean in Sudan, Afgans in Pakistan, Tibetans in India, Salvadoriand in Honduras, Cambodians and Laotians in Thailand, Mozambicans in Malawai, Anglolans in Zaire. However, incarceration of large number of asylum seekers in Hong Kong is a unique social and political phenomenon. A very limited information is available to the researchers and general community regarding the living conditions in the refugee detention centres. Most of the refugee detention centres are considered as a security issue by the governments rather than a grave humanitarian issue. When the asylum seekers are not detained they are assigned to remote international borders or to areas generally inaccessible to the general public. This section describes the day to day life of the asylum seekers and their transition in the detention centres.

Camp management practices and it's impact on the life of the detainees, the general profile of a camp, social service facilities in a camp, camp amenities, how the asylum seeking community is organised in the camps, survival strategies of the asylees as well as strategies developed by the asylum seekers to cope with the consequences of ethnocide, such as various economic activities in the camp, role of religion, psycho social problems in the camps in general, and the role of community development activities in the camp are discussed in relation to the process of ethnocide is discussed in this chapter.

The process of community disintegration and the roots of this process are explored as well.

Separation and segregation of asylum seekers itself contribute to the process of community disorganisation and demoralisation. This process has both individual and group consequences. The most important observation made is about the direction of change. The changes taking place are self destructive and negative. Mostly, this phenomenon is worse than the situation they experienced in their own country. The Vietnamese asylum seekers are legally, socially and institutionally segregated and separated from the Hong Kong population. Asylum seekers are under the administrative detention as per the Immigration laws of British - Hong Kong Government. Though, detaining a person without the benefit of legal trial is against the basic principles of the English Law.

The detention centres (generally referred to as camps) are in the suburbs or in uninhabited outlying islands. In general, the Hong Kong public is largely unaware of the life or living conditions in the detention centres. The press and the public are barred from the camps. Only the camp administration staff, United Nations High Commissioner for Refugees (UNHCR) officials, few religious persons and some social service agency staff are allowed to visit them during normal office hours. UNHCR and social service staff leaves the camp after office hours.

The immigration laws under which the Vietnamese are detained are based on the British Prison Laws with certain amendments. The detention of asylum seekers is against the basic spirit of 1951 Convention on the status of refugees, and International Covenant on Civil and Political Rights (ICCPR). The Comprehensive Plan of Action (CPA) that was proposed by the United Nations general assembly to control the unrestricted flow of humanity from Vietnam during the late 1980s does not authorise detaining asylum seekers. The British-Hong Kong government's social ostracism of asylum seekers is often orchestrated through the xenophobic public utterances of the appointed members of Hong Kong law making body. The British-Hong Kong government has passed necessary regulations to bring migrant workers from other overseas countries to ease acute labour shortage. But any suggestion to employ the Vietnamese was met with rejection.

Forty two percent of the asylum seekers in Hong Kong were under eighteen years old. The immigration ordinance allows imposing a condition on any refugee that he or she shall not become a student in a School, University or other educational institution. Unlike rest of Hong Kong, the law does not require child asylees and refugee children to attend school. The camp schools are not registered or supervised under the Education Ordinance of Hong Kong. The quality of education offered to the refugee children is questionable.

Differential management practices in Hong Kong detention centres

The Vietnamese are under the administrative detention in the following detention centres. Chi Ma Wan Detention Centre (Upper and Lower Camps), Hei Ling Chau Detention Centre, Green Island Reception Centre, Whitehead Detention Centre, Argyle Street Detention Centre, Lo Wu Detention Centre, Tai A Chau Vietnamese Holding centre, High Island Detention Centre, Nei Kwu Chau Detention Centre, Victoria prison and Sek Kong Detention Centre.

Even though all the detention centres come under uniform rules, the daily management pattern varies from camp to camp. The difference in the daily administrative practice has a profound impact on the life situation of people living in the detention centres. Depending upon the administrative practices, the level of community participation and the pattern of participation varied. So does the ability of the population to cope with the stress of being a detainee. In the camps managed by the Correctional Service Department (CSD), and the Hong Kong Housing Service for Refugees (HKHSR), there is an elected community representative structure. But in the camps managed by the police, the community leaders are appointed after a police verification of the candidates. The Hong Kong Police department, Hong Kong CSD, and HKHSR are the key administrators of the refugees, asylum seekers and the asylum seekers who are determined as non-refugees.

The Civil Aid Society, a largely volunteer group is also involved in the running of some of the small camps. The overall co-ordination of the refugees and asylum seekers is under the administration of the Security branch of British-Hong Kong Government. The differential management practices in the camps also affect the basic rights of the camp residents. The management practices vary from the relative freedom in Tai A Chau camp to the complete segregation of the asylees in the camps based on gender, separating husbands, wives and children, and locking them up in huts after sunset in Lo Wu, and Green Island camp. In some camps, the management confiscates even music systems, pocket radios and other personal items.

The physical changes experienced by the asylum seekers are, a new place to live, mostly a bed space in a crowded three-tier bed system without any privacy or personal space. A family or group of five live in a bed space of 8 ft. by 6 ft. by 3 ft; crammed with all their belongings. Usually only a thin cotton curtain separates them from the next family. For several asylum seekers this space has been their home for five to six years. They are not even able to stand up in their bunk space. Even Hong Kong's criminal prisoners have space to stand up in their cells.

The bed space itself is assigned by the camp administration. Asylum seekers have very limited or no option regarding the selection or use of their space. In most cases there is no special provision for the elderly, disabled, women or families with small children. Most asylum seekers have little or no personal possessions. During winter all of them are exposed to the severity of the weather. When the summer heat rises to 40°C, the metallic Nissan huts are no protection against the heat. In at least five centres the asylum seekers are locked in their huts during night, ostensibly for their own security, but with little regard for their safety in case of a fire or an emergency. They are confronted with new diseases. The spread of HIV virus is a real threat. Officials from the Department of Health reported 106 new cases of venereal disease out of a total of 400 people seeking medical treatment in 1991, in the Whitehead Detention Centre holding 22,888 Vietnamese asylum seekers (SCMP, August 25, 1992).

Deteriorating nutritional status and extremely limited self-care facilities contributed to the lowering of health standards. The nature of overall biological changes experienced by the refugees under detention is unknown. The medical facilities and access to proper and relevant information is always a concern for the service agency staff and the asylees themselves. On June 28, 1990, a Vietnamese woman, mother of a small child, died on her way back to the High Island Detention Centre after being discharged from the Prince of Wales Hospital, where she had been sent as an emergency case earlier in the day. A number of witnesses reported that it had taken five minutes to resuscitate her when she fainted in the police truck, which was carrying her back to the detention centre. Despite her repeated pleas to take her back to the hospital, the Police refused to do so. Apparently she did not have the correct referral papers (Davis, 1991).

The UNHCR gag order and its impact

There is no scope for the asylum seekers to organise themselves politically and gain political power to influence decisions related to their own future. All forms of communication channels with the outside world and between themselves and different sections within the camps is controlled. The service agency staffs are ordered to make sure that access to the telephone is controlled or supervised. Even some of the Humanitarian Aid and Social Service Agency

Personnel unplug their own telephone instruments and carry it with them while they are away from their offices. Added to the revised guidelines from the UNHCR in consultation with the lead agencies and Security Branch, a new clause (item 12) has been added to the guidelines for the operations of NGOs in detention centres. 'Individuals who are working in the detention centres under the auspices of the assistance program should treat any information received directly from the centre residents or other sources with confidentiality'. This includes matters relating to the claims for refugee status of asylum seekers. Relations with the media should be consistent with the media policies of respective agencies. Normally the authorisation from the head of an agency is required before staff or volunteers can talk to the media (HK BO: UNHCR REF NO: AS/0142 (502). Most interestingly this document was signed by the UNHCR social service co-ordinator.

UNHCR itself highlighted the value of information as protection in many of the UNHCR documents. Information is both a resource and a tool for the protection of refugees. It is the resource that alerts governments, international agencies and private groups to the needs of refugees. It is often the tool that persuades such entities to act and convinces the members of the public to support their action. It may also help refugees choose the most appropriate decisions about their life and future (UNHCR, 1993). When UNHCR Hong Kong decided to gag the agency staff to control the flow of information from within the camps, it also effectively sealed off an important prerequisite for the protection of refugees in Hong Kong. This was the most decisive action, which accelerated the process of ethnocide in the camps.

The new regulation effectively restricts the possibility of an asylum seeker getting legal or moral support from outside. It has muzzled the few vocal, agency staff. All personal mail is censored by the camp administration before it is distributed. Often some of the material is confiscated. In some of the CSD run camps, radios, newspapers, magazines and cameras are prohibited. Any such item kept by the asylum seekers is liable to be confiscated. Most ironically, the humanitarian halo of the UNHCR will prevent any effective scrutiny of its actions in Hong Kong. Most tragically, the UNHCR implemented a series of policies in Hong Kong, particularly from 1998 onwards, which has contributed against the best interest of the refugees and asylum seekers. As the rewt interest defind by the refugees. The professional administrators of UNHCR in Hong Kong were beyond any form of accountability to the international community or to the refugees.

Economic changes faced by the asylum seekers are from no economic resources to forced unemployment, underemployment or new forms of employment with token or no payment at all. A few asylum seekers who were lucky enough to get a job with the agencies or with the camp administration were entitled to get a maximum salary of HK$180 per month (approximately US $22 in accordance with the prison terms).

The cultural changes in the detention centres are: a new language is accrued or the importance of one's own language changes or diminishes. Cox, while discussing about the impact of migration on children observed considerable evidence of difficulties emerging when children are obliged to switch their language - when their cultural norms are not reinforced or even devalued by those around them or experience conflict within or without the family between their cultural norms and those of significant others. In some children this can create great confusion and suffering resulting in serious emotional difficulties, intellectual retardation and disturbed personal relationships (Cox, 1990).

Freedom for religious practices

It is often claimed that there was no denial of religious freedom in the camps. However, in reality religious practices are restricted or limited. The camp residents have to make several petitions to retain their religious freedom. In August 1992, the Sek Kong Detention Camp Management denied the Catholic group their freedom to attend their weekly Holy Mass. They had to make several petitions to the camp management, and UNHCR, for permission to gather for weekly mass. The following is the letter from the catholic community, signed by 26 representatives of the community addressed to the camp authorities.

On behalf of Catholic representatives in SKDC we present this petition for your consideration with good wishes for your health and thanks to you for having allowed us to gather in the school to attend the mass every Saturday for the last three years. After a meeting with the representative from the welfare section and the Catholic Chaplain Fr. Peter Lam and Catholic sister Marinei last Monday (Aug. 3, 1992), we were told that from now on we will not be able to attend the weekly mass as usual. The Catholic Church instructs its faithful to attend the Mass weekly and such an instruction is part of the six main commandments of the church. We, the Vietnamese Boat People suffered religious persecution in Vietnam and were many times prevented from gathering together to exercise our religious duties. We were very glad to be **able to breathe the air of religious freedom in Hong Kong by being able to** gather together to pray. This has been the only source of consolation to endure the hardships of our present life and the uncertainty of our future.

Because we have only one priest who can speak Vietnamese (according to the changed arrangements only one priest is allowed at a time to enter the camp for religious practices), each section will have to wait for three weeks before attending Mass again. We know we will have a religious service conducted by the Sisters every week but it is different from attending the Holy Mass. Besides, the community huts are also used in the morning by other religious groups and we do not know if the place will be really allocated to us and we would like not to enter into conflict with other religious groups or be left standing outside in the summer heat.

We have always tried our best to keep good discipline for the sake of camp security while participating in Holy Mass and we consider that we haven't done anything wrong which would break the camp regulations. So, we respectfully present this petition for your consideration in order to accept our request to continue attending Mass weekly by gathering all the Catholics from the three sections at the school. So as we will be able to fulfil the requirements of our Catholic faith and exercise our Catholic faith and our religious freedom. [Signed by 26 representatives from all the sections]

Often new religious affiliations are formed. Some of the Christian Zealots used this opportunity to preach and covert them into Christianity. A large number of religious conversions have been reported from the camps. Most interestingly these religious groups were out of the UNHCR frame of reference, and they were not required to attend the mandatory inter-agency co-ordination meeting. The Security Branch of the Hong Kong government gives permission to some of these Christian evangelical groups.

Reinforcement of cultural identity is an integral part in sustaining self-esteem. In the detention centre context, very often, the service agency staff and the camp administrative staff ridicule Vietnamese identity, intentionally or unintentionally or as a control tactics 'to keep the asylees in their place'.

Access to education is limited for the asylum seekers, or substandard education is offered. Access to new or any kind of technology is limited or controlled. The possibility of elder generation transferring their rituals and belief systems to the younger generation is also limited or restricted. Asylum seekers social relations, inter-group and intra-group relations were deliberately left to deteriorate. New forms of group conflicts have been emerging and patterns of social dominance have changed. Group allegiance is formed on the lines of North-South, and provinces, districts of origin, and so on.

To return or not to return

There was also tension in the camps between those who had opted for voluntary repatriation and those who were unwilling to return to Vietnam. In several cases, spouses and or siblings had different opinion regarding their return to Vietnam. Hence, this resulted in one party returning without a partner. Group conflict became a way of life. On February 3-4, 1992, in the ensuing riot between two groups in Sek Kong Camp, 24 Vietnamese, including women, children and elderly were burned to death and about 100 were hospitalised (this case is narrated in detail in the following chapter). Another major source of tension within the camps was in keeping the asylum seekers together with the asylum seekers who were determined as non-refugees.

A Vietnamese woman, Ms. Tran, who challenged the Government's screening process in Hong Kong High court but settled the case with the government lawyer along with eight others shortly before the judgement, was stabbed by fellow residents when she was returned to the White Head Detention Centre. A Vietnamese man with a broken fluorescent light stabbed her and her husband after an altercation. Just before judge Mortimer was to make a ruling on their case, the group of eight people who challenged the government's screening policy, agreed to end the case in exchange for a new interview with the Refugee Status Review Board (RSRB). This was brought about through a secret negotiation with the asylum seekers by the camp management to 'save the face' of Hong Kong government, But only two were granted refugee status. During the court hearing Ms. Tran claimed that she had been persecuted for 25 years in Vietnam for being a devout Catholic. But the RSRB rejected her claim for refugee status.

The group was shunned and criticised by fellow asylum seekers for accepting Government's offer of a second appeal hearing rather than proceeding with their judicial review. Many observers believed that the landmark case might have resulted in a ruling that would force the administration to review all the screening procedure. Most major conflicts between the camp management were reported in 'Hei Ling Chau Report' by the Justices of the Peace (JPs) Denis, Chang khen-lee and Edward Hamilton enquiry report on the CSD assault on a large number of asylum seekers and the death of an asylum seeker in SKDC police beating.

Life in 'Tiger Cages'

Some of the researchers on Hong Kong camp life reached the conclusion that **violence on women and children is mostly perpetuated by their fellow asylum** seekers (for instance MacCallin, 1993). I am not denying the fact that violence is often perpetuated by the asylum seekers on others, but such portrayals often evolve out of a stereotyped understanding of asylum seekers and the violence in the camps. The best protection an asylum seeker can get in the camp is often from their own neighbours and support network. But the constant movement of asylum seekers from one camp to another deliberately discouraged formation of such support network.

Day to day violations of individual rights and harassment by the camp authorities was often under reported. As a camp worker, I have come across innumerable cases. Mr Tran Quoc Tuan's case is presented to explain the nature of such day to day violations of individual rights. Most of the camps have a detention facility within the detention camps to segregate the 'violators of camp rules'. In Sek Kong detention centre this was known as the '*Tiger Cage*'. The tiger cage is 2m by 5m separately fenced enclosure right near the main gate of the detention centre in the immediate vicinity of the camp command post. One day when I went to work at SKDC as usual, I saw Mr Tran Quoc Tuan (VRD 236/91, F/No 8821, Hut B7 Section B SKDC) in the *Tiger Cage*. I looked into this case, as this was an example of violation of individual rights in the camps.

There was no water supply on May 22, 1992 in section B of SKDC. Since morning the residents of section B were requesting the camp management to go to section A to get water for morning ablutions. At about 8.30 a.m., one young girl who was waiting near the gate between Section B and Section A, with a bucket, repeatedly asked for permission to go the other section to get water. The policeman at the gate got annoyed with this. As the girl was inside the gate he spat on the girls face. Mr. Tran happened to come to the gate at that time and he saw what had happened, and verbally challenged the policemen from inside the fence. As a culmination of a series of events it landed him in the '*Tiger Cage*'. The details of the event was written by Mr Tran in his letter to various service agencies requesting help from them to be released from police custody.

At 8.30 in the morning on May 22, 1992, when I went to the gate of section B I saw a policeman was shouting at a girl. I did not know the reason of the fight. When I went closer to the gate I saw the policeman spiting on the girl's face. The angry girl shouted back at the policeman in a foul language. He opened the gate and rushed towards the girl and slapped her and pushed her down into the dirty slime and went back to his position outside the gate. The girl, in tears, got up from the mud and slime and went to the gate to read the badge number of the policeman. This infuriated the policeman again. He rushed in and pushed the girl into the puddle again and dragged her out through the gate. When I saw this, impulsively, I felt I must do something to stop this. I went to the gate and tried to release the girl from the policeman's grip. When he began shouting at me in anger, I got frightened and tried to get back to the door. The policeman chased me to Section B and I began running to escape from the police.

While running, I slipped and fell. The policeman then beat me on my back. Responding to the wireless message from the policeman some other police also joined him. They lifted me up, by pulling my hair. They handcuffed me and took me to the camp administrative office. I sat there for three hours facing a wall, without permission to move. The police gathered some people from the camp to give evidence against me. They asked them to narrate the incident. They photographed and transferred me to the nearest police station. A police complaint was lodged against me. They fingerprinted, photographed and questioned me again. They forced me to squat on the floor with out moving, throughout the night.

The following morning, I was again transferred to another police station. They read the charge-sheet to me, accusing me of assaulting a policeman and obstructing his duty. They kept me in custody for another two days, waiting for the court hearing. At the court, I was asked whether I assaulted any policemen. I denied this allegation. I also told the court that I would like to go back to Sek Kong so that I can attend my school. The court also asked me to narrate the incident. The court adjoined without a decision and the next trial was set for September 25, 1992, and I was taken back to the SKDC 'isolation section'. I am at the 'isolation section' since then.

Individual disorientation

Inability of certain asylees to cope with the camp situation turns their attention to self-destruction activities. A proportionately high number of suicides and attempted suicides were reported in the camps. These attempts may be a desperate cry for help from an acute sense of hopelessness. About 30 trained caseworkers offer counselling on an average to 1,200 clients every month indicating their level of mental health situation.

Some of the psychological changes noticed among the asylees are: their value systems are changing, individual abilities are deteriorating, and motives for social relationships have qualitatively changed to selfish or manipulative. Perception regarding self-identity is also rapidly changing. Child asylees in detention who are without parents or immediate legal guardians (about 4,500 such children are in Hong Kong) are the most vulnerable group. Internationally accepted norms of children's rights are denied to this group. Even though the CPA and the UN convention of the rights of the child consider anyone below the age of 18 as a child. In Hong Kong detention centres the child asylees (without parental care) is considered as child, if only they are below 16 years of age on the day of the refugee status determination interview with the immigration department.

The psychological and intellectual impairment of children due to incarceration will come to light only years later. By then the irreversible damage would already have been done to thousands of children. All aspects of life in the detention centres are under public glare. There is no privacy for a couple to air their differences. The disagreement often takes place in the open, thus, reducing the possibility of reconciliation. Moreover, spouses are often a convenient scapegoat to target one's own frustrations due to uncertain incarceration. An alarming level of spouse abuse is also being reported.

'Marriage or cohabitation for protection' is a process by which a young single woman can buy protection. Many women depend on this form of protection rather than the official protection mechanisms of law and regulations. 'Marriage of convenience' is often arranged and looked upon as an escape route to get out of indefinite detention. There are various incidents of dissolution of traditional marriages (which are not officially registered) in favour of marrying someone from a resettled country so that they could escape from the detention centres.

Teenage pregnancy and the Medical Termination of Pregnancy cases are exceptionally high among the child asylees (especially among children without parental care). According to the Family Planning Association of Hong Kong, the number of legal abortions performed in the Vietnamese detention centres increased by 127 per cent to 246 in 1991. In 1989 there were 37 abortions.

In general, culturally appropriate family planning facilities are not available for anyone other than the 'officially married couples'. The Family Planing Association of Hong Kong decides who should be the beneficiary of the family planing services. In some camps the Family Planing service unit announces the names of the prospective female clients over the public address system to approach the clinic for family planning services. During 1990, the birth rate of Vietnamese asylum seekers was 55 per 1000. During 1991 it was 32. And in 1992 it is expected to be 30. Comparing to the birth rate of 12.8 for 1000 in Hong Kong, the birth rate in detention centres is very high.

Separation and segregation of asylum seekers and the subsequent factors contribute towards the process of community disorganisation and demoralisation. This process has both individual and group consequences. The most important observation I have made is about the direction of behavioural change. The changes taking place are self-destructive and negative. Mostly this phenomenon is worse than the situation they experience in their own country.

Glimpse of freedom

As an anthropologist/community worker in the camp, I was aware of the consequence of rigid separation of refugees from the outside world. Often I explored the possibility to break such segregation in whatever way I could 'legally'. One of the strategies I evolved was to use my personal rapport with some of the camp managers to exploit a loophole in the detention policy. Under the discretion of the camp manager, asylum seekers are allowed to go out (with escort) briefly during the daytime. The police managed camps were more liberal in allowing such 'outings'. I was instrumental in organising several brief 'outings' for the children, elderly and the community leaders from the Sek Kong Detention Centre. Once after such a trip to a local amusement park, The Ocean Park, especially, organised for the elderly (this luxury materialised because of the generosity of the park authorities and a local parish priest) the representative of the elderly group wrote a prose to show their feelings towards freedom. Mr. Ngoc Lau on (Midnight) 23 March 1992 wrote:

We have no words to avail to show our gratitude to you, for organising a trip for us to go out. I am only an asylum seeker, trying to compose a few words to express our love to you. You gave us a precious memory. A memory to cherish all my life.

HERE FREEDOM:
There is only a little, but enough a precious moment.
We suffered so much in our lives.
Miseries in life, in sea, miseries in our trip
But today we had a chance to see, to hear happiness.

We are old and asylum seekers in a strange country.
Our fragile frames are detained...
Suddenly we saw greenery...
The sea...

I feel like a human being...
I am a visitor...
Let me run up to the mountain...
Let me run down to the sea...

The shark from under the ocean waved at us
Wait a minute shark you want to come with me?
Let me take a 'snap' of you.
Now I feel you are better than many human beings.

Shark how old are you?
Your circus is marvellous.
You can look at the cloud
You can sing and play well...

I could hear the birds singing
from the top of the mountain.
The greenery is so wonderful
The peacock dance to the tune of the waterfalls.

Oh poor birds in the cages.
You are like me, I have nowhere to escape.
I do not open my lips inside the barbed wire.
But you can.

And the sun set...
I am back in the detention centre.

Profile of a detention camp

The detention centre is not only a community of Vietnamese asylees, it is also an area of interaction between two other forces - the camp administration and various social service agency staff. The roles and functions of all these actors are interdependent and influence the outcome of the 'detention culture'.

I chose Tai A Chau detention centre as a case study for a profile of a detention centre mainly due to my access to the camp as a camp level worker. Even though I had an option to work in other camps, I selected Tai A Chau, primarily because I was curious to see the impact of relative freedom (to move around in the island during the daytime) on the social conditions of the asylum seekers and how they utilised this facility. Even though it is perceived that there was freedom very few people opted to move around in the island.

Most of them were confined to their bunks most of the time. In effect there was not much difference between other camps and Tai A Chau camp. Tai A Chau also had a history of riots when the Royal Hong Kong Police maintained the camp.

Tai A Chau is an hour's 'speed boat' ride from Central, Hong Kong. It is a hilly, barren, barely habitable patch of rock measuring less than half a square mile. Situated at the edge of Hong Kong's territorial waters, the native fishermen abandoned the island due to scarcity of fresh water. A Hong Kong company, the 'Hong Kong Land' bought large sections of the island some years ago to develop Tai A Chau as a holiday resort, but the plan was dropped because of financial problems. Today, it is converted into a beautifully landscaped island. A custom-made drainage system, water, electricity and communication cables are linked to the island as part of the 'infrastructure development'. The residents are asked to contribute free labour to de sledge the small fresh water pond. It is being developed into a duck-breeding farm. The asylum seekers under the supervision of the camp management landscaped a large section of the island.

'The Hong Kong Land' should be the happiest people in allowing the Vietnamese to use the island. In return, they got the island developed as a resort at public expenditure, and at the cheap labour of asylum seekers. During 1990, the authorities spent HK $230 million to develop the island with water, sewerage system and all weather huts to house the Vietnamese (the UNHCR was expected to pay the bills). The new residents were about 8,000 Vietnamese asylum seekers. Since 1989 this island was a shelter for the asylum seekers, however, during that time the asylum seekers were kept in makeshift tents.

Table 6.1   TAC Camp Population Summary by Sex and Age Group as of January 31, 1993

Age	Male	Female	Total
Under 1	169	157	326
01 - 05	580	546	1126
06 - 15	910	724	1634
16 - 29	2103	1704	3807
30 - 39	767	749	1516
40 - 49	293	179	472
50 - 59	63	42	105
60 - over	48	37	85
Total	4933	4138	9071

Even though, the island is declared as a detention centre and administered under the same immigration detention rules, the unique geographical aspect allowed the residents more freedom than many other camps. Except the earlier days of commissioning, the camp residents were allowed to move around the island during daytime.

In many aspects Tai A Chau is not a sample of a typical Hong Kong Detention Centre. The camp is divided into four sections holding about 2,500 people in each section (Table 6.2 population by area). A private company, the Hong Kong Housing Services for Refugees (HKHSR) manages it with a small detachment of Marine police.

Table 6.2   TAC Detention Centre Population Summary by Area as of January 31, 1993

Area	No of residents	Escape	KTVMTC	Total
A	2332	8	29	2295
B	2266	7	37	2222
C	2176	5	20	2151
D	2297	4	29	2264

HKHSR Limited was established in Hong Kong solely for the purpose of providing accommodation facilities for the Vietnamese. The same company is running the only refugee centre in the territory, the Pillar Point Refugee Camp. An executive director under the supervision of the board of directors manages the camp. A senior manager based at the camp is running the day to day management of the camp. A deputy senior manager, who is also in charge of projects and recreations, assists the senior manager. A regulatory manager, technical and administration managers assist the deputy senior manager.

There are assistant managers for food and beverages, logistics, project and recreation, hygiene, maintenance, administration, and welfare issues. Each department has a sizeable number of clerical staff and Vietnamese asylum seeker staff, (Refer Fig 6.1 for organisation chart of Tai A Chau Detention centre). The residents and the service agency staff deal mostly with the welfare department. Welfare department is responsible for a wide **spectrum of services; asylum** seekers' visits to other camps, hiring welfare workers, burial, **cremation arrangements, tracing of asylum seekers, posting of notices, visits** to the huts, counselling on family disputes, marriage and divorce applications, birth and death certificates, identification and foster care for unaccompanied minors, status registration, co-ordination with the clinic on medical cases,

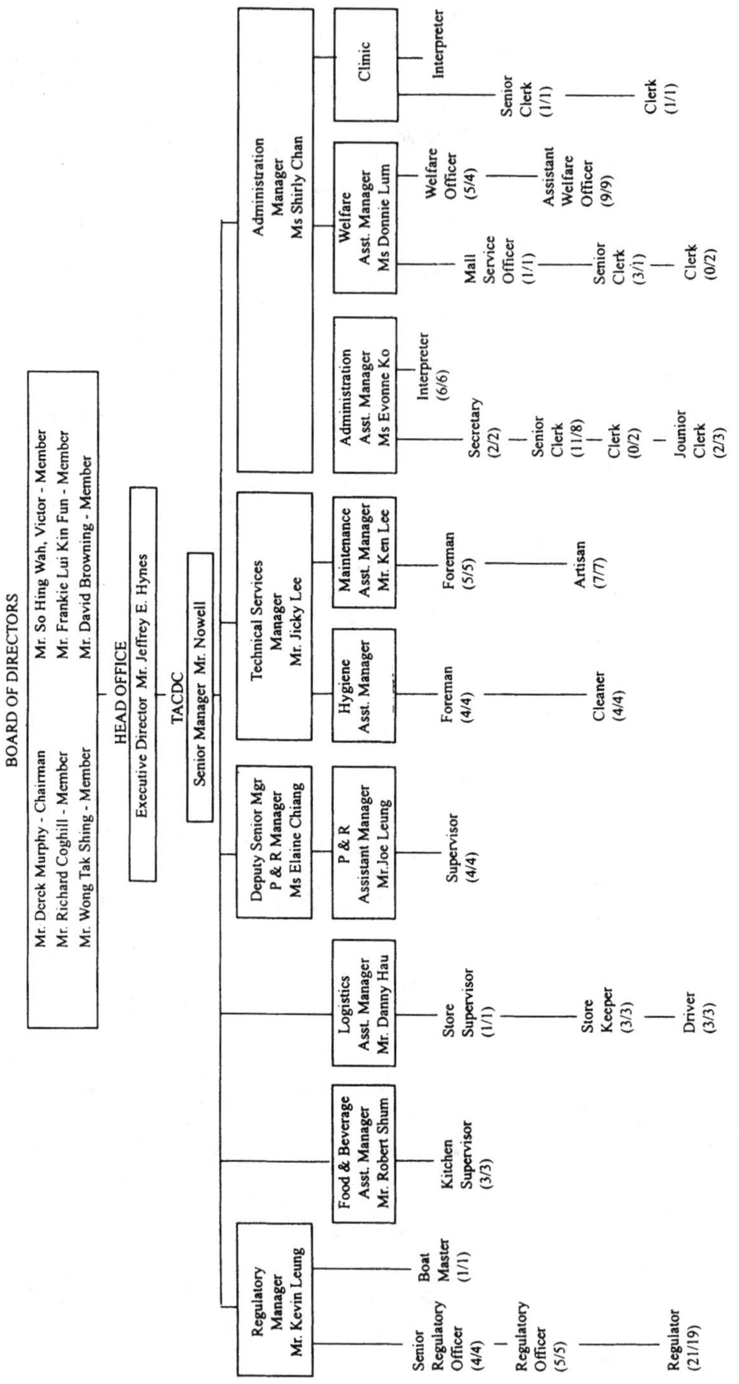

BOARD OF DIRECTORS

Mr. Derek Murphy - Chairman   Mr. So Hing Wah, Victor - Member
Mr. Richard Coghill - Member   Mr. Frankie Lui Kin Fun - Member
Mr. Wong Tak Shing - Member   Mr. David Browning - Member

HEAD OFFICE

Executive Director Mr. Jeffrey E. Hynes

TACDC

Senior Manager Mr. Nowell

Deputy Senior Mgr
P & R Manager
Ms Elaine Chiang

Regulatory Manager Mr. Kevin Leung

- Senior Regulatory Officer (4/4)
- Regulatory Officer (5/5)
- Regulator (21/19)
- Boat Master (1/1)

Food & Beverage Asst. Manager Mr. Robert Shum

- Kitchen Supervisor (3/3)

Logistics Asst. Manager Mr. Danny Hau

- Store Supervisor (1/1)
- Store Keeper (3/3)
- Driver (3/3)

P & R Assistant Manager Mr. Joe Leung

- Supervisor (4/4)

Technical Services Manager Mr. Jicky Lee

Hygiene Asst. Manager
- Foreman (4/4)
- Cleaner (4/4)

Maintenance Asst. Manager Mr. Ken Lee
- Foreman (5/5)
- Artisan (7/7)

Administration Manager Ms Shirly Chan

Administration Asst. Manager Ms Evonne Ko
- Interpreter (6/6)
- Secretary (2/2)
- Senior Clerk (11/8)
- Clerk (0/2)
- Jounior Clerk (2/3)

Welfare Asst. Manager Ms Donnie Lum
- Welfare Officer (5/4)
- Assistant Welfare Officer (9/9)
- Mall Service Officer (1/1)
- Senior Clerk (3/1)
- Clerk (0/2)

Clinic
- Interpreter
- Senior Clerk (1/1)
- Clerk (1/1)

Figure 6.1   Organization Chart for TAC Detention Centre

keeping daily movement register, escorting patients, briefing of pregnant women and patients, deployment of interpreters, out-patient transportation arrangement, hospital visits, bed allocation, transportation and distribution of donations, issuing purchasing permit, welfare administration, money remittance, identity card issuing, redemption of confiscated items, residents property registration, and mail services are some of the daily routine work done by the welfare department of the camp.

The social service facilities in Tai A Chau camp

Access to adequate social service facilities could reduce the negative consequence of the effect of ethnocide. In this section an assessment is carried out to ascertain the level of social service facilities available in Tai a Chau detention camp. UNHCR, International Social Services (ISS), Caritas, Community and Family Services International (CFSI), Jesuit Refugee Services (JRS), Save the Children Fund (SCF), Hong Kong Christian Aid for Refugees (HKCAR) and the Hong Kong Health Department are the agencies offering services to the residents of Tai A Chau camp.

The International Social Services (ISS)

ISS is an international voluntary agency mainly involved in the area of education for the underprivileged all over the world. The Hong Kong branch of ISS was established in 1958. ISS Hong Kong branch under the auspices of UNHCR was responsible for working with the asylum seekers (Vietnamese migrants according to ISS documents) in the areas of education, skill training, and recreation. At Tai A Chau, the ISS is located in the school block outside the camp confines and focuses primarily on education and recreational issues for children and adults. ISS is operating five education programs in Tai a Chau with the help of four professional staff (outside staff) and 170 Vietnamese staff.
1. The school is divided into two levels: Primary (grades 1 to 5) and secondary (grades 6 to 10). Based on the 'UNHCR curriculum' the school offers two-language instruction, Vietnamese and Chinese.
2. The adult education program is offering courses in English, Chinese and typing.
3. Extra curricular activities (EXCAP) program: offers recreational and skill development for students in the areas of culture and art, as well as cultural

studies. Children are encouraged to be involved in organising games, outdoor activities, art classes and sports according to their interests. The group activities offered under this program are swimming, sports, video programmes, embroidery and toy making, and music and arts.

4. Teenage peer group program: seeks to attract groups of young people who are not attending school. This program offers activities in the area of personal and mental development. The peer group program offers the following group activities. Embroidery and drawing classes, sports group, music group, dance group and writers group.

5. Music education program in co-operation with Caritas: this program draws on the talents of Vietnamese musicians in the camp, to organise and conduct music activities within the camp.

The Caritas

Caritas is an international social service agency operating in many countries around the world as an arm of the Catholic Church. Since 1979, Caritas Hong Kong has been providing assistance to the Vietnamese population living in both open camps and detention centres. The areas of services offered by Caritas under the auspices of UNHCR are education, social welfare assistance, recreation and training. In Tai Ah Chau, Caritas has focused primarily on providing services in the area of welfare and recreation. Library, dance class, aerobic classes, handicrafts, beautician courses, hairdressing, dress making, soccer games, basketball games, regular video shows, and activities for the elderly are the programs conducted by Caritas. The Caritas library stocks over thousand old books and magazines in English, Chinese and Vietnamese. The camp residents can borrow the books by depositing their camp identity card as a deposit. The Caritas dance and aerobics program attracted several women in the camp. Eight dance classes and eight aerobic classes of about 30 to 40 students are enrolled in the program. The program is of three-month duration. Beautician course, women's hairdressing course and dress making courses are also popular among women in the camp. The beautician course admitted 15 students. The duration of the course is one month. Two batches of hairdressing courses offer two months training for 15 students each. Apart from programs for women, sports' training is also offered to the residents. Four teams of soccer, four teams of basketball and volleyball are trained by Caritas. The Caritas Tai Ah Chau program was run by two full time professional staff with the assistance of several asylum seekers.

The Community and Family Services International (CFSI)

CFSI is a social service agency providing assistance to the Vietnamese asylum seekers and other displaced persons in South East Asia. CFSI was offering social development program for the Vietnamese asylum seekers and the refugees in Hong Kong under the auspicious of UNHCR. Casework service and community development programs are the two important aspects of CFSI work in Hong Kong. CFSI in general support people help themselves to improve the quality of their lives during their time in the detention centres. CFSI assists individuals to cope with personal, family and social problems. Advocacy, family reunion, cases of single women, cases of elderly, unaccompanied minors, marital problems, child abuse, spouse abuse, mentally and physically handicapped, sick, rape victims, attempted suicides, victims of violence are some of the cases handled by the CFSI case workers.

CFSI community workers assists the community to develop community structures through community organisation. CFSI ensures community participation in community affairs through their assistance in developing elderly groups, religious groups, veterans groups, and special interest groups. The representatives are encouraged to represent their interests of the community to the camp management and to the service agencies. Community education is another part of CFSI community development work. Hygiene campaigns, health care issues, alcohol abuse, domestic violence are discussed in various community forums to create awareness about these issues. Five professional social service staff and 22 para-professional staff run the CFSI programs in Tai Ah Chau camp (a detailed discussion of the role of CFSI in the camps is presented in Chapter VIII).

The Jesuit Refugee Services (JRS)

JRS is an international social service agency under the auspices of the Catholic Church. In Hong Kong, JRS offered 'pre-screening' legal assistance to the asylum seekers. JRS offers information about the Hong Kong government immigration procedures and help people to prepare their cases to be presented to the immigration officers.

Save the Children Fund (SCF)

The save the Children Fund (SCF) an international child welfare agency is operating in all the refugee camps and detention centres in Hong Kong. It primarily focuses on providing health care and development support for children under 6 years of age. SCF had two programs at Tai Ah Chau; Pre-school and Well baby clinic. Pre-school are for children of in the age group three to five years, to prepare them to enter in primary one. Children are assisted in learning basic writing, reading, painting and music. Well-Baby clinic focuses on child health care. The clinic also provides services for the elderly, children less than 5 years and their mother, handicapped mothers, and pregnant women. Health education is also provided under this program, where hygiene, health, sex-education and family planning are also dealt with under the program. Five professional staff and several Vietnamese staff run the SCF programs.

The Hong Kong Christian Aid to Refugees (HKCAR)

HKCAR is a local Christian social service agency established to provide assistance to refugees in Hong Kong. It operates in all the detention centres in Hong Kong providing services in the area of work and training. This includes running shops, supervising factories, and operating clothing workshops and conducting vocational training courses. At Tai Ah Chau, HKCAR provided vocational training programs. HKCAR was running a clothing workshop with 20 pedal sewing machines. Sewing and pattern making classes are conducted for the teenage, intermediate and advanced levels. In addition a community-sewing program is also offered by HKCAR. Free hair cutting and training are conducted in conjunction with Caritas. A small business training class, computer classes, handicraft training is also provided by HKCAR. HKCAR organised regular visits of dentists to the camp.

The Clinic

The Tai Ah Chau health centre is operated by the Health department of Hong Kong to provide medical services to the Vietnamese asylum seekers. The centre is located just outside the camp compound and is equipped to provide medical treatment for most general health problems and equipped with a 15 bead ward. If problems arise of a more specialised or serious nature, the clinic can refer these cases to specialised out patient hospitals in Hong Kong. For emergency cases a Helicopter evacuation facility is also available to transport patients from the island to Hong Kong.

Medical consultation is available for the patients from the section A and B in the morning and in the afternoon for the patients from section C and D.

Prior to going to the clinic, patients have to get a registration slip from the camp welfare department. The registration for the section A and B commences at 9.00 AM and for section C and D, is at 1.00 PM. Specialised antenatal care, dentistry, postnatal care, family planning and optometry services are also available on a limited scale. A team of six doctors mans the clinic round the clock.

The Camp Security

A private company, 'Centurion Security Company' is in charge of the general security of the Tai Ah Chau camp. The private security guards man the gates and the ferry pier. Their area of operation is generally restricted to the outside aspects of the camp security. The security staffs are generally trained and experienced in industrial security rather than dealing with refugees. Quite understandably the relation between the security staff and the camp residents are not always smooth.

The rift between the security staff and the community occurred because of certain incidents in the past. (alcohol was the flash point for the conflict.) Some camp residents maintained 'residual anger' towards some of the members of the 'Security Team'.

The 'Regulators'

The camp management also had their own security guards known as 'regulators'. These regulators or the security guards had no training or sensitivity to the needs and problems of the Vietnamese asylum seekers. The regulators often do not wear uniforms and disguise their ID cards with leather jackets that resembles HK Government immigration department's ID cards, posing as immigration officers. The 'regulators' were also often acted as Hong Kong police and 'law enforcers' in the camp. As all the regulators are the local Chinese, they could easily manage to intimidate the asylum seekers.

Camp amenities

Water and sanitation: Providing water facility for a population of 10,000 is not always an easy task. The problem was lack of pressure in some taps, especially, in sections C and D, which subsequently affected the sanitation. Only three or four bathrooms are fully functional. Wastage of water is another problem due to missing taps. There are no hot water bathing facilities for the sick and the elderly. During winter this creates additional pressure on the hot water boiler system. Quite often long queues are formed in front of the hot water boilers. In each section there are three boilers, two for drinking water and one normally for bathing.

Food: Catering to about 10,000 people has its own logistics and management problems. It is alleged that the quality and quantity of food is not according to the standards set by the Hong Kong government. The vegetarians suffer more than others due to the poor quality of food. My informants reported that children suffer due to mal-nourishment as a result of the poor quality of food. The secretary for security, in consultation with the UNHCR, decides the quantity and quality of the rations for the asylum seekers. But there is no daily monitoring system to check the quantity and quality of the food. According to the security department a four-scale diet is implemented for the detainees (refer table no 6.3 for details of the camp diet).

Table 6.3   Supply of rations for Vietnamese asylum seekers detained in Hong Kong*

Item no	Description	Weight / quantity
1	Diet Scale A (Vietamese Boat people of 1 year and above, Two hot meals per day each containing)	
a	meat, fresh / forzen and wholessome beef (boneless)	85 g / meals 2 meals / week
	Pork (bonless) average 50 per cent lean	6 meals / week
	chicken wings (1 no weighing 95 - 110 gm / head / meal)	2 meals / week
	Tinned luncheon meat	2 meals / week
	Tinned fried dace with or without salted black beans or	2 meals / week
	Fish fresh 112 gm / meal	2 meals / week
b	Fresh seasonal green vegetables any one kind of vegetable must not be delivered more than 3 times a week	280 gms
c	Salt	14 gms
d	Chili	04 gms
e	Yue low	04 gms
f	Corn flower	05 gms
g	Oil for cooking	28 gms
h	Chinese tea	03 gms
i	Preserved vegetable	14 gms
j	Ginger or onion or garlic	07 gms
k	Bean products (fried cured balls / bean stripes / bean paste, bean curd soya bean)	14 gms

*   Three scale diet is aviable for the asylum seekers detained in Hong Kong, however only one scale is presented here.

Source: Security branch, SRD 807/1/C, 27.3.1990.

Even though, an elaborate menu exists, the camp residents or their representatives have seldom seen a copy of their ration allowances. The actual distribution of ration in relation to the statutory requirements is often debatable. The 1991 nutritional survey conducted by Save The Children Fund (SCF) for children under five years (N=1002) in the detention centres identified acute malnutrition. 7.1 per cent of the children under study were suffering from acute malnutrition, 26.8 per cent were suffering from mixed malnutrition and 20.5 per cent are suffering from chronic malnutrition. According to this study, malnutrition (67per cent) occurs more frequently between six and 24 months. Approximately 74 per cent of the malnourished children spent more than half of their life in the detention centres. Only 7.8 per cent spent less than two months in the detention centeres. About 30 per cent of the malnourished children have chronic disease, mostly chronic infectious diseases. Scabies and chronic diarrhoea are common among these children. The nutritional status of the children in detention centres is lower than the nutrition status of children in Vietnam (SCF Nutritional Survey in Detention Centres, 1991).

Community organisation in the camps

The first impression of any detention camp is total anarchy. Children run around, youngsters mill around aimlessly, grown-ups just sit idle in their bed bunks and the camp presents a picture of total confusion. However, in all the camps certain system has been organised for distribution of food, allocation of provisions, distribution of living space, to solve the day to day problems of sharing water, space and limited resources. The camp management exercises a considerable influence in deciding who would be the residents of Tai Ah Chau, unlike many other camps. The selection procedure was carefully monitored and any potential trouble-makers were excluded. Often the North Vietnamese were generally excluded, ethnic Chinese Vietnamese were preferred the Vietnamese (Table 6.4, population summary by regional groups). Thus Tai Ah Chau has a large concentration of ethnic Chinese-Vietnamese asylum seekers. This ethnic factor has implications in management functions. The HKHSR employed local Chinese staff and they can have a better communication with the camp residents.

Often, when new staff were recruited to the camp service agencies, the relatives of the already existing staff were preferred. Mostly single men were discouraged, because they were perceived as potential trouble-makers. When people were moved to Tai Ah Chau, the camp management deliberately assigned bunks through a purposive random selection. Already existing

Table 6.4   TAC Population Summary by Regional Group as at January 31, 1993

Place of Birth	Total no
South VN	5773
Central VN	2775
North VN	523
Total	9071

networks were deliberately discouraged. People who had previously been together in the same hut or in the same block were discouraged to flock together.

The primary nature of community organisation is in the form of informal networks. The community texture continues through cleaving and forming community cleavages. The social attachments existed in the camps were linked with the date and circumstance of arrival, occupational adherence, political cleaves, religious cleaves, age and sex network, kinship and ethnic network were also contributed to the camp structure. Camp management deliberately discouraged any form of such cleaves in the camp.

The camp administration has developed a form of community organisation for their own convenience. The camp administration and the agency staff acknowledge a community representative structure based on limited community participation. Hut leaders were nominated by the camp administration. The four 'areas' in the camp are further divided into four blocks/halls and 80 hall representatives are appointed by the camp management with equal representation of men and women. All the representatives were paid a token amount by the camp management. Monitoring food distribution, hygiene, general discipline in the huts, distribution of clothing and other donations are part of the responsibility of the hut leaders.

Apart from the 'hut leaders' there were other 'community leaders' in the camp. As a community worker in the camp my responsibility was to organise such groups and convey their concerns to the camp management. There were leaders of Chinese teaching group, traditional Chinese dance and music group, women's group, handicap persons group, elderly persons group, boy scouts and the scout animators, *Nungs* group, war veterans group, revival church, Vietnamese church, Catholics, *Quan Am* temple committee, the Buddhists, the Buddhist family group and the Master *Ching Hai* group. Recognition of these 'community leaders' was generally limited to the camp service agency staff and the camp residents. The camp management was reluctant to acknowledge the leadership role of these representatives. Yet these community leaders yielded considerable influence on the camp population.

The UNHCR representatives and the social service agency representatives met the leaders of various groups and the hut leaders every month to discuss various community issues. The camp community development workers were also constantly in touch with all the community leaders. The camp management normally invited 16 area representatives, UNHCR representatives, camp community worker (in this case myself) and religious group representatives for a monthly meeting.

Survival strategies in a detention camp

The survival strategies developed by the camp population are a testimony of their resilience. Even though the case study may portray the asylum seekers in a bad light, nonetheless, it is important to understand the strategies developed by some of them, if not all, to beat boredom, to get things done in the camp, to generate a small income, to present themselves differently, and in general to survive. Most of the survival strategies are very much similar in all the asylum seeker camps in Hong Kong. The only difference is in the scope of activities. The strategies presented in this study are not in any particular order. These strategies act as counter measures for survival from the onslaught of ethnocide. In essence, ethnocide contributes to the systematic assassination of the self by attacking the physical, mental and the social well being of the asylum seekers detained in the camps. Such a process is perpetuated in a systemic and structural level rather than by individuals. How much individuality the community or the individual could assert was the key point in deciding the contradiction between the process of ethnocide and the effort of the asylees to counter such efforts in whatever way they could in the detention context. They created a series of activities such as organising micro-economic activities in the camps, through barter, cash transactions, production of alcohol or exchange of services.

Micro-economic activities in the camp

Even though, any form of economic activities in the camps are restricted by the Hong Kong government, an active 'informal micro-economic' system operated inside most camps. Staff payments, remittance from abroad, agency programs, donations from informal sources and transaction between the outside staff and the residents were some of the source of income for the asylum seekers. The most important income source was the salary paid to the

Vietnamese staff by the agencies and the camp administration. The detention centre laws stipulated a maximum pay of HK $180 per month. The economic resources recycled through the transactions between residents who were involved in a number of economic activities.

Independent teaching was a well-respected and widespread economic activity. There were classes in English, Cantonese and Vietnamese. English classes were in great demand. HK $ 30 per month was the charge for teaching English per student in the camps. At a time there were about 40 to 50 English classes. Each class had about 30 students. For Vietnamese and Cantonese language class, the numbers enrolled was small, and the charge was HK $20 per student.

The number of 'informal shops' (the shops sold a few cigarettes, specially prepared food, coffee mix, biscuits, eggs, etc.) varied according to the availability of items for sale which are mostly smuggled in by various sources. Bringing any 'saleable' item into the camp itself was an economic activity. Residents brought these items to the camp when they went out for medical or legal reasons. The only hurdle was to smuggle them in through the security inspection at the ferry pier, which was often lax. Winemaking was the most lucrative and organised economic activity.

Organising gambling, offering protection for the gamblers, settlement of disputes, arranging space, doing errands, making special soup for customers, selling cigarettes to gamblers were some of the economic activities related to gambling. Making money by arranging telephone services was the privilege of a few who had access to social service agency telephones. The service charges varied according to the destination and the duration of the call. A local call can be as expensive as HK $5 to HK $10. Selling ice from various social service agencies' refrigerators was another form of economic activity of a few. It was used for the iced coffee sold in the coffee shops in the camps.

The profits from the 'telephone service' and the sale of ice (from the refrigerators of the service agencies) did not necessarily go to the agency employees. A substantial 'cut' had to be given to the 'organiser' at whose instance the services were offered. Some of the residents owned a music system, mostly given by relatives' abroad. Such a system with a good collection of cassettes was offered on 'hire' in the coffee shops to attract more clients. HK $20 was the normal hiring rate for a night.

Sexual liaison for monetary benefits was also practised discreetly by a few women. The clients were both from 'staff' and the residents. The only difference was that the 'outside' customers had to pay more.

Making hammocks and fishing nets from woollen clothes or from genuine ropes (if available) and making stationary child prams with bamboo sticks obtained from brooms were skilled economic activities (HK $15 for each). Tailoring, making dresses, hair dressing were also income generating skilled activities. Tooth Filling, and tooth extraction were practised only by the 'experienced' residents. If any of the residents were interested in keeping some of their camp situation in permanent memory, they could utilise the services of camp photographers for a small service charge.

HK $100 was the rate for 'helping' somebody to prepare their 'story' for immigration department refugee status determination procedure, for translating documents, repairing electronic equipment, repairing locks (it was more time efficient and quicker for the agencies to rely on the 'resident locksmiths' than the repair department of the management as only one packet of cigarettes was the service charge). Making fish sauce and washing clothes were some other activities, which generated some resources.

There were also enterprising fishermen in the camps. Their craft and gear were the fishing lines and nets made in the camps. The net is cast after clandestinely swimming far into the sea. The 'fishermen' sell their catch to the residents and also some times to the camp staff. Often the camp residents lose to the economic power of the camp staff in purchasing fresh fish!

Selling information to the police

It is alleged that the police intelligence network operated through the paid informer system developed by the police in the camps. The recruits were mostly from the pool of persons who already had a brush with the law enforcers. Charges against them were often soft-pedalled. In exchange, they had to work as camp informants. In effect, some of the law-breakers become informers so that they could keep up their other activities like running 'gambling joints' and maintaining links with the alcohol makers. Mostly, the one who crossed the path of the informers were booked as law-breakers. The advantage of this system was that the police had a regular source of 'controlled information' and also maintained a 'controlled intervention'.

Money transactions

Formal and informal money transaction facilities existed in the camps. The camp residents were expected to do all the 'official money transactions' through the 'Revival church workers' as they were the only ones 'permitted' to do the money transaction services by the camp management. However, informally, both Catholic and other Protestant groups were also willing to cash bank drafts, cheques and money orders. Reportedly some groups offered a better deal for money transactions. Often the transactions took a week or so. If somebody was in desperate need for cash, one had to 'sell' the bank draft or cheque to someone from the camp.

The US economic embargo on Vietnam had an impact on the money transactions in the camp. The major US bank 'Citibank' did not encash any draft addressed to a Vietnamese asylum seeker (again, if you have a Vietnamese name you can't cash your draft at Citibank) if the amount is more than US $300!

Consumption and distilling alcohol

One of the most fascinating aspects of camp life was the ingenuity of the asylum seekers to distil home made alcohol. It was also an interesting expression of 'creativity' in the camp. The most tangible indicator about the level of alcohol use in Tai Ah Chau camp (and in other camps) was the quantity of the alcohol seized by police. Reportedly police seized and destroyed about 100 gallons of alcohol or 'distilled wash' every week. Apparently, alcohol abuse was a source of family conflict, debt and violation of camp rules. Brewing, consumption and selling of alcohol were against the camp rules. Several family conflict cases reported to the caseworkers were related to alcohol abuse. Fighting under the influence of alcohol was a major source of tension in the camp.

Often camp property was damaged to collect materials for distilling alcohol. Illegal tapping of electricity for making alcohol caused - electric fuse blowouts, 'black outs'. Blackouts caused other problems related to the camp security. In addition, illegal taping of electricity was also a fire hazard. Water pipes were often vandalised for alcohol making, which lead to water distribution problems. Minors, young adults and children who were deprived of parental care were the potential victims of alcohol abuse in the camps. Some teenagers got in trouble with the law after consuming alcohol were transferred to Upper Chi Ma Wan prison as punishment. These children carry criminal records when they leave the camp. Groups of youngsters who sit around drinking alcohol during the night gradually turn into a noisy crowd as the night progresses, causing disturbance to other residents.

The process of making alcohol in Tai Ah Chau camp

In Tai Ah Chau camp two processes of alcohol making are employed. One is the 'Electrolysis Method' and the other is the 'Distilling Method'. The raw material for both the processes is the same. A large quantity of rice and 'yeast culture' for fermentation is needed. A large plastic bucket (a rubbish bin is mostly used for this purpose), a plastic or metal pipe of one or two metres (water pipes are vandalised for this purpose), a few metres long electric wire, and a long, thin metal plate a few inches long. I had the privilege of witnessing the process of alcohol production several times and some of the camp members patiently explained to me the process and also were generous to offer me free sample! The home made alcohol tasted almost like strong Vodka. Even though alcohol was available in Sek Kong camp I never had an opportunity actually to witness the production process in that camp.

Electrolysis method: The electrolysis method is more hazardous due to the use of illegally tapped electricity. The production process is carried out inside the huts. The main raw materials for making alcohol, rice, can be collected through friends or relatives who queue up more than once for their share when rice is distributed or they collect the leftover food from the huts at the end of the day.

Three or four 'wash basin' measures of rice are mixed with a small amount of yeast culture and water in large plastic buckets. This 'wash' is kept for few days for fermenting. When the 'wash' ferments the 'submarine' the cathode unit for the electrolysis is inserted into the wash. The bucket will be closed tightly with only one exit pipe for collecting the alcohol vapour. The alcohol vapour is cooled in running water. The running or 'dripping' water is arranged with the simple device of another bucket with water and a thin pipe, to let the water drip at the 'alcohol vapour exit pipe'. The alcohol, condensed out of the alcohol vapour is collected in 'Coke bottles' ready for consumption.

The alcohol produced through this process is less popular and cheaper in the camp (HK $30 for 1.25 litre Coke bottle) as there are sediments of metal particles, especially due to the presence of the lead particles. The 'consumer demand' for a better quality alcohol has led to a more sophisticated type of distilling. The most important production hassle of this process is that the entire production unit can be confiscated and the production team could easily be identified and punished. One of the safety nets used by the entrepreneurs is that they seldom use their own premises for distilling. Mostly the production is done at someone else's premises in order to escape detection. It is alleged that 'alcohol entrepreneurs' often bully the residents to part with the safe premises for producing alcohol. If the production unit is confiscated and the 'owner' of the space is arrested the real entrepreneur can escape.

Distilling method: The raw material is the same for the distilling method. The distillery apparatus is also almost same except for the container, which should be metal instead of plastic. Firewood is used for the fermented 'Wash' instead of electricity. Hillside hideout is a favourable place for this process. The production and distribution system of a 'hillside distillery' is better diversified than the 'production units' running inside the huts. The 'hillside production units' are diversified into observation post teams to keep watch. The production team, distribution, sales team, and transport team, brings the alcohol back into the camp. It has been reported that the 'staff of hillside production team' spends a long time outside the camp. They often come back to the camp for food or raw materials only.

The end product of 'hillside distillery' is assumed to be pure distilled alcohol, which is favoured more by the camp residents, so the price is more than the other type of alcohol (HK \$40 per 1.25 litre coke bottle). Hill fire is a hazard of this process. Trees and shrubs are cut down for firewood, which is detrimental to the conservation needs of the Island. The strategy adopted by the brewers is to send different people around the huts to collect the leftover rice at the end of the day in order to avoid detection. When some of the hut leaders tried to intervene they were reminded that 'their authority ends by midnight and the RHKP is responsible for law and order in the camp after midnight'.

Gambling: Gambling was a very popular activity in almost all the camps to cope with the boredom in the camps. Card games is also an avenue for gambling. 'Bridge' is very popular in the camp. The betting is only for small stakes. '*Mah jong*' is played by a few and the betting on '*Mah jong*' is very low. It is reported that '*Xi - Phe*', '*Bau Cau*', and '*Tai Xiu*' are the high stake games in the camp. Both men and women play '*Xi Phe*'. Some women are known to be experts in the game. According to the respondents of this study, thousands of dollars are circulated through this game. '*Xi Phe*' is played by four or five people at a time and mostly controlled by a few members in the community. Normally the 'game controller' takes care of the investments of the game. Without the sanction of the 'game controller' it cannot be played in the camp.

The 'game controller' makes the initial investment in the game by contributing a large amount of cash as floating capital, the craft and gear of the game. Mediation in settling bets, controlling quarrels and liasing with authorities, arranging a place for the games are the other functions of the game controller. Two women 'game organisers' - when they failed in recovering gambling debts approached the game controller to enforce payment. The game controllers enforce payment by various means, either by allowing payments to be made in instalments, and/or by publicly humiliating the debtor at his / her 'work place'.

Sometimes taking a loan from a loan shark pays a gambling debt. In one instance a couple lost all their savings generated through the informal economic activities by gambling. The wife tried to commit suicide by taking whatever medicine and tablets she could lay her hands on. She ended up in hospital for treatment. It has been reported that during the festival time the incidence of gambling and debt goes up. In the past, there was conflict over gambling debts, but nowadays the game controllers enforce the payment of gambling debt and prevent open fighting.

Credit, debt and loans in the camps

Camp residents tend to be indebted because of alcohol consumption, gambling, buying extra food for children, spending on clothes and cosmetics for special occasions, such as meeting with the immigration officer, consuming coffee, cigarettes, buying stamps for sending letters to relatives, or any other activity, which involves monetary transactions. In order to break the monotony of the camp life people develop many stratagems to pass time, which invariably leads to indebtedness.

Most of the camp residents had to do with the used clothes distributed through the camp management. These clothes are brought through the donation campaign run by various Hong Kong social service agencies. Some residents do get a new pair of clothes through their relatives. Some of them are willing to sell them for a price. Wearing a neat and well-pressed dress is often an opportunity to assert one's individuality and that to maintain one's self-esteem. Even though, the price one has to pay is often high. The use of cosmetics by women is often taken for granted. Most of the women in the camp were under intense pressure to maintain their femininity by using some amount of cosmetics. In this process they get indebted. Often debt leads to conflict and spouse abuse.

When one woman resident in the camp (who was working with an agency) owed a large amount of debt, the best option she had was to get a transfer from Tai Ah Chau. She was discreetly transferred to White Head detention centre with the support of her employer, who was not aware of the real motive for her request of transfer (in the employing agency, it was known as a case of an alleged sexual harassment).

Some of the camp's evening 'underground coffee shops' had to be closed down when the proprietors lost their capital due to large number of creditors. Camp residents take loans to run small shops, to repay debt incurred to small shopkeepers. A mother can reinforce her role as a care provider by taking extra care of the child even though she has to face difficulty in that process.

Medicines could be bought, mostly antibiotics and pain killers from the informal shops in the camp. Patients feel that sometimes they need to have an additional dose over and above the camp clinic doctor's prescription, or buying the medicine inside the camp can save time and energy of walking to the clinic and waiting in the queue with a cold or a headache. Rituals related to life transition are often a reason to borrow money. Some of the residents have to take care of the post-funeral rites of their relatives or friends. Even if the loved ones of the residents die in Vietnam or elsewhere, the relatives have to arrange for a memorial ceremony at least as a token. Marriage is another social occasion, which demands financial resources, subsequently leading to personal debt. It is reported that the interest on the personal loan charged is ten per cent a month!

Practice of religion in the camp

Reinforcement of cultural identity is an integral part in sustaining ones' self-esteem. Often religion plays the role of cultural identity. A sizeable number of religious affiliations exist with different levels of influence, resource base and contacts with the outside world. Often new religious affiliations were also formed. However, religious practices were restricted or limited.

Religious freedom is seriously restricted and controlled in subtle ways. In several camps there is no place for religious worship. Residents are discouraged from religious practices through indirect means. They are asked to queue up before the commencement of religious practices, are escorted to the place of worship, subjected to head count at the place of worship. The priests are expected to get all security clearance in advance to enter the camps. Some religious teachers and monks are denied permission to enter the camps. Religious education is discouraged. Often these restrictions are enforced under the guise of camp security.

Vietnamese Buddhist: One of the largest groups of the community is the Vietnamese Buddhist. The difference between the Vietnamese group and the Chinese Buddhist is ritualistic - in terms of worship. The way the prayer is chanted, the language used for prayer and the rituals are different. For example, offering meat is forbidden in Buddhism but not in the 'Kwan Yin' tradition.

Chinese Buddhist: The religious text used for prayer is different from the Vietnamese Buddhist and the rituals are also subtly different.

Kwan Yin worshipers: '*Kwan yin*' is a mixture of Buddhism and ancestor worship. Their main difference from other Buddhist groups is that they offer meat in *Kwan yin* shrine. Nung ethnic groups mostly practise Kwan Yin. The new temple is associated with this group. The perception of the camp residents is that the new shrine on the hill was allowed to be constructed by the '*Kwan yin*' group due to their proximity to the camp management. Other groups' request for space for worship was met with resistance from the camp management.

The management insisted that all other Buddhist group could use the shrine as a common place of worship. It may be irrelevant to say that each group has to accommodate the other group by sharing the space of worship.

The Catholic Church: The Catholic Holy Mass is conducted every Tuesday in the community TV room. Daily prayer and catechism classes are organised by the believers themselves. There are about 400 Catholics in Tai Ah Chau.

Revival Church: The Revival church worship is conducted every Saturday morning at the Workshop area. There are about 100 followers of the Revival Church group. Operations of all the religious groups are generally through the camp management, except the revival group. This group has managed to carve a special permission from the security branch.

The Christian Ministers Alliance (Good News Church): The CMA group conducts their prayers every Sunday morning. The numbers of followers are reported to be about 150.

Ancestor Worship (Chinese and Buddhist): Both Chinese and Vietnamese tradition of ancestor worship is practised by several people. However, they seldom manage to get fresh fruits, vegetables and other offerings, which are essential for the rituals.

Cao Dai: The Cao Dai religious group is organised by Mr. Ngo Van Chieu. They are mainly of South Vietnamese origin. In the camp they have a small group of followers (Cao Dai loosely translated means highest position). They practice special rituals, but the camp condition does not permit them to practice those rituals.

Hoa Hao: One of the most recent leaders of Hoa Hao, fiercely anti-Communist (Huynh Phu So) was assassinated by the Vietminh. This is a Buddhist sect with the influence of Zen that was established by Phat Thay Tay An. Both Cao Dai and Hoa Hao groups have only a very small number of followers in the camp.

Religion in the camp provides an opportunity for the residents to form community networks and community solidarity. Community fabric is maintained through religious affiliations. A sense of belonging, a sense of power and purpose and legitimacy for any group activity are the other functions of religion in the camps. Camps are also a breeding ground for religious fundamentalism. The religious sphere offers one of the safest means of experimenting with ones' leadership and organisational skills.

The psycho-social issues in the camp

The camp management and the service providers and the camp residents often perceive the psychosocial needs of the community differently. As a community worker in the camp one of my responsibility was to monitor the psychosocial problems in the camp. However, whenever I tried to do a formal assessment of psychosocial problems through in-depth interviews, observations and through focus group discussions, often the same unresolved issues like the following surfaced. The following is the sum of community perception on community problems and needs in Tai Ah Chau camp. From a service providers' point of view this may not constitute a profile of psychosocial problems in the camps. During a community consultation on community needs in the camps, the camp residents prepared the following list as their priority issues, which deserved immediate attention.

- Inadequate quantity and quality of food
- Inadequate water supply
- Many taps and flushes in the toilet were often out of order
- No buckets were available for collecting hot water during winter
- Food is not suitable for elderly, (often half baked/cooked)
- Not enough doctors, patients have to wait in long queues
- Elderly and children require warm clothes in winter
- Ophthalmic and dental care is required
- Request for reading glasses by the elderly
- Current distribution of undergarments for women is not adequate
- Request *Congee* for the elderly
- Request roofing for the cooking area
- Lighting inside the dormitory is not adequate

- Rats are rampant in the camps
- Bunk beds required repairs
- Staircases need repairing
- JRS should inform the community about the details of screening,
- No proper place for people to wash clothes
- ISS teachers lack responsibility in teaching
- Students sleep in the class and play outside with the fire
- Camp shops sells spoiled eggs, high price for certain goods, and goods are of old stock
- Increase the quantity of vegetables sold in the camp
- Some of the stoves in the cooking area need replacing

Working with the 'Community'

Even though the role of community workers in the camp was acknowledged and funded by the UNHCR, the scope of working with the community was ambiguous, which led to several discussions and deliberations by the community workers (at least one Community worker for 5,000 population was the norm accepted by the UNHCR in Hong Kong). Most of the discourse on the scope of community work in detention centres evolved through discussions among the community workers, the Vietnamese (asylum seeker) para-professionals and other camp workers. The result of such an exercise is incorporated in this study to highlight the scope of community work in the camps. Besides, such intervention plays an important role in maintaining the integrity of the community against the consequence of ethnocide.

In order to speculate the scope of 'community work/ community development' (CD) strategy in Detention Centres, one has to make an attempt to clarify the concept under discussion. Is CD just another social welfare effort or is it just a neutral community intervention? If so, the apt expression shouldn't be social welfare or community work initiatives. Social welfare is just an umbrella concept, which includes a wide spectrum of involvement from charity, distribution of old clothes to medical assistance to clients. The term community work denotes a neutral involvement, which lacks any direction. Community development efforts are goal oriented, often targeted towards behavioural and structural changes with both qualitative and quantitative dimensions.

Community development is generally understood as a social intervention for achieving certain tangible changes a society. Often, the scope of community development is identified as planned social engineering. A community development approach is often used for achieving greater participation from the 'client' community. Community development workers are perceived as agents who bring about this change. The target community or the service delivery agency or the dominant political forces may set the objective of community development (social engineering).

For any meaningful discussion, community development is identified as a process by which a community identifies it's own problems and finds out a manageable solution through a mutually accepted process for all the agencies involved. This definition is not a comprehensive one and does not encompass all the variables of this aspect. But this is a statement, which might give certain direction to focus our attention on the discussion on community development in a detention camp setting (Ref. fig. 6.2 for a community role metrix).

LEVEL of INTERVENTION \ TASK	AGENT OF AUTHORITY	CHANGE AGENT	INFORMATION GIVER	POWER BROKER	ADVOCATE	CONSULTANT	SOCIAL ENTREP RENEUR
individual	X	X	X	X	X	X	X
family	X	X	X	X	X	X	X
interest groups	X	X	X	X	X	X	X
community leadership	X	X	X	X	X	X	X
community network	X	X	X	X	X	X	X
agency wide	O	O	O	O	X	X	X
camp management	O	X	O	O	O	X	X
other agencies	O	X	O	O	O	X	X
CFSI field office	O	O	O	O	X	X	X
larger society	O	X	X	O	X	X	X
O= no role to play				X = an assigned role to play			

Figure 6.2   Community Work Role Matrix

How the community development goals are set is an important aspect in the success or failure of the program. It is assumed that if the community development goals are set through a process of dialogue between different groups involved, the success rate may be higher. Whatever may be the mode of setting community development goals, the primary objective of community development is to enhance the participatory profile of the community in problem solving and problem identifying. The next important aspect of community development is the nature and extent of community structures evolved in order to enhance community participation.

An effective community organisation strategy is imperative in order to activate the function of the community structures. The possibility of community organisation and community action strategy is another important factor, which contributes to the success or failure of the intervention. Community development strategy is essentially an approach, an attitude towards a recipient community. A host of factors contribute to the success and failure of the program.

The impact of community development work on camp life

Empowerment of the target population to deal with their own problems is the ideal goal of CD strategy. Yet how far asylum seekers are allowed to be empowered in the camps are a moot question. Community participation is the key for empowerment. The concept of 'participation' is one of the areas, which attracts a wide audience of academicians, social service practitioners, and students of community development. The concept of development participation has many dimensions and can be approached in a variety of ways. Andrew Pearse and Mathias Setifel (1979) has suggested six dimensions.
a) Participation as an encounter
b) Participatory groups and movements
c) Participation as individual experience
d) Participation as a program or project
e) Participation as a policy contributing to national development
f) Anti-participatory structures and ideologies

In this discussion the concern is about the issue of Participation as a program or a project, specifically refugee participation in social assistance projects. Lance Clark (1987) identified four important benefits of refugee participation. According to Clark, participation enhances normal coping process, it is cost effective, and participation leads to self-sufficiency, and promotes protection.

The psychological benefits of refugee participation are identified as: promoting self-esteem, help in rebuilding self-confidence, reduces feelings of isolation and reduces lethargy, depression and despondency. The cost effectiveness of refugee participation lies in the fact that it would help to avoid many mistakes in project formulation and project implementation. Refugees themselves are in a better position to comment on their needs. The internal protection problem of a refugee community often stems out from a relative anomaly of the members of the community. Refugee situation breaks the normal community protection mechanisms. The community feeling is the first victim of the refugee situation. Community participation encourages more areas of communication channel between the community and the agencies.

Strategies of working with the 'community'

The process of CD approach begins with a stock taking of existing power relationship and identification of community power structures within the community. This includes identifying regional affiliation of the community, past critical experiences of the community (for example a bitter riot) existence of traditional power structure, identifying influential persons, and relationship with the management (refer to figure 6.3 for a schematic presentation of relationship between community work and leadership).

This can be achieved through a purposive interaction with the community members. The community worker has to make sure he has achieved a reasonable rapport between the worker and the interpreter, if an interpreter is involved in the process. It will also be necessary to brief the interpreter about the objectives of this exercise. If already a certain level of community participation is achieved, and the worker is new to the community, the worker has to pay attention to understand the situation accordingly. The next step is to identify the interest groups within the community.

The major part of the formal community development plans for the first quarter of 1993 was in relation to the formal leadership structure. The existing formal community leadership structure operated through persons elected/ appointed by the camp management and the community. There was a need to follow up with the proposals submitted to the camp management and UNHCR regarding the modification of the existing leadership structure through greater women's participation, regular consultations, possible training programs, formal election of new leaders and through regular contacts with the leaders.

A more representative community leadership structure was required to facilitate a community leadership system for broader participation. Proposed services and activities for the CD work was: Advocate for more participatory role, possibility of implementing modified community leadership structure, participation of women in community leadership structure, training for formal leaders and regular needs assessment, individual contacts.

Implementation strategies

a) Advocate for the need of participatory leadership in community structures through inter-agency meetings, and meetings with management.

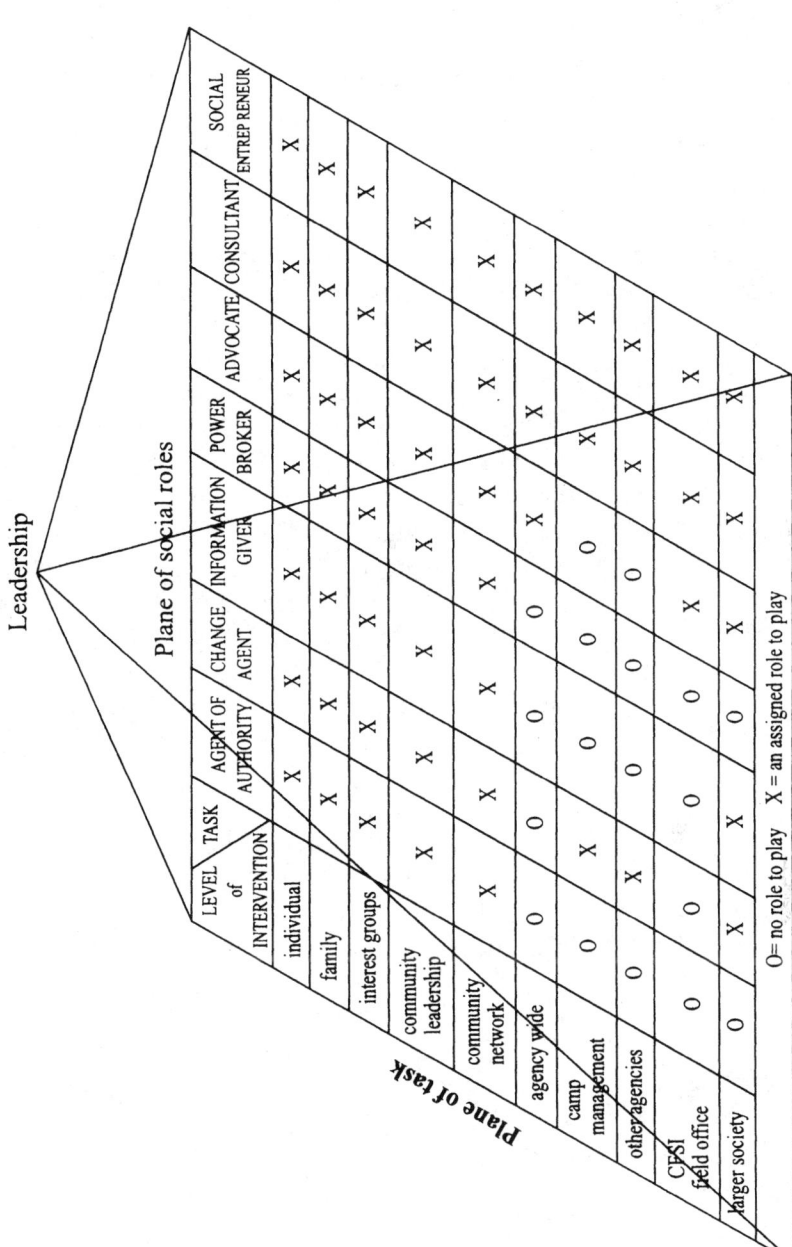

Figure 6.3   Community Work and Leadership Matrix

b) Conduct a community education program on need for community participation.
c) Discuss with the existing leadership the need for female participation in community leadership structure.
d) Training for the community leaders - community leadership, self-help issues.
e) Document all the activities for reference.
f) Prepare a list of all the community leaders and make it available to all the agencies. Encourage the agencies to consult the leaders about their activities.

Women's representation: The level of women's participation in camp level decission making was very minimal. The following changes were proposed to the consideration of the camp management in order to enhance the level of participation. In all the sections there will be a womens club/group organised with the help of CFSI Para-professional staff. This different group will represent different age group. All the women representatives will be elected by the women of each section. As part of an on going community development efforts, CFSI will impart training in the form of leadership training, consultation, and resource person's inputs will offer regular training for the group leaders and members. In each section, one CFSI para-professional is assigned to assist in organising womens group.

Services and activities: Establishing womens group in all the sections, conducting womens group meetings, organising training for the women leaders, conducting election of womens leaders, advocacy towards women's participation in community structure, establish and maintain women's self-help groups, and conducting a needs assessment., were the activities and services provided by the CD staff in the camp.

Implementation strategies:
• To conduct training programs for women leaders;
• To establish women's group in all sections;
• To encourage regular meetings of women's groups; elect women leaders in all the sections;
• Promotion of special interest groups, recreation, income generating skill development;
• Prepare a list of women leaders in the camp and make it available to all the agencies.

Working with Youth: CFSI in collaboration with ISS ran a youth development programme in order to achieve organisational development for youth of both sexes in the camp. The CFSI input was in the form of leadership training and human resources development through enhancing organisational development.

Services and activities: Facilitation of a youth group, training for leadership development, recreational and cultural activities, and needs assessment of young women were provided.

Implementation strategies: Organising regular youth group meetings, leadership training for youth, needs assessment of youth.

Unaccompanied minors: Community development input for unaccompanied minors was in line with the overall development program for the UAM. It included organisational development, group activities and training programs, camp level advocacy, ongoing needs assessment were other areas of CD input.

Services and activities: Needs assessment, training, case referrals in cases which required attention, childrens group activities, recreation, follow up on progress of education, follow up on health care, and facilitate general education.

Implementation strategies: Conducting regular needs assessment, follow up on needs assessment, conducting leadership training, regular group meetings, and organising follow up on recreational and educational needs.

Care givers: A care giver collective was formed in each section in order to strengthen their mutual support system and supportive networking among the care givers.

Implementation strategies: Organising care givers group, arranging care givers meetings, education for care givers on child development issues, recruiting and monitoring of care givers, needs assessment, updating the filing system.

Handicapped: Community development input for the handicapped strengthened the mutual support group of the handicap. Camp level advocacy, policy suggestion to be other areas of CD involvement.

Activities and services: A collective for the disabled for their mutual support was developed, case references, needs assessment, activities, referral for appropriate skill development and training was provided.

Implementation strategies: Organised regular activities for handicapped, conducted need assessment referral cases, which needed special attention and advocacy for the special needs of the handicapped in the camp.

The elderly: Old people's organisational development and mutual support network was strengthened. Camp level advocacy, policy consultations are other areas of CD involvement.

Description of services and activities: Establishment of mutual support groups, regular activities, needs assessment, advocacy on special needs of elderly, maintaining a list of elderly in the camp.

Working with the religious groups: (Catholic, Protestant and Buddhist groups) Religious groups to be integrated into the overall community forum. Individual consultation with the community leaders and monks are to be maintained. Integration of religious leaders into the community forum to be aimed at. Religious leaders to be encouraged to play active role in community affairs. Informal consultation and insformation channels to be maintained by the CD staff. In addition, facilitation of inter-religious dialogue and co-operation to be the goal.

Activities and services: Consultation with the religious leaders was conducted, carrying out needs assessment, facilitating inter religious interaction, religious groups representation in community forum, facilitation of religious activities, establishing information, community education channels through religious groups, and maintaining a list of community leaders. The Buddhist groups request for training in social service training will be supported through a multi module training program.

Community education and service information: Community education on issues identified by the community to be carried out. Agency service information and access to agency to be facilitated through advocacy, consultation and negotiation.

Activities and services: Facilitating service information to wider audience, compiling information on service facilities, exploring the possibility of camp newsletter, and conducting community education on identified issues.

Community participation: Community development strategy was aimed at enhancing overall community participation profile, through community organisation, community education, facilitation, and advocacy. It has also proposed to have community participation at inter agency forums.

Activities and services: Proposing community election for community leaders, preparing a plan for community election, encouraging community activities, collaborating with voluntary agencies and management in community, activities, creating avenues for community participation, working towards the participation of community representative in inter agency meetings.

Facilitation of creative expressions: Artistic and creative expressions to be encouraged through community development channels. This was facilitated through individual attention and providing platform to those capable in order to encourage the expression of community feeling.

Activities and Services: Providing avenues for expression through a 'Wall Paper', camp newsletter, and through cultural means, for example, theatre.

Community needs assessment: Regular psychosocial needs of community in general and specific needs of the groups was conducted as part of CD efforts in the camp.

Activities and services: Needs assessment report was prepared quarterly, follow up action was carried out on the needs identified by the residents. Needs assessment report was prepared, which was the basis for all the programs. A document on community profile was prepared along with a community resource information booklet. Paraprofessionals were recruited and training programs carried out.

Community development initiatives in the camps give an opportunity for the asylum seekers to exercise some of their basic rights as a member of a civilised society. Often the camp administrators and the policy makers look upon this process with suspicion. They feel that any sort of initiative was an hindrance to the 'durable solutions' they planned for the asylum seekers. Right of the target population to participate in any deliberations which affect their lives seriously in principle has been promoted by various international agencies, yet this remains a lip service in case of the Vietnamese asylum seekers detained in Hong Kong. Closing down all the community development initiatives and cutting down the services in Hong Kong camps was an example of this process.

Conclusion

As we have noted earlier pain and suffering are not simply individual experience of the asylum seekers, which are actively created and distributed by the social order itself (Das, 1994). This chapter narrates the linkages between the social order and the basis of individual misery, pain, the social process and the pathways through which pain and misery are contrived as an extension of the social structure itself.

This chapter contributed towards a better understanding of the life situation of the asylees in detention camps. The detainees developed various strategies to carry out their day to day life in the camps and to cope with the process of ethnocide. Asylum seekers are caught between their desire for an integrated culture and the forces contribute toward the disintegration of culture. Most of the camp structures contribute towards the disintegration of their culture. In practice, camp management practices contributed towards the disintegration of social and cultural life of the detainees. Social service facilities in a camp are the rare outside element, which could have contributed towards a resemblance of social integrity.

How the asylum seeking community organises or are allowed to organise in the camps has a lot to contribute with the coping ability of the community and to reduce the effect of ethnocide. Facilities for practising religion also have substantially contributed to the cultural integrity of the community. The micro economic activity in the camp is yet another symbol of lingering resilience of the community to face adversity.

7 Violence in the Camps

Introduction

The overall situation in the detention centres was like a time bomb ticking slowly. The inhuman duration of administrative detention and a combination of factors like mandatory and forced repatriation of the 'screened out' asylum seeker led to senseless violence and consequent loss of human lives. Violence within the camps was often an indication of the level of frustration of the detainees and a symptom of stress. This chapter elaborates the various aspects of violence in the camps, which is presented as the cause and consequence of the process of ethnocide in the detention centres.

Authors such as Frederick (1980), Berren, Beigel and Ghertner (1982), Beigel and Berren (1985) and Shah (1985) have discussed the effects of violence on human beings. However, very little has been written on violence in the detention camps and the impact of violence on the camp life. In the context of Hong Kong refugee camps, camp management used camp violence as a tool of social control. In the aftermath of violence, with holding appropriate intervention to diffuse violence in the camps was used by the camp authorities to discredit the asylum seekers by portraying them as violent people on the media. Often, the police version of the 'violence' was given to the media and independent verification of such incidents by the media was denied.

The detention of refugees and asylum seekers severely disturbed the social control mechanisms, cultural values, social network, and self-identity. Maurice Eisenbruch (1991) referred to this situation as cultural bereavement. Harrell Bond (1986) in her study of Ugandan refugees observed that 'the symptoms associated with unrelieved crisis or stress include *explosive, violent behaviour* (emphasis added), profound depression, loss of personal identity, depersonalisation, psychosomatic symptoms, and sometimes psychotic withdrawal'.

As noted by Kunz (1981), there is a tendency to view all refugees from Vietnam as a homogeneous group, despite major ethnic and ideological differences. Urban South Vietnamese, illiterate rural fishermen from North Vietnam and ethnic Chinese Vietnamese were all bundled together under the same label and were offered the same services. If this situation were not carefully monitored through community participation, it would have been volatile. This can best be expressed in the words of Yossef S. Ben-Porath (1991), 'given the high degree of stress and distress, coupled with a sense of helplessness, it is not surprising that scapegoats were identified and abused in the camps'.

According to Frederick (1980) the five phases of Human-Induced violence are the initial impact, acceptance/respect for perpetrators, interaction between victims and perpetrators, disintegration or termination of perpetrator's control and acquiescence/surrender. But camp violence presents another dimension, the role of legal guardians, who can and could have prevented human-induced violence through proactive intervention, but knowingly withheld such intervention.

The typology of violence in Hong Kong camps included:
a) Violence between individuals
b) Violence between small groups and factions
c) Violence between northerners and southerners
d) Violence between police and the asylum seekers
e) Violence by the asylum seekers to the police
f) Violence by the police on asylum seekers
g) Violence between groups with the tactical understanding of the police.

To best explain different kinds of violence, two specific case studies have been selected to explain the process of violence in the camps.

Violence in the White Head Detention Centre (WHDC)

The White Head detention Centre (WHDC), described as the biggest jail in the world opened in January 1989. Uniformed Correctional Service Department (CSD) staff who manages all the prisons in Hong Kong managed the various refugee camps in Hong Kong.

This detention facility had an initial population of 4,000 people in April 1989. But by October, the population increased to 10,000 and by June 1990, the number swelled to about 24,000. At any given time about 50 per cent of the population were women and children. White Head was one of the first detention camps custom-made for detaining the Vietnamese. The camp was divided into 10 sections, of these, nine sections were occupied by the people from North Vietnam one section was occupied by South Vietnamese asylum seekers. Access to each section was controlled. The criterion for assigning a section to an asylum seeker was based on ethnic group and district of origin.

WHDC was a highly crowded place with very limited common space. A hundred people lived in each dormitory hut and there were about 25 huts per section. The residents were allowed to move around only in their own sections. It was estimated that in certain sections each person had only 3.0 square meter of space available for themselves.

As the population at WHDC increased the problems also augmented. Deteriorating physical conditions, increased level of violence, heightened level of tension, attempted mass escapes, and rioting became a daily affair. In some sections, gangs were exercising their power to intimidate other asylum seekers. It was alleged that they received the patronage of the CSD staff. Often crude weapons, sharp metal objects, metal pipes, improvised wooden clubs were manufactured in the camp for both defensive and offensive purposes.

During late 1991, WHDC experienced wave after wave of 'violence'. This case study is based on one of such incident. Section three had experienced five days of continuous violence between members of '*Hong Gai*' group and '*Minh Dong*' groups. The fight broke out at 2:00 AM caused by an argument between two people over which TV channel to watch (Chinese or English). The argument continued till they reached their own huts in the Section. Friends and relatives of arguing parties also joined in the fray. This commotion led to drawing of home made weapons they had stocked earlier.

People were rudely awakened from their sleep by the screaming and subsequent fighting. When the violence broke out, police used teargas to control the agitators but not with much result. Next morning the CSD, UNHCR and CFSI staff initiated a negotiation with the two warring factions. However, the initiatives were not successful because the '*Minh Dong*' group was not ready for negotiation. Later, they agreed to negotiate on the condition that the venue of the negotiation should be near to their huts so that their friends and relatives would protect them if the other group attacked them.

During the negotiation each group insisted that the other group should move out to another section. But neither group was willing to do so. '*Hong Gai*' group argued that since they were the bigger group they could not move. They insisted that the smaller group '*Minh Dong*' move out. They argued that they had moved out of Section four recently due to an earlier incident. They insisted that it was fair for the '*Hong Gai*' group to move out this time so that the CSD would not be seen as favouring them all the time.

Not much was achieved from the series of negotiations (11 meetings) during the five days of fighting. People were willing to negotiate during the day in the presence of the agency staff and resumed fighting in the night when the service agency staff and UNHCR representatives were not in the camp. In the end, CSD decided to move '*Hong Gai*' group to High Island Detention Centre (HIDC). The Hong Kong Police and the HIDC camp management were not willing to accept a big number of people at a short notice. Finally, CSD managed to move the 1,200 '*Ming Dong*' group to High Island. In return, White Head CSD accepted 1,400 '*Hong Gai*' group from the HIDC for Section three.

Two hundred and forty people were arrested for the violence and nine were kept in isolation, which included the chairman and deputy chairman of the 'peace and order' committee. Allegedly the CSD was reluctant to arrest the leaders of 'peace and order' committee because they were said to be very helpful to the camp management in their 'combing operations'. Arresting the 'peace and order' leaders was part of the condition agreed during the negotiations. However, the camp management implemented this decision only when the service agencies insisted on it.

The violence was an outburst of simmering discontent among the population. Most of the people were very tense due to the possibility of forced repatriation. '*Minh Dong*' and '*Campha*' groups felt that CSD favoured the '*Hong Gai*' group on several occasions. Apparently the 'trouble makers' wanted to have full control over the community which meant more jobs, money and privileges to their group.

Eight persons were injured, including an unaccompanied child. The injured were moved to the hospital. One of the warring groups used the school premises as their 'control centre'. Electrical installations, school facilities, chair and windows along with the blackboards and other school equipment were damaged in the conflict. Schools were suspended for two weeks for repairs forcing children to stay in their own bunks.

Police combing operation resulted in damaging personal belongings of the asylum seekers. Many residents were severely traumatised emotionally, especially those who had lost their friends or relatives in the ensuing violence. Each group feared retaliation and kept awake during nights. They felt safe to sleep at daytime. Several peoples sleeping pattern was drastically altered. Several families were separated from their immediate kith and kin. All cleaning operations were suspended for several days resulting in heaps of rubbish littered all over the camp.

CSD response to camp violence

According to the Chief security officer of WHDC, violence in the detention centre can be divided into 'small scale violence' and 'large scale violence'.

The methods and the strategies adopted by the camp management to contain the violence depend upon the nature of the violence involved.

According to the CSD 'small scale violence' includes fistfights involving small number of participants, child abuse, spouse abuse, assaults, rape and wounding others. In these kinds of small-scale violence, an initial investigation was carried out to assess whether the people involved were in danger or not. The offenders were then relocated temporarily to a special unit pending in-depth inquiry. Often punishment was dispensed immediately without necessarily following any legal procedures. The security officer often claimed that 'the offenders were presented to the disciplinary board and the punishment was dealt with according to the severity of the offences'. The punishment varied from a maximum solitary confinement of up to 28 days to suspension of privileges for three months, and in serious cases, the matter was referred to the police.

Gang fights, mass fighting, mass escape attempts, and factional conflicts were classified as 'large scale violence' by the CSD. The camp management strategies to deal with large scale violence was to immediately activate the 'intelligence network' in the camp to locate the trouble spot. The responsible parties were then arrested and segregated pending further enquiry. In serious cases, the offenders were sent to Upper Chi Ma Wan Detention Centre for not more than six months.

During factional conflicts different groups were separated to different sections. More stringent security measures were adopted after a large-scale violence. The detention centres were further divided into smaller sections and more barbed wire was added. Hidden cameras were installed, mass discipline, control of equipment, and frequent search operations was adopted as a response to the violence (CFSI staff training report 17.02. 1992).

Violence in Sek Kong Detention Centre (SKDC)

The violence erupted in the context of an extreme deprivation, anxiety, confusion, and unmet expectations of the residents. The following were some of the psychosocial needs expressed by the 'community leaders' prior to the violence.
• Problems with rats, cockroaches and mosquitoes
• Problems with the toilets, which were inadequate, broken and overflowing
• Lack of adequate drinking water
• Lack of general hygiene in the camp, ankle deep slime
• Lack of any meaningful activities for women

• Request for Vietnamese books and magazines
• Problems with medical care and access to the clinic
• Elderly and pregnant women had to wait in the queue for food, water and health care
• Insufficient hours available for medical care
• Unmet need for personal garments and toiletries for women
• Unmet need for a place of worship, and incense for offering
• Request for information on the screening procedure
• Request for postnatal care
• Issues of domestic violence and marital conflict
• Request for winter clothes for children and the elderly

Like any other asylum seeker detention centres in Hong Kong, Sek Kong Camp was also segregated from the outside world with high barbed wire fences. Inside the centre the living arrangements were prepared on a contingency basis. Each corrugated tin hut accommodated approximately 300 people. They were accommodated in tin huts with three tier bunk beds and were expected to share the communal bath and toilet facilities. A cluster of six to seven huts was grouped in one section, which was again segregated. Filth and rubbish was scattered around the camp, which added to the misery of daily living conditions.

There was no medical facility available within any of the Sections in Sek Kong. If anybody needed medical attention he/she had to approach the guard at the gate. If the guard was satisfied, the patient would be allowed to go to the clinic area, which was beyond the primary perimeter fence, and inside the secondary perimeter fence. Many authors, researchers, and social service assistance agency staff identified a high level of anxiety and stress experienced by asylum seekers in Hong Kong detention centres. Cultural unawareness, and insensitivity to the needs and characters of the different groups within the community proved to be an additional factor contributing to the 'Pressure Cooker Situation'.

Overall services available to a single elderly woman or an unaccompanied minor boy or a girl was similar. Likewise, a handicapped person or an able bodied young man received the same services. Each one had to equally compete for hot water, food, and access to medical centre and the overall facilities. The level of access to the camp resources varied from group to group. The closely linked Catholic and Protestant community had more access to international support and communication. The Chinese speaking Vietnamese had better access to the camp administration. The English speaking urban

Vietnamese had better access to the service agency staff. This effected the community structure and community participation profile.

The South Vietnamese had better 'purchasing power' within the camp because of the fact that a large number of Southerners who had already resettled in other countries were willing to send money to their relatives and friends in the detention centres. Because of various socio-political reasons the North Vietnamese in general did not have any additional revenue within the camp. Distilling liquor from rice was one of the main 'illicit income generating programs' which they practised despite frequent inspections by the camp administration.

The event

The Sek Kong incidence was one of the most vicious conflicts that ever happened between the North and the South Vietnamese asylum seekers in the Hong Kong. On Lunar New Year eve of 1992, violence erupted between factions in Section C and Section D in the Sek Kong Detention Centre (SKDC), which resulted in arson and gang warfare. Twenty-four 'Boat People', 12 children, and 12 adults were burned to death, 139 were injured in the fire and the fighting, 13 were missing and 192 were detained to face rioting charges.

Expose of the Incident

I was working in the camp till late night on the eve of Lunar New Year. My 'office' was in Section C, the same section where the incident occurred (the office was destroyed in the ensuing fire). I was attending a Lunar New Year get-together of the asylum seekers who worked as paraprofessionals and interpreters with me. When I left the camp there was no indication of a build-up towards violence, even though I had seen two men quarrelling. My interpreter told me that they were quarrelling over an alcohol debt. The next morning I was woken by a call from one of the 'friendly' police officers stating that something terrible had happened in the camp and 'you better hurry up'. As I lived near the camp it was easy for me to reach the camp at 6.10 am. I was allowed to enter the camp. Later, the camp was sealed off for all the service agency staff.

The first incident I noticed on entering the camp was that of the police removing charred human bodies from the remains of the completely gutted Section C. My immediate priority was to locate the asylum seekers who worked with me as interpreters and paraprofessionals. I had a hurried briefing of what had happened from my interpreters and paraprofessionals. Some of the policemen with whom I had a good working relationship also briefed me as to what had happened. Even though, I was aware of the need to document what I had heard and what I was seeing, it was impossible for me to do so then and there. The following account was written the next day of the incident based on my interviews with the asylum seekers and the police. Subsequently, I was also called upon to present the account of the incident to the enquiry commission set up by the Hong Kong government and the police internal enquiry commission.

During the time of the incident, SKDC was managed by the Royal Hong Kong Police and had approximately 10,000 Vietnamese asylum seekers and 830 people who had volunteered to return to Vietnam.

Sek Kong camp was situated in an old airfield, where the asylum seekers were held in five sections, known as Section A, B, C, D and E. The UNHCR and the camp authorities decided to construct a 'Voluntary Repatriation Centre' right in the middle of the camp in Section C. This section was segregated from the other sections with separate barbed wire and metal sheets. Voluntary agencies were asked to move their offices from Section C prior to the opening of Section C as a 'Voluntary Repatriation Centre'. The volunteers were both from the North and South Vietnam, even though all the North Vietnamese were held in Section B, and the other sections were for the South Vietnamese. However, Section A was partially for the Chinese Vietnamese. In Section D there were also a few 'Chinese Cambodians'.

On the eve of the traditional Vietnamese New Year 'Tet' (around 7:00 p.m.) one South Vietnamese man in Section C, hut number two, was apparently confronted by a North Vietnamese man from hut number six, asking him to settle the amount owed to him. This amount was due because of a transaction involving rice liquor brewing. They argued, quarrelled and fought with each other. Both of them got injured in the ensuing fight, but the northerner was more injured than the southerner. The police intervened and both of them were taken to the clinic. The people from the other sections heard the commotion and the police announcement on the public address system asking people to go back to their own huts. However, the 'residents' of the other sections did not know the reason for the fight, nor the number of actual victims. Some people from the other sections perceived and speculated that there were a large number of casualties.

When each party came back to Section C after receiving first aid they apparently started canvassing among their own group for a revenge attack. Metal pegs which were used for removing rice from the wood rice distribution buckets, bed posts, small home made knives and wooden clubs were collected in preparation for self-defence and offence if required.

The police instituted a weapon search in Section C around 1930 hours. After the search it appeared that the Southerners fearing retaliation from Northerners shouted for help to Section D. Responding to the shout for help, residents from Section D began gathering at the gate near Section C. All this time the police guards posted at the command post situated near the main gate were witnessing the build-up from an elevated platform with an overview of the camp.

It is said that the Northerners from hut number 5, Section C, gathered at hut number 6, collecting stones and other available materials expecting a reprisal from the Southerners. At about 2130 hours on February 3, 1992, a group of Northerners apparently charged into hut number 2 (Southerner's hut) with whatever weapons they managed to get their hands on. The Southerners shouted for help to Section D, where people were already milling near the gate 'C' in anticipation of trouble. They were still not clear about the exact details of what was going on at the other side of the metal wall. Around 2200 hours they managed to push open the gates and race into Section C. A small number of police came to the scene through the perimeter path between Section C and D and tried to force the people back into Section D. However, one policeman was reportedly hit by a rock thrown by the people, and the police withdrew for reinforcements.

Some women and children from Section C managed to escape to section D and E. The residents of Section E were alerted by the noise and shouting from other Sections. The gates of Section E also apparently gave way under pressure. Some people from Section E rushed into Section C to rescue their relatives and friends. Some of them also went ahead because of curiosity and others simply utilised an opportunity to walk through the gates.

The Northerners of hut number five, Section C, escaped to hut number six avoiding the crowd. The people in hut number six apparently closed the metal door of their hut from inside and reinforced the door latch with metal wires from inside, hoping that the Southerners would not be able to attack them. When the hut was set on fire many people were trapped inside the huts.

The increased violence was allegedly organised by a small band of people from Section D who distinguished themselves with a white band tied around their head and wrists. The perpetuators of the violence circled hut number six, Section C, with whatever weapons they could lay their hands on. Some people climbed on the roof of hut number six and opened the steel roof and threw blazing blankets inside. Those who were on the ground broke the window glasses (there were no bars on these windows). The people inside the hut tried to protect themselves by using the bedsteads as weapons. The crowds circled hut number six and asked the women and children to leave the hut in order to take revenge only on men. But some people inside the hut apparently did not allow them to escape hoping that the women and children could shield them from the mob outside.

The plywood bunks, hardboard boxes, clothes, and curtains separating the bunks caught fire instantly. The melee and the stampede following the fire was made worse because of the latched door. A small number of people who had positioned themselves near the front door of hut number six beat anybody who tried to escape through the door, all this was happening under the watchful eyes of Hong Kong Police.

The fire service alert was given at 2355 hours. Nine fire engines from the nearby Pat Heung fire station reached the scene at 0001 hours. The fire services were not able to approach the scene until 0134 hours. After the fire was controlled and put off there were charred belongings and dead bodies. All the metal frames of the bunk beds were twisted and tangled.

A team of more than 100 detectives launched a criminal investigation immediately. The fire services department also set up a three man team to investigate the cause of fire. The British-Hong Kong Police (Vietnamese management section) conducted their own investigation.

Crisis intervention

My first attempt was to contact the paraprofessional staff in all the sections in order to make a quick assessment of the situation. The police had already sealed off Sections A and B. However, we were allowed to enter the primary sterile areas and through the fence we could talk to the refugees. It was revealed that one of the paraprofessional staff from Section C was missing and there was no way to ascertain about his whereabouts at that time.

This initial contact was useful for further work. This assessment provided a fair picture of the possibility of mobilising the paraprofessional staff and their locations. They articulated the story in a fairly vivid manner. The first phase of intervention succeeded in establishing individual contacts with some community leaders. The environment was charged with emotion. No information was available of the actual events. Rumours regarding the possible revenge attacks from other sections, exaggeration of the number of deaths were circulating freely. Even though it was a holiday, most of the regular CFSI staff employed at the SKDC managed to reach the camp by 9:00 a.m.

The camp management gave the first briefing at 9:00 a.m. on February 4, 1992.

CFSI set up an informal task force team immediately. The program co-ordinator and the supervisors alerted the staff from other locations. Some of the staff were dispatched to the hospital where a large number of victims were admitted. They were admitted in various hospitals and nobody kept a track of the patients or the hospitals they were admitted into.

It was estimated that about 200 people including children, elderly women, were partially burned and injured. Most of the victims were under severe shock and confusion. Some of the children who were separated from their parents had taken refuge in the administrative area. The immediate task of the staff was to assess the situation of the people who were staying in the open without any food or water since the incident.

Some of the CFSI staff visited the hospitals and managed to compile a list of the Vietnamese who were admitted in the hospitals. This list was faxed to the temporary co-ordination unit at SKDC. It was the only available list of patients in hospitals. Meanwhile the list of children left alone in the administrative area was prepared. The list of patients in hospitals was used to reassure the residents about the whereabouts of their relatives.

There was no private place available for gathering the basic information regarding the patients. This exercise soon turned into a group counselling. The staff was forced to confirm the death of immediate relatives of some of the clients in the presence of other relatives who did not know the whereabouts of their family members. This added to the bewilderment and shock.

Meanwhile tension was mounting inside the camp. The North Vietnamese section of the camp feared attack from the Southerners and vice versa. Even though access to the sections was limited, CFSI staff managed to get into various sections very expeditiously. Community leaders used this opportunity to clarify their own fears of attack from other sections. To a large extent reassuring the community leaders was instrumental in diffusing the tension building in the camp.

Due to the different lines of authority operating in the camp during the crisis situation total confusion prevailed. The regular police force, the criminal investigation department and the police tactical unit operated somewhat independently making their own decisions. This created confusion about access to different sections in the camp by the CFSI staff. Some police allowed the social service staff into the camps but some did not. Even though the assessment of CFSI staff did not indicate any possibility of violence against the service agency staff, the police and camp administration was not willing to allow the staff access to the camp residents citing security reasons.

During noon, a truckload of people discharged from the hospital was brought to the camp. All of them had been discharged from the hospital after receiving only basic first aid care. Some of them had serious burns and injuries. It was deplorable that the local public health authorities discharged the victims in such a condition. The camp service staff immediately lobbied with the camp management to take back those persons who were obviously seriously injured and were in need of urgent and proper medical attention.

All the injured were wearing clothes, which were either burnt, full of dirt, or bloodstains. It was a gruesome scene. The arrival of the new victims discharged from the hospital created a fresh wave of emotional outburst and pandemonium. The people who were squatting on the ground stood up and surged towards the new arrivals looking for their relatives. Some others began to cry hysterically.

Meanwhile, the police criminal investigation team pressed into action. They took control of the situation and established their authority. They cordoned off all the sections and began a 'head count'. All the people were asked to squat in the open space in front of each hut, segregating women, children and men. All the men were subjected to an identification parade. This parade in Section D went on till late in the evening.

Some of the CFSI staff who left in the evening were called back to the camp again at 2200 hrs in order to pacify and to counsel some of the women who had become hysterical on seeing their husbands being taken away by the police. When the CFSI staff went into the huts late at night, many people were on the brink of an emotional breakdown, particularly, some of the pregnant women who were without any relatives or friends and whose husbands had been whisked away by the police. For some other residents, this experience had a 'triggering off' effect. They suffered 'flashback memories' about their escape from Vietnam and their experience with the Vietnamese military and security forces.

All the front line service staff experienced severe stress, and stress related symptoms. On the third day the front line staff were asked to take a compulsory day off from the camp. Another team of staff replaced them in order to cope with the stress. A Critical Incident Stress Debriefing (CISD) session was instituted for the benefit of all the staffs who were involved in the situation.

The Hong Kong government instituted an independent inquiry into the incident. The findings of Mr. Justice Kempster though presented in a bureaucratic jargon clearly indicated that the police had lost initiative in securing the life of the asylum seekers during the Sek Kong incident. The following were the findings and recommendations of Mr. Justice Kempster on the Sek Kong incident.

FINDINGS of Justice Kempster

(1)   Section C of Sek Kong Detention Centre where the tragedy occurred was evacuated. The incident contained, priority was given to maintaining the fence and segregation barriers and reinforcements awaited as required by police internal guidelines.

(2)   In the absence of troop carrying helicopters on standby the movement of reinforcements could hardly have been more rapid.

(3)   At 2330 hours on 3rd February, as part of a concurrent operation involving two groups of 12 and 17 men respectively (29 in all), the police were prepared to re-enter Section C, which they had left at 2300 hours, to restore order. Due to an incursion from Section B they did not do so albeit CS gas was used. By 2350 hours 60 officers and by 2355 hours 70 officers in all were available to restore order, to watch Section B (the incursion from which had by then been contained) to guard the other segregation barriers and the perimeter and to man the Command Post.

(4)   No further CS gas was used and no further attempts were made to re-enter Section C between 2342 hours on February 3rd and 0012 hours on February 4th by which time the number of available officers had risen to 142.

(5)   Everyone involved, whether or not conversant with the Vietnamese language, knew that as from 2300 hours on February 3rd inmates of Section C were at grave risk of injury to life and limb.

(6)   There was a substantial stock of CS gas available to the forces of law and order throughout the incident and it was known that the arrival of PTU (Police Tactical Unit) platoons with further supplies was imminent.

(7)   At no stage after 2353 hours was the officer in command, who had to borrow a respirator, aware of the presence of or, in any event, able to communicate with the constables on the container mentioned in or vice versa. Had he learnt of either of the messages reporting fire in a hut in Section C, which they transmitted by beat radio, I am quite convinced that he would have immediately given the order to use CS gas and re-enter Section C. He took such an action only when, at 0013 hours on February 4th, he saw inmates of Section C being grievously assaulted in front of his very eyes.

(8)   Between 2325 hours and 2353 hours not one officer was effectively in command at Sek Kong.

(9)   The only effective observation post from which all that was happening at Section C could readily be seen, was the top of a container to which

two observers had been posted. Due to the absence of communication between those observers and the officer in command and his immediate subordinates, its value was greatly diminished.

(10) In the circumstances described and with the benefit of hindsight it is apparent that while the protection of life must have been regarded as a principle objective the initiative was not swiftly seized or held by the Police. Nor was law and order restored as quickly as possible as required by the Police internal guidelines. Signs capable of interpretation as weakness were permitted to appear. Had the Police again fired CS gas at 2355 hours and re-entered Section C the tragedy might well have been averted. As it was the crowd had reformed and re-grouped and the attack on hut six resumed after the firing of CS ceased at about 2342 hours.

Recommendations of Justice Kempster Commission

(1)   Having regard to the bereavement, injury and consequent bitterness and hatred which is the legacy of the incident, Vietnamese from the North should not, until the climate has improved, be housed together with those from the Centre and South of that country. Further sub-division may be called for - as has been found necessary at White Head. This was the effect of the order confirmed by your Excellency on the morning of February 4th.

(2)   The fears, anxieties and uncertainties experienced by inmates of the centres would be relieved and their understanding of the wider world, of Hong Kong and of the choices open to them enhanced by:

(a)   Films, with soundtrack in the Vietnamese language, graphically describing those choices and showing current living and working conditions in Vietnam.

(b)   Written or oral announcement in the centres about the convictions of Vietnamese in the Hong Kong Courts and the sentences imposed (the 'camp newspaper' produced at Hei Ling Chau could serve this purpose).

(c)   Delaying the isolation of volunteers and their removal from familiar surroundings until shortly before expected dates of departure from Hong Kong.

(3)   In all centres where Vietnamese migrants are confined facilities should be provided to allow them to engage in remunerated productive work. Space for 'factories' may well become available if the number of new arrivals remains at a low level and the process of voluntary repatriation

continues. The provision of work should be the first priority and the closure or alternative use of centres the second.

(4) In any event a reduction in the population of White Head should take precedence over the closure of, say, Argyle.

(5) Sufficient staff should be employed markedly to accelerate the screening process.

(6) All police and CSD officers liable for call to the scene of disturbance at a detention centre, whatever their rank, should be issued with respirators. Officers liable to take command should be equipped with respirators suitable for use with radio-telephones.

(7) Available at each detention centre should be:

(a) Spare respirators including at least two suitable for use with radio telephones.

(b) Spare 'beat' radios tuned to centre channel.

(c) Spare 'sabre' radios tuned to appropriate regional channel.

(8) Any officer assuming command in a situation of disturbance should, as a matter of routine, be in possession of an appropriate respirator and of 'beat' and sabre radios. He need not carry a mobile telephone as well.

(9) An observation tower or towers sufficiently high to command a view of the whole of each centre should be reconstructed in sterile areas. Officers equipped with 'beat' radios should permanently man such tower or towers. Early in this enquiry I considered the utility of searchlights of the type employed on Stone Cutters Island to maintain the integrity of the magazine but the provision of the assured supply of electricity which they require would in itself render the artificial lighting at Sek Kong at least, adequate.

(10) At all centres' barrier fences between sections, gates and locks should be inspected and, where necessary, reinforced, strengthened and replaced.

(11) The protection of life and limb should take precedence over the prevention of escape. Police and CSD directives should make this plain.

(12) In the event of a disturbance, giving rise to a reasonable apprehension of danger to life and limb and when insufficient personnel are available at once to quell it, CS gas should be used without hesitation. Albeit the whole centre may be affected, its use should be continued until sufficient men have been mustered to permit re-entry without unacceptable risk to police or CSD officers as the case may be. Order should then be restored firmly and with determination.

I have no recommendation to make as regards the Fire Services.

No doubt a number of these recommendations, some having financial implications, have already been anticipated. Further, I accept that the judgement of the officer in command at the scene of a disturbance must not unduly be fettered. He must, however, be clear in his mind as to the priorities'.

One of the striking tragedies of this incident is that immediately after this incident the UNHCR officials went to the media and to the camp population campaigning the importance of repatriation in the context of camp violence. Some people did decide to repatriate voluntarily after this incident, including some of the perpetuators of the violence.

Even though camp violence was increasingly perceived as a serious problem in the camp, no concrete efforts were made by any of the stakeholders. UNHCR or Hong Kong government did not make any concerted effort to avoid the situations of violence and neither did they implement the suggestions of Justice Kempster's recommendations. However, the nature of camp violence itself has changed over a period of time. The Hong Kong government began using force to move the residents from one camp to another and to move the asylum seekers for forced repatriation to Vietnam.

Many independent observers also expressed concern about the violence in the camps. Refugee Concern, a local refugee advocacy group was one of them. Refugees Concern was a voluntary advocacy group of concerned lawyers and refugee welfare workers. They took up several issues of the refugees, including an independent fact finding on the nature of violence in the camps. The following is one of their critical reports on camp violence.

Report On the Selected Aspects Of The Administration's Attack On The People Of Section 7, White Head, And UNHCR's Betrayal Of The People Of Section 7 *(From Refugee Concern to the Government Inquiry).*

This report is not intended to be a comprehensive account of the issues that must be addressed by the Inquiry, rather, it is intended to draw attention of the Inquiry to some of the selected issues.

The Administration intended to use unnecessary and excessive violence

From the information we already have, it is clear that the Administration intended to use unnecessary and excessive violence against the Vietnamese people in Section 7 (and those in the adjoining Sections 6 and 8 who also suffered teargas attacks). This we know for the following reasons.

1. There were other ways in which the move of a group of people from one camp to another could have been, and in the past, has been undertaken. None

of the alternatives open to the Administration were attempted. Arbitrary violence against defenceless men, women and children was employed as a first resort and not as a last recourse. One example of when alternative measures were successfully employed was in 1993. The people in Section 1 at White Head were told that they were to be dispersed amongst different sections of the camp.

(Perhaps 1,000 of the 1,500 people in Section 7 during the April 7 attack were detained in Section 1 in 1993 when the administration ordered this move). They protested the move, believing that it was a means for the Administration to target them for punishment and removal. The community leaders and others who had been active in demonstrations felt that their personal safety might be endangered by such a move. After the first few weeks, solidarity amongst the people in Section 1 protesting the move broke down and the vast majority of the people voluntarily left and were moved to other sections of the camp. After approximately 4 weeks, only 300 of the 2,500 people remained in section 1. Even they volunteered to leave the Section. However, the CSD refused to allow them to move peacefully. The CSD moved in and forcibly removed the remaining people from Section 1.

No force was used to move 85 per cent of people

This is an extreme example. The vast majority of moves from one camp to another are undertaken as a routine measure without any use of force. The closure of Nei Kwu Chau earlier this year is just one example.

2. We have now received approximately 200 individual accounts of the April 7 attack from Section 7 victims. According to the letters the victims have written, and through the conferences with them, they have consistently stated that, they were not aware before 6:20 am, when the first round of teargas was fired and mace was sprayed, that they were expected to leave the Section to move to the High Island Detention Centre.

Nor could the Vietnamese people be expected to so quickly grasp what was happening. We believe that this is the first time ever that the Administration had undertaken a transfer of such a large number of people from one camp to another without giving them any prior warning. The people in Section 7 had not expected that they would all be required to make such a move.

The facts of the situation are that the Administration attacked these people with gas before they were properly informed as to what was happening to them and what was expected of them. The 1,500 people of the Section could not comprehend clearly what was happening and what was expected of them within 28 minutes at 6 a.m. in the morning when they were expected to leave immediately to be transferred to High Island. No remotely reasonable administrator could have expected that such an understanding could be accomplished amongst 1,500 people within a span of 28 minutes.

3. The Administration states that the first rounds of tear gas was fired (and mace sprayed) within 28 minutes of riot officers entering Section 7. They have stated, inaccurately as the Inquiry will already be aware, that they used the 28 minutes to engage in negotiations with the people of Section 7. There were no such negotiations. But, even if the Administration's claims were true, no remotely reasonable administrator could possibly believe that 28 minutes provided enough time for a person to wakeup, get dressed, dress their children, discover what was going on and what was expected of them, pack all their possessions and leave the Section, not to mention have time to participate in negotiations.

4. No remotely reasonable administrator can claim that 28 minutes of negotiation, even if such negotiations had taken place, is a long enough time to determine that negotiations are completely without hope of achieving their desired ends, and against defenceless men, women and children.

5. The Administration cannot legitimately claim that a single person would have left the Section to be moved to High Island if they had been properly informed about their options. The fact that not a single person left the Section before the first rounds of teargas were fired and mace sprayed is itself evidence that the Administration never intended to make any effort to use 'no or minimal force'. And this must have been clear at the planning stages of the operation, to use widespread and unnecessary violence.

The Administration deliberately created a climate of fear prior to the April 7 attack and then falsely claimed they had 'Lost Control'.

In its public statements following the attack, the Administration played upon the false stereotype of the Vietnamese people as being violent, claiming that there was a need to go into Section 7 with great force to avoid a violent response. This is completely false.

There is no history of people being moved from one camp to another responding with violent force against the people charged with moving them. The Vietnamese people are well aware that if they did attempt to use force to resist riot officers, they would be met with a force thousand times greater than anything they could muster. For example, the riot officers are armed with assault rifles and presumably would not hesitate to use them if they felt in any way threatened. There is a history of people resisting forced repatriation, but this is a completely different situation.

Not surprisingly, there were no reports in the wake of the April 7 attack any physical resistance to being moved. The Secretary for Security, Mr. Alistair Asprey confirmed this at the Legco Security Panel hearing on April 19. The vast majority of people left the Section peacefully soon after the first rounds of teargas was fired and mace sprayed, when it was clear to them that this was what was expected of them, without even collecting their life belongings. They had no intention of making any resistance to the move whatsoever. Nor did the small number of people who climbed onto the roofs of Section 7 to escape tear gas that was fired into their huts, physically resist their removal when they came down. Most of these people, particularly the women and children, were either too traumatised or too scared to come off the roofs earlier, partly because they had witnessed riot officer assaulting others who had climbed down.

In the weeks prior to the attack, there had been indications that the CSD was planning some sort of operation. This was widely perceived to be a retaliatory action aimed at those engaging in peaceful demonstration to protest against the unjust screening practices and forced repatriation. Several hunger strikers had already been removed to Upper Chi Ma Wan. More importantly, battalions of riot officers were conducting an unprecedented number of 'routine searches' on sections at White Head. This was seen as a precursor to more serious action and as intimidation to discourage the continuation of the peaceful demonstrations.

The Vietnamese people had experienced the heavy-handed tactics of riot officers in previous operations. Invariably, the officers were not held accountable for the violence of their actions on previous occasions. Just one example of this is detailed in JP's Report on the 1988 Hei Ling Chau incident.

Accordingly, so called 'drills' had been conducted by the Vietnamese people in section 7. These 'drills' were not to practice armed resistance to a move from one camp to another. They were not to practice armed resistance in any sense. Rather, these 'drills' involved forming human chains of people around those who were peacefully at hunger strike and who it was believed would be the target of any riot officer. No violent action was planned, only passive resistance. Once again, it would make no sense for the Vietnamese people to fight with the heavily armed police force with any force of their own. Even if these 'drills' were considered to constitute a threat to security, negotiation with community leaders is a far better alternative than the use of widespread, arbitrary violence.

The Administration is aware of the history of the lack of resistance on the part of the Vietnamese people over the past six years, particularly in the context of a simple move from one camp to another. They cannot legitimately claim that they overestimated the resistance that they would face. The Secretary for Security at the Legco Security Panel hearing stated vaguely that their 'intelligence sources' might have got it wrong.

The reality is that the Administration in the weeks leading up to the April 7 attack deliberately created a climate of fear in White Head. They made it clear that an operation involving riot officers, known from past experience to use excess violence for which they are unaccountable, was being planned. The Vietnamese people believed that such an action would target those conducting peaceful protests. Very minor measures involving practising passive resistance to the planned operation was conducted in Section 7. The Administration then used this to claim that they had 'lost control' at White Head. Under this false and deliberately orchestrated pretext, they conducted the most violent and unnecessary paramilitary operation in the recent history of Hong Kong.

The targets of this violence were not only the peaceful demonstrators in Section 7, but the defenceless men, women and children of Section 7 who were not involved in the protests, and also every Vietnamese asylum seeker being detained in Hong Kong. Since enrolment for voluntary repatriation was very low and a target date of the end of 1995 for the closure of the camps was envisaged, the attack was intended to be a clear warning that the Administration would use arbitrary violence against those refusing to voluntarily return to Vietnam.

This was not a riot situation

Commissioner of the Correctional Services Department, Mr. Eric McCosh was quoted as stating that the operation had been planned for two months, at the press conference he held on April 7. The Secretary for Security stated at the Legco Security Panel hearing that this specific operation had been planned for two to three weeks prior to April 7. Whichever account is most accurate, the operation was clearly planned well in advance, underlining the fact that the situation at White Head was not an emergency. The Vietnamese were not rioting nor had they planned for any uprising. Certainly, the only justification for even contemplating the use of force involving the gassing of 1,500 defenceless men, women and children were unjustifiable.

The Inquiry must expose why and how this attack was planned, and who was involved; what the Administration's motives were for planning to use violence. Only then will the full picture of a deliberately planned, intentionally violent attack on defenceless people be brought to light. Only then, will the people high-up in the Administration, who planned this attack can be brought to account and the future administrators would then plan any future operations in accordance with the rule of the law.

The UNHCR is not a fit and proper monitor

The UNHCR's mandated role is to monitor and protect refugees and asylum seekers from abuses. Not only did the UNHCR fail to suggest alternatives to the planned operation at White Head of which they were forewarned. Besides, the UNHCR failed to monitor the operation as it was taking place. But the UNHCR's Chief of Mission, Mr. Assadi, gave encouragement to the April 7 attack, both implicitly and explicitly, before and after the attack. Soon after the demonstrations against unjust screening and forced repatriation began in February, Mr. Assadi was quoted in the local media to the effect that these people were exercising their human right to freedom of speech and expression. Such human rights are of course, guaranteed by several United Nations instruments.

The tone of Mr. Assadi's public comments however, changed within a few weeks. On March 4 he stated that the demonstrations could not continue and that the Administration would be forced to move against the peaceful demonstrators if they did not end their protests soon. Such action, he stated would be 'understandable' (Rachel Clarke, 'Aid workers fear strife in camps' Eastern Express, 5/6 March 1994).

The chief of mission for the United Nations High Commissioner for Refugees in Hong Kong, Jahanshad Assadi, said if the demonstrations continued for much longer, there might have to be a change in approach by authorities. (Mr Assadi) 'I think it will be counter-productive and overkill if they persist with these hunger strikes and demonstrations'. 'If they continue for weeks and weeks I would imagine that things would change, something would have to give and things may not remain as calm as they have been'. If the demonstrations and hunger strikes continue the authorities may want to resort to other measures, that would be understandable, they cannot allow it to continue for six or seven weeks Assadi said.

This must have been interpreted by the Administration as: if Mr. Assadi did not explicitly state it to Administration, that the UNHCR would not object to, indeed advocated, action being taken against the people peacefully demonstrating. In effect, Mr. Assadi, on behalf of the UNHCR gave the administration green light to use force. Regarding the attack on section 7, this was UNHCR's first betrayal of the Vietnamese people and of its role of providing protection to asylum seekers.

Mr. Assadi has consistently maintained that he and others in the UNHCR did what they could to prevent the Administration to take action against them. This of course was not true. The Administration was not forced to act against those peacefully demonstrating. It chose to act in the hope of achieving other desired ends. Moreover, not once did Mr. Assadi meet the Administration to state that it would be completely unacceptable from the UNHCR's point of view and in terms of internationally recognised human right standards to use force to end peaceful protest. All of Mr. Assadi's public statements in the lead up to the April 7 Attack supported the Administration's alleged need to take action to end the protests.

Twelve hours prior to the April 7 attack, Mr. Assadi learned from the Refugee Co-ordinator Mr. Brian Bresnihan, that the Administration was planning a major operation against the people detained in Section 7. He was told that the operation was simply intended to transfer people to High Island and that involved the use of 1,250 riot officers.

To any organisation performing a legitimate monitoring role, this should have rung alarm bells, but not so for Mr. Assadi. He did not question the need for such a transfer, nor did he suggest alternative ways in which to transfer the people (which was previously effective), without the need for battalions of riot officers. When asked by a Member of Legco's Security Panel, why he did not suggest an alternative approach to Mr. Bresnihan on April 6, Mr. Assadi evaded the question without giving any direct answer.

The size of the operation, the time for which it was planned (6 a.m.) and the motives behind using these tactics to effect a simple transfer must have indicated to Mr. Assadi that this operation would at the very least involve a large amount of force against the Vietnamese people. Mr. Assadi's failure to question the need for the transfer and to suggest alternative means by which such a transfer could be peacefully effected was the UNHCR's second betrayal of the Vietnamese people and its role of providing protection to asylum seekers.

When speaking to the Refuge Co-ordinator on April 6, Mr. Assadi did not request that UNHCR Officers be allowed into Section 7 to explain to the Vietnamese people that this was a simple move from one detention centre to another. He was content to have battalions of riot officers who knew nothing of the Vietnamese people's lives to wake them at 6 a.m. to tell them to pack their belongings and move. The failure to even attempt to be a mediator was UNHCR's third betrayal of the Vietnamese people and of its role in providing protection to the asylum seekers.

On the morning of the April 7 attack, the first UNHCR 'monitoring' officer arrived at White Head at 9:30 a.m., some three and a half hours after the operation began. This of cours,e was after the major part of the attack had taken place and when approximately 1,100 of the people from Section 7 had already left the Section. Mr. Assadi knew that the operation was scheduled to begin at 6 a.m. and took no steps to ensure that UNHCR monitors were there to observe it and, characteristically, temper the actions of the riot officers. At the Legco Security Panel hearing, Mr. Assadi stated that the UNHCR officers appeared at White Head at the 'usual' time of 9:30 a.m. for three reasons. First, because he was not sure that monitor's would be allowed into the camp. (It seems he simply forgot to ask Mr. Bresnihan when he was informed of the impending operation!). Nonetheless, UNHCR officers clearly should have been there when the operation began in the hope that they would be permitted to enter White Head and monitor the situation. Moreover, the Administration has always recognised the UNHCR's right to monitor operations. The administrations forewarning to Mr. Assadi that the operation was to be conducted is a reflection of this. (In an in-house UNHCR 'interview', the transcript of which was released in late April, Mr. Assadi made very shrewd attempt to disguise the truth regarding why no UNHCR monitors were present when the operation began). He is quoted as stating:

They (the Government) also informed me (on April 6) that UNHCR and NGO staff would not be allowed into the camp 'for their own safety'........ Upon hearing this news, I immediately informed my staff and a meeting involving a large number of my staff (including field staff) was convened to discuss our response. We agreed that we would, nevertheless, try to enter White Head on the following day, even on the pretext of trying to carry on with our normal work. This would enable us to at least know better what was going on with the transfer of the Section 7 population. Upon attempting to enter White Head, all our staff- with the exception of two- were barred from entering. Of the two who were allowed in, one was confined by the authorities to his office, and the other was allowed to watch events from a distant hilltop. By then, it was 0930-0945 hours, and the operation was well underway (as from 0600 hrs).

Mr. Assadi in his 'interview' attempted to create the impression that Mr. Bresnihan had told him that no UNHCR monitors would be permitted to enter White Head. Indeed it was true that no general UNHCR staff and other NGO staff were to be permitted into White Head on April 7, but this is completely distinct from UNHCR officers being permitted to monitor the operation. The Government has never prevented the UNHCR from monitoring an operation, as that is the UNHCR's mandated role.

Second, Mr. Assadi stated that there was Security concerns if UNHCR monitors were present. This is difficult to understand. UNHCR monitors can, and when they eventually entered did, remain outside the Sections where the Vietnamese people were detained. Was Mr. Assadi concerned that the UNHCR monitoring officers would be mistaken by the riot officers for Vietnamese people and also arbitrarily assaulted?

Third, Mr. Assadi stated at Legco that another reason he did not have UNHCR monitors there before 9:30 a.m. was because the Vietnamese people might 'put on a bigger show' to say 'look what is happening to us'. This was a disgraceful remark. The Vietnamese people did not need to put on any 'show'. They were systematically and arbitrarily assaulted with gases and truncheons for no justifiable reason. Mr. Assadi knew the strength of force with which the riot officers were going into Section 7 and that at the very least, violence against the Vietnamese people was a distinct possibility. It is the UNHCR's mandated role to protect asylum seekers from abuses. Mr. Assadi's failure to ensure that monitor's were on the scene when the attack began was the UNHCR's fourth betrayal of the Vietnamese people and its role in providing protection to the asylum seekers.

When the UNHCR officers did finally arrive and two were allowed into White Head, one was confined to his office, apparently on the orders of the Administration. This Deputy Field Officer, amongst others, resigned from the UNHCR. The other UNHCR more senior 'monitor' stood on the hill at White Head, some considerable distance from Section 7, without any visual aids. He was not in a position to clearly see what was taking place in many parts of Section 7. Nor can only one monitor possibly observe what was taking place between 300 to 400 Vietnamese people who remained in the Section and the battalions of riot officers. The lack of adequate monitoring was

UNHCR's fifth betrayal of the Vietnamese people and its role of providing protection to asylum the seekers.

Mr. Assadi contradicted his testimony at the Legco Security Panel hearing on April 19 regarding the number of monitors the UNHCR requested to be permitted to enter White Head. At Legco he stated that given that the UNHCR monitors did not arrive at White Head until 3 to 4 hours after the operation had begun, there was little point in requesting more than two monitors be permitted to enter. Whereas, in the UNHCR 'interview' Mr. Assadi stated that he requested that all the UNHCR staff be permitted to enter White Head and that only two were permitted. Once again, he attempted to create a false impression of UNHCR's (lack of) effort to monitor the operation by disguising in language the distinction between general UNHCR staff and those performing a specific monitoring role.

Following the attack, the people of Hong Kong had to rely on statistics released by the CSD and Administration. Those figures were grossly inaccurate and misleading, and the UNHCR was in the best position to know this and was obliged to set the public record straight. Numerous members of his field staff told Mr. Assadi that the number and seriousness of casualties were far greater than that being stated by the Administration. According to reports from UNHCR field staff, Mr. Assadi was dismissive of their reports, preferring the figures released by the CSD. At the Legco hearing, Mr. Assadi defended this by stating that there was information coming from all directions that needed to be verified. This is both a slight on his field staff and a farce. If he wanted to obtain accurate casualty statistics, all he had to do was enquire of the British Red Cross in High Island Detention Centre and the Department of Health.

In any case, the UNHCR made no independent report, and it took robust journalism for the Administration to admit that it had misled the public. The failure of the UNHCR to provide a public and independent report that was based on reality rather than Administration propaganda was its sixth betrayal of the Vietnamese people and its role of providing protection to the asylum seekers. On the day following the attack, Mr. Assadi made public statements that offered no hint of criticism of the April 7 attack. Instead he implicitly supported the attack, stating that he had told the Vietnamese people that they were forcing the Government to take 'drastic action' and that the attack was to be expected much the same as he had stated one month earlier.

'...this is what I was telling the Vietnamese refugees might happen if they did not stop their hunger strikes and demonstrations. They are compelling the Government to take drastic action' (Rachel Clarke, Eastern Express, 8

April 1994). At Legco Mr. Assadi claimed that on April 8 he quietly raised some concerns with the Administration regarding the operation. Exactly what those concerns were and how far they ranged remains unclear. What is clear is that he certainly did not make a formal objection or protest to the Administration regarding the attack as a whole.

On the afternoon of April 8, a meeting was held at the UNHCR headquarters in Hong Kong with field staff from White Head. To the dismay of UNHCR field staff, Mr. Assadi stated that what had happened at Section 7 would 'look like a picnic' compared with what was to follow. He told his field officers to do some 'soul searching', and if they could not face the prospect of further violent attacks being perpetrated on the Vietnamese people, then perhaps they should leave the UNHCR. There was clearly no intention on Mr. Assadi's part to ensure that no such attacks would occur in the future. On the contrary, he was of the view that even more brutal attacks would follow. Mr. Assadi did not question the legitimacy or appropriateness of the attack but rather reiterated that the Vietnamese people had forced the Administration's hand by conducting prolonged (peaceful) protests.

Mr. Assadi explicitly supported the attack by justifying it in reference to the peaceful protests, by refusing to criticise it, and by being satisfied that further attacks would take place that would make the April 7 'look like a picnic'. Mr. Assadi's support for the Administration's attack was the UNHCR's seventh betrayal of the Vietnamese people and its role in providing protection to the asylum seekers (Since 19 April, Mr. Assadi had consistently attempted to portray his support for the April 7 attack by making observations. His argument is apparently along the following lines. When he stated on March 4 that it was 'understandable' and necessary for the Administration to take action against those people peacefully demonstrating, he was not really advocating that action be taken but merely observing that the Administration would take action. Similarly, when on the day of the April 7 attack. Mr. Assadi stated that he had warned the peaceful demonstrators that this sort of action would likely occur if they persisted and that they were 'compelling' the Government to take drastic action. He was not really saying that the Government was forced to take this sort of drastic action but rather that he thought the Administration would take drastic action).

It has been reported to us that on Sunday, 10 April, Mr. Assadi continued to publicly support the attack in a television interview that was seen by a number of asylum seekers. He apparently stated, among other things, that he believed that the attack would boost voluntary repatriation rates. Once again, in the absence of any comment criticising the attack, his comments support, and are seen as supporting the attack.

Mr. Assadi did some heavy back-pedalling at the Legco Security Panel hearing on 19 April. There he made his first public criticism of the attack but only under the weight of widespread public outrage, intense and critical media coverage, the robust expression of concern by the Members of the Legislative Council's Security Panel and the Administration's calling of an Inquiry. At Legco he maintained that not only was he 'shocked' by the violence of the attack but he could 'not understand how any decent organisation or human being could support the operation'. He also changed his position on voluntary repatriation. At Legco he suddenly stated that such an operation would be counter productive to encouraging people to voluntarily repatriate, not the reverse.

In his initial comments, Mr. Assadi's supported the attack saying that it would serve the Administration's purpose of lifting enrolment for voluntary repatriation. The implicit support entailed in these comments for the use of further such attacks was the UNHCR's eighth betrayal of the Vietnamese people and of its role to protect the asylum seekers. In the final analysis, the upper echelons of the UNHCR have proven that the Organisation is not a fit and proper monitor for the Vietnamese people; that rather than being their only defence against abuses, the UNHCR is itself a player in those abuses.

As a result of the UNHCR's support for this attack and its failure to make even an attempt to protect them from the Administration's abuses, the Vietnamese people have lost any faith that they had previously had in the organisation. To prevent further such attacks and abuses, the Inquiry must recommend monitoring alternatives to that of the UNHCR.

Conclusion

It appears that over a period of time the Hong Kong government refugee bureaucrats have learned to use violence systematically against the asylum seekers as tool of refugee management. Some independent agencies traced the relationship between camp violence and the role of Hong Kong Police. A report by the refugee rights advocacy group, 'refugee concern' about violent incidents in the camp clearly mentioned that it was an attack on the asylum seekers, and that the UNHCR betrayed the asylum seekers' interests' in the context of increasing violence against them by the Hong Kong government and the police. Indiscriminate and increasing use of tear gas was used by the police against the asylum seekers detained in the camps.

A multitude of factors contributed towards making the camp a violent place to live. Prolonged and unjustified detention of a community in itself is a violent act. Structural violence is often overlooked by the camp management and researchers in assessing the roots of violence in the detention camps. In order to understand the nature and cause of violence in the asylum seeker detention camps, a general consideration should be given to the historical background of the population. The communist indoctrination influenced the thinking pattern of several people in the camps. In the camp situation some of them cannot look at others without suspicion. Existing police informant network strengthened this suspicion. The South Vietnamese felt that they deserved a better life and the world owed it to them, the Northerners were coming in between to steal this opportunity. Whereas the Northerners felt that they had slogged all their lives under the communist influence and now it was their chance to experience freedom.

The immediate provocation for violence was often attributed towards issues related to unsettled dues of organising escape from Vietnam. The escapees were expected to pay to the boat organiser. In some cases, people promised to pay after they reached their destination, or they paid only partially. Once they reached Hong Kong, the boat organisers tried to redeem their dues, which often lead to violence. Limited food, water and provisions resulted in intimidation during their voyage to Hong Kong. The residual grudge is another factor for the violence in the camps.

The environmental factors of the camps were a breeding ground for violence. Often community networks based on ethnic and primordial sentiments became cleavages as well as source of power. Perpetuating violence in the camp was an exercise of power. The perpetuator controlled the situation by forcing the camp management and the service staff to attend to the situation immediately. Often, the victims were the weak and powerless in the community. The contribution of the environmental factors in perpetuating violence in the detention centres can be summarised as the violence due to spatial intrusions, monotony and external factors (Suedfeld, 1977). Administrative practices like tear gassing the crowd, even when there were unprotected children in the crowd, forcing the community to squat in the hot sun, forcing them for regular physical searches was another form of violence. In a nutshell the phenomenon of camp violence is a cause and consequence of ethnocide took place in the detention camps.

8 The Silence of the Power Brokers

Introduction

This chapter explores the function and role of social service intervention in Hong Kong detention centres in relation to the process of ethnocide taking place in the detention centres. The main theme explored here is how 'helping intervention' influences the outcome of the social process that takes place within the detention centres. The main focus here is on the role of CFSI and other NGOs that offered social service assistance to the asylum seekers.

Social services are a helping intervention in any crisis situation. When clients perceives the intervention as one of disservice and ignores or reject the services, the service intervention becomes just an intervention to maintain the interest of other social players and not the clients. In this situation the helping intervention ceases to be a service intervention. Social service enables clients to cope with critical situations or events either in groups, and or as individuals. However, helping intervention is not a value neutral involvement.

The objective of the client is not always concurrent to the objective of the service agency and it's sponsors. It is often an area of conflict between the client, the agency and the sponsoring agency. 'Intervention' in refugee assistance is just another emerging arena for the professional 'service intervention'. It is necessary to critically evaluate the function and role of service intervention in assisting the clients and it's impact on the social changes taking place in the detention centres.

The UNHCR and Hong Kong governments understanding of services to the asylum seekers

According to the statement of understanding reached between the Hong Kong Government and UNHCR, concerning the treatment of asylum seekers, the Hong Kong Government and the UNHCR jointly considered the need for services in all centres for the asylum seekers, refugees and persons determined not to be refugees. When a need for a particular service was identified it was provided by the voluntary agencies determined by the UNHCR following a consultation with the Hong Kong Government.

The UNHCR and the Hong Kong Government gave contracts to the following agencies to carry out assistance programs for the Vietnamese refugees in Hong Kong. The Hong Kong Housing Services for Refugees (HKHSR); Agency for Voluntary Services (AVS); Hong Kong Christian Aid to Refugees (HKCAR); Medicines Sans Frontiers (MSF) - Belgium; Save the Children Fund (SCF); Community and Family Services International (CFSI); Caritas; British Red Cross Society(BRCS); and International Social Services (ISS) - Hong Kong Branch, to carry out assistance programs. Community and Family Services International was mainly dependent on the UNHCR for resources. All the other agencies working with the refugees had access to resources other than UNHCR sources.

CFSI was offering counselling and community development services for the asylum seekers in all the existing camps in Hong Kong. SCF was offering services for the children, and ISS was offering educational services for the asylum seekers. Hong Kong Caritas was assisting the asylum seekers with limited social assistance and recreational activities, whereas the HKCAR was offering vocational training for the asylum seekers. Hong Kong government Health Services and MSF provided medical assistance to the asylum seekers.

Camp administrative offices, social service agency offices, and medical facilities were often outside the perimeter of the primary fencing of the detention centres. In order to get access to these services, asylum seekers had to convince the gatekeeper that they had a genuine need to consult the service staff. They also had to negotiate several metal gates or narrow staircases before they could reach a service agency's office.

Though half a dozen agencies were working at any given time in any asylum seeker camps, only a limited number of camp residents were utilising these services. The service agencies' survival in the camp was often dictated by the survival needs of the agency itself and how best they could cater to the interests' of the funding agencies. For instance, any of these functions were not fulfilled by the agency, or if it was perceived that they were not capable of fulfilling the functions, the existence of such an agency would have been in trouble (refer to table 8.1 for a list of agencies involved in refugee services under the auspices of UNHCR and their area of involvement).

The service agencies deliver a host of programmes like child welfare, community development work, counselling, recreational activities, education, medial care, family planning services and occupational training. One of the most common denominator of all the agencies was their reluctance to introduce the element of community participation in their projects. Often the participation of the community was limited to 'service recipient' function.

Table 8.1   List of agencies and services offered by them

AGENCIES	SERVICES
AVS	Assistance in resettlement
AMS	Medical assistance
CARITAS	Financial assistance
CAS	Management of refugee centres
CFSI	Social services
CSD	Management of detention centres
ESF	Education services
HKCAR	Management of refugee centres
HKFPA	Family planning services
HKHR	Management of refugee centres
IOM	Assistance in resettlement
HKRC	Tracing relatives
JVA	Assistance in resettlement
ISS	Education for children
MSF	Medical assistance
OXFAM	Financial assistance
RKHP	Management of detention centres
SCF	Child care
TREATS	Recreation for children

The service delivery agencies were offering a valuable service to the asylum seekers. They offered a 'helping hand' and a sympathetic ear to the asylum seekers during their utmost difficult period in life at the detention centres. Yet, in order to maintain the service delivery role of the agencies most of the service agencies were asked to 'tow the line' by the camp administrators with the tactical support of the inter-governmental humanitarian agency, the UNHCR.

The primary objective of the UNHCR and the camp administration was to repatriate all the asylum seekers back to Vietnam at the earliest. For them the criteria to assess the effectiveness and the relevance of any services were to assess how much the agencies were contributing to their objective of repatriation. Because, according to their agenda no other programmes were of importance. Some service agencies meekly accepted it, some protested vehemently initially but gradually obliged to tow the line. Service agencies were the silent witnesses of the massive human rights violation and the subsequent process of ethnocide of the asylum seekers on a daily basis. Nevertheless, the agencies were extremely careful in not upsetting the refugee administrators.

During 1988-89, at the beginning of the detention policy, Save the Children Fund (SCF), a British child welfare agency threatened the refugee administers that they would withdraw from the detention camps in protest against the inhuman detention policy. Hong Kong Housing Services for Refugees (HKHSR) was the only private limited company entrusted to run a detention centre with the help of a private security company and the Hong Kong Police. The HKHSR was always an obedient and silent partner in lieu with the refugee administrators. They never objected to the detention centre policy nor any other polices related to the treatment of the asylum seekers.

Even though the International Organisation for Migration (IOM) and Joint Voluntary Agency (JVA) did not have daily presence in the camps, they arranged for the asylum seekers to move from Hong Kong, by means of voluntary repatriation, or by resettling them in another country. However, they also never expressed their reservations about the British Hong Kong government refugee policy.

At least a minimum level of bureaucratisation is essential or is a pre-requisite for any institution. Unless high precision is taken by the leadership, the social service objectives will be dominated by bureaucratic structures. Vision of people involved with the institutions, ideological position of the staff and leadership, objectives of institution, and the internal mechanisms of the institutions are some of the factors which play a crucial role in influencing the goals of the social services in 'total institutions'.

The constant exposure to the detention centre conditions exerts both professional and personal strain on the social service delivery capabilities of the agencies and the staff. Often, the social service agencies' exposure to the acute 'totality of institution' setting, force them to deflect from their professional objectives of the social service delivery process.

The dilemma of professional social workers in bureaucratic structures could be explained as a process of learned incapacity. Learned incapacity is an inability of a professional to discharge his or her professions functions in a given situation, due to the extreme high professional demand of the situation which is beyond the coping capacity of those professionals.

In general social workers in bureaucratic structures adopt measures in keeping with the perceived roles of bureaucratic structures which may significantly differ from the actual requirement of the clients or social conditions. According to Dewey 'occupational psychosis' is a 'pronounced character of the mind'. This psychosis develops through demands put upon individual by the particular institutional set-up of her/his occupational role. Basically this creates some sort of ambivalence. One of the major demands of a bureaucratic set-up is discipline. Maintenance of discipline and 'results' can be effectively done only if ideal patterns of social services are buttressed by strong impersonal attitudes, which however, put a profound limitation on service providers' competence and performance. The 'trained inability's' of the social workers in influencing the life of the asylees significantly in the detention centres are not essentially an individual problem. It is clearly derived from structural sources. This process is briefly explained by Robert Merton as this:

1. An effective bureaucracy demands reliability of responses and strict devotion to regulations.
2. Such devotion to the rules leads to their transformation into absolutes. The rules no longer coincide with a relative set of purpose.
3. The inflexibility of bureaucratic rules interferes with its ready adaptation under special conditions
4. Those who draw up the rule may not be willing to deviate from the rules
5. Thus the very elements which conduce towards efficiency in general produce inefficiency in specific instances.

Another feature of bureaucratic structure is the stress on depersonalisation of relationships, which is against the social work principle of individualisation of the clients. In a total institutional context individual variation of cases and the peculiarities of individual cases are often forced to be overlooked (Refer to Fig 8.1 for a comparison of values of total institution and values of Social Service).

Table 8.2   Comparison of values of 'total institutions' and values of social service

Values of Bureaucracy/Values of total institutions	Values of social service
Discipline	Self discipline
Efficiency	Human concern
Impersonal	Personal
Hierarchical	Collective
Legal jurisdiction	Parental jurisdiction
Formal	Interdependency
Specific roles	Dynamic roles
Authoritarianism	Charismatic
Secondary groups	Primary groups
Pragmatism	Idealism
Maintenance of status quo	Reform, change
Quantitative achievement	Qualitative achievements
Limited objectives	Vision oriented
Frozen structures	Flexible structures

A case study of CFSI

During early 1981 the Community and Family Services International (CFSI) was established by a group of Filipino and American refugee assistance professionals employed at the Philippine Refuge Processing Centre (PRPC) in Batan, Philippines. At the request of the UNHCR in April 1989, CFSI began developing service delivery systems for the refugee camps and centres in Hong Kong. Since 1990 CFSI started offering its services of refugee assistance operation programmes to the Southeast Asian region. However, CFSI was shortly asked to wind up its programme and operations in Hong Kong with effect from August 1993, by the UNHCR, the sole funding agency of CFSI. The UNHCR cited 'changed priorities' for their particular request.

Community and Family Services International (CFSI) offered a comprehensive social development programme for the Vietnamese in Hong Kong detention centres. CFSI was the only social service agency that offered services to all the Vietnamese centres in the territory.

The overall objective of the Social Development project agreed between UNHCR and CFSI was to continuously assess and address the psychosocial needs of the Vietnamese refugees and asylum seekers and persons determined as non-refugees in Hong Kong. This intervention was expected to be carried out through therapeutic interventions including training, community organisation, and community development efforts. The active community participation was presented as the central feature of the project. The target population of the project was the refugees and the asylum seekers and asylum seekers determined as non-refugees in Hong Kong. Mentally ill, sick, the disabled, victims of violence or abuse, those in acute personal crisis, and mentally handicapped were the active cases of the CFSI. The overall co-ordination and monitoring of the project was undertaken by the UNHCR Social Services Co-ordinator and the UNHCR Field officers were designated monitors at the camp level.

Community development component and casework component are the two strong points of CFSI contribution to the Vietnamese community work in Hong Kong. CFSI employed and trained 180 Vietnamese paraprofessional staff along with about 40 professional case workers and community work staff supervised by four area supervisors and one programme co-ordinator, one project director, one paraprofessional co-ordinator and office staff. A training unit was developed to train the paraprofessionals in carrying out assistance programmes for the Vietnamese population in the detention centres and refugee centres.

Community development services, research, counselling for vulnerable persons, minors, training and support management services were identified as CFSI service intervention in the camps. Community development teams were employed at all the sites comprising of one professional staff and five paraprofessional staff, per 5,000 population. The overall objective of CFSI community development intervention was to develop, support and maintenance of resources within the community.

Community Development workers were instrumental in developing and maintaining camp profiles through surveys and updated statistics, continuing assessment of service needs and sharing information with other NGOs in the camps. The community leadership structure was developed and enhanced. Identification of existing community structures and alliances were achieved. Organisation of sectoral meetings, facilitating the process of representative leadership, liasing and advocacy with other agencies and camp management to promote community organisations were some of the achievements of the CFSI. In addition, they also offered training for the community leaders, community education, the development of an effective information and communication system were some of the other achievements of the community development efforts of CFSI.

An overall guideline for CFSI Community Development (CD) work

According to CFSI, community development is a set of community intervention strategies to achieve certain tangible behavioural and structural changes in the client population. The goal of Community Development is to develop an organised community actively involved in service delivery. The guiding principle of Community Development work is to ensure maximum community participation, maximum use of community resources, complimentary nature of CD and Case-work, collegiality of professional and paraprofessional staff and active role of paraprofessionals in service delivery. The objectives of CD work were:

a. *Psychosocial needs assessment*: CD workers were expected to do the psychosocial needs assessment of the camps they were working in. The components of psychosocial need assessment were socio-cultural, demographic characteristics, community needs assessment and resource identification. The tasks involved in CD work were conducting need assessment surveys, developing need assessment tools and methodology, developing a reporting system of community needs, planning projects and programmes to address the needs, identification and mobilisation of resources and follow-up. The indicators of the tasks achieved were camp profiles, need assessment reports, profile of community needs, and resource inventory list and follow up actions.

b. *Development and enhancement of community leadership structures*: CD workers in consultation with all the concerned agencies were expected to work towards developing/enhancing community leadership structures. The essential components of developing/enhancing community leadership structure were based on analysis of existing power structure, acknowledging and changing the existing power structure, if required, community organisation, facilitating venues for community participation, and developing skilled community leaders. The tasks involved in enhancing/ developing leadership structure were identification of power structure and interest groups, identification and enhancement of positive structures, soliciting consensus, and support for desired goals, formation of interest groups, promoting and advocating community participation and providing training for community leaders. The indicators of the task achieved were description of power structure, established community structures, consensus building exercises, organisation, development and elections, community participation at various levels of decision-making and implementation of specialised training modules.

c. *Community participation in service delivery*: Facilitating community participation in service delivery programmes was an important element of CD work in the camps. CD workers tried to evolve avenues for community participation. Essential components in the process of enhancing community participation in service delivery system were community participation in needs and issues identification, community participation in planning, implementation and evaluation. The most important tasks in this area were to evolve community participation strategies in need assessment, strategies for community planning and developing a participatory evaluation methodology. The indicators of the tasks that was achieved were list of issues, needs of various groups, community plan of action, identification of priorities and time schedules for activities and programme reports.

d. *The community advocacy*: CD workers were expected to promote the interest of the client community by all possible avenues. The important components in community advocacy were the identification issues and developing an advocacy strategy. The tasks involved in community advocacy were planning and evolving an appropriate strategy. The indicators of the tasks achieved were documentation on issues and reports on results.

e. *The community education*: CD workers were expected to play the role of community educators. The essential components of community education were identification of issues and consultation on issues. The important tasks involved were list issues, plan community education and implementation strategy. The indicators of the tasks achieved were community education needs list, community education materials, community education reports and results.

f. *The staff training*: The CD staff were sensitive to the staff training needs and the needs were periodically articulated by identification of training needs, developing training tools and methodology, mobilisation of resources and implementation of training sessions. The indicators of the tasks achieved were training plans, reports and documentation.

g. *Involvement of paraprofessionals in service delivery*: The CD staffs were also expected to involve the paraprofessional in all the possible areas of service delivery system. The tasks involved were facilitation of training, service delivery systems, and specific assignments to the staff, supervision of paraprofessionals and staff evaluation. The indicators of the tasks were training plans, documentation and reports, service delivery systems and regular supervision reports.

h. *Communication and information systems*: The CD staff was also involved in evolving appropriate communication strategy in the community. The tasks involved were to provide means and access to information, documentation of information and experiences. The indicators of the tasks achieved were newsletters, meetings, reports and other communication channels.

i. *A set of possible community development activities*: Accepting camp specific diversity, a set of CD intervention strategies was proposed. For each camp, the staff, camp representatives, agencies and the CFSI management evolved specific CD involvement strategy. Working with community groups included, developing sectoral interests, vulnerable self help groups, income generation, identification of groups, need assessment, advocacy, leadership development, planning, monitoring, and evaluation. Problem solving within the community, resource mobilisation, organising recreation, social and cultural events were also part of working with community groups. Developing community structures involved, conducting community elections, organising community forum, developing camp committees, advisory committees, programmes for community leadership development, consultation, conflict resolution, negotiation, planning, and community participation. Community education programs involved orientation for new arrivals on health, hygiene, and safety. Education on substance abuse, peace and order, organising skill development training, organising newsletters, legal education. Education on social issues, general information, resource identification, community relations and education on community responsibilities were the other components of community education programmes. In addition, counselling services teams were employed at all the camp sites. These teams consisted of professionally qualified counsellors and eight paraprofessionals for each 2,500 population. The overall goal of casework was to provide preventive and protective therapeutic services to promote optimum psychosocial function of the individual and families.

CFSI actively contributed towards identifying the unaccompanied minors, mentally ill and mentally handicapped. Offering services for the unaccompanied minors was one of the strong areas of CFSI work in the camps. CFSI assessed all the children in Hong Kong without parents to determine the nature and quality of existing care giving relationships with an adult. Through supportive counselling the individual psychosocial needs of each child was identified and specific case plans were developed. The individuals who were unable to function adequately in the camps were identified through community outreach and referral mechanisms. The case plan for these individuals are individual counselling, group work and therapeutic interventions, facilitating access to the services and community based rehabilitation programmes.

A training unit was developed to provide basic service training for the paraprofessionals. The professional staff's training needs were met through regular training on supervision skills, training in dealing with child abuse cases, domestic violence, and sexual abuse and crisis intervention.

Response of other NGOs

A large number of NGOs were involved with the Hong Kong asylum seeker issues. International and local NGOs from different political perspectives were responding to this situation. Some were involved in service delivery on a daily or regular basis. They were the Justice and Peace Commission of the HK Catholic Diocese, Oxfam Hong Kong, Refugee Concern Hong Kong, and Amnesty International. These agencies consistently played a strong advocacy role for better human right conditions for the asylum seekers in Hong Kong.

The justice and peace Commission of the Hong Kong Catholic Diocese published their views about the Vietnamese asylum seeker issues in 1990.

According to the commission, since the introduction of the closed camp policy, the measures introduced by the Hong Kong government in dealing with the Vietnamese had been by and large inhumane. It is an irony that in the process of braving the waves in search for freedom, the first aberration that these innocent Vietnamese people had to face was an indefinite period of detention in a cramped and prison like condition.

Justice and peace commission was also instrumental in sending an open letter to the foreign Minister of the British government against forced repatriation signed by 17 other local groups and NGOs. During November 1992 the commission members met the refugee administrators and they were assured that the service provision for the asylum seekers would not be cut. But during early 1993 it was announced that all the service provision would be scaled down drastically.

The Refugee Concern Hong Kong (RCHK) was a group of refugee camp workers and concerned individuals who shared the desire to facilitate awareness and constructive action, to ensure welfare of the Vietnamese refugees and asylum seekers in Hong Kong. The most critical and important contribution of RCHK was their study on children living in detention centres entitled 'Defenceless in Detention, Vietnamese Children Living Amidst Increasing Violence in Hong Kong' (1991). The RCHK report was based on a research study and a campaign against detention. Interestingly enough another agency, CFSI, was also instrumental in conducting a research on the effect of detention on children. However, unlike RCHK, CFSI used the results of the study to campaign and to promote repatriation of the Vietnamese asylum seekers back to Vietnam. Moreover, the CFSI study had nothing to say about the policy of detention of the refugees in Hong Kong.

Amnesty International's (AI) role on Vietnamese refugee issues was often dictated by the international secretariat. AI's concern was mostly related to the procedural aspects of screening process rather than the human rights violation of the asylum seekers in the full context. Significantly enough, the AI did not acknowledge the political implication of the refugees' detention in Hong Kong. Amnesty International expressed its concern about the ill treatment of the asylum seekers in detention, forced repatriation and the procedural aspects of screening. Yet the AI was reluctant to denounce the detention policy in clear terms and to accept the reality that the asylum seekers detained in Hong Kong were detained for the political convenience of the UK Hong Kong government and were political prisoners of the UK-Hong Kong government. No specific campaign was ever initiated by the AI to invite international attention to the plight of the refugees detained in Hong Kong (perhaps taking on British human rights violation abroad may not be a viable option for fund raising for the AI in the UK, or are they really impartial to the international policies of the UK government?).

Conclusion

Some of the international NGOs have done some intense lobbying and advocacy work for the rights of the detainees. Lawyers committee for human rights and the women's commission for refugees jointly made a submission to the United Nations working group on arbitrary detention of the asylum seekers. 'Asia Watch' is another agency, which was strongly opposed to forced repatriation and the detention policy.

Normally it is very unlikely to dismantle an active programme, which was implemented in a volatile situation like in the Hong Kong camps without any adequate reasons. If the real issue were financial problems, UNHCR, deciding to take over the social service component would never have occurred. The way and the manner in which CFSI Hong Kong programmes were terminated by the UNHCR deserve a closer look. This might give an insight into the role and function of the service intervention in refugee assistance and the scope of humanitarian intervention itself.

Community Family Services International operates on the notion of 'a person in an environment or ecological perspective'. 'A major CFSI service commitment is environmental modification, particularly of the social element' (Muncy, 1991). Even though in public the agency put up a face of progressive stand on environmental modification in the camp, any attempt by the staff to do such interventions were severely reprimanded by the management.

As an agency CFSI never articulated its concern about the prolonged detention of asylum seekers and the need for environmental and structural modifications of the camp regime. Whenever the agency raised its concern, it was to 'educate' the Vietnamese to go back to Vietnam. The CFSI director visited Vietnam as a consultant to the Special Committee of UNHCR, just before she took her assignment with CFSI. This visit to Vietnam was to investigate the alternatives available for the care of children, whose parents were dead, missing or for some reason unable to provide care, along with other terms of references. In effect, her trip was to explore and identify the orphanages in Vietnam to send the orphan children back from the Hong Kong camps, which was in the 'best interest of the child'! Her main findings and recommendations were 'for children to return to Vietnam whose parents were dead, missing or unable to provide care'. The approach of this kind of recommendation was that the Vietnamese authorities would try to trace extended family members who would be prepared to accept the child. For those cases where extended family members could not be traced, it was however, in the child's best interest to return to Vietnam. It was proposed that in such cases funding an extension of the Birla children's home in Vietnam be considered, which could take in the returnees from Hong Kong. It was also stipulated that regular funding of this home was to be brought up to the same standard as that of the S.O.S children's village to enable to accommodate the returnee children from the Hong Kong camps (Report on joint Mission to Hanoi, 1990).

This statement was an indicator of the direction of all CFSI activities in the camps. All service intervention was subtly geared towards sending children back to Vietnam by any means. All such efforts of CFSI to continue its programmes in the camps by trying to please the UNHCR became futile in the end. The agency was asked to close down its programmes. Even though the publicly cited reasons for the closure of the agency was given as financial problems. The actual reason for this closure was the perception of certain refugee administrators that CFSI was not contributing adequately in encouraging the asylum seekers to go back to Vietnam. Besides, CFSI was also instrumental in developing community structures in the camps, which were a source of strength to the Vietnamese in their desperate attempt to stay in Hong Kong.

CFSI was gradually changing its initial role as a social service intervention agency to an effective social service bureaucracy, deviating from the best interest of the client to protect the best interest of the Hong Kong refugee bureaucracy. In that process CFSI moved dangerously close to the role of UNHCR, threatening the relevance and role of UNHCR itself. The professional jealousy and insecurity of some of the UNHCR field staff also contributed towards the downfall of CFSI. In their desperate struggle to keep the momentum of voluntary repatriation going, the field staff indiscriminately began looking for scapegoats. CFSI was a convenient scapegoat to explain the sagging momentum of voluntary repatriation.

The global image of UNHCR as a Good Samaritan for the refugees was severely tarnished in the Hong Kong camps. UNHCRs active involvement in voluntary repatriation and its tactical support to the UK-Hong Kong government in carrying out forced repatriation was the cause of UNHCRs tarnished image in the territory. In the field situation, CFSI was identified as the 'good guys' and the UNHCR as the 'bad guys'. Information from the camps reached the office. Some of the CFSI staff's holier than thou attitude toward UNHCR irritated the field staff severely. The CFSI involvement with the community structures was another area of conflict. For the Hong Kong UNHCR, the concept of community participation was the voluntary participation of the asylum seekers in going into repatriation flights without any questions. The community development component of CFSI's activities was actively discussed, debated, criticised during the entire first half of 1992 without reaching any consensus. "The term 'Community Development' itself had been questioned by UNHCR because of a perception that community development was aimed at consolidating the existing camp populations and perpetuating them in Hong Kong"(Warburton, 1992). CFSI was asked by the UNHCR to consider changing the title and job description of the community development workers to community liaison workers. As a compromise CFSI agreed to change the title of the Community Development staff as that of group of social workers.

However, it was too late to salvage the agency. The UNHCR demanded to close down the activities of CFSI with effect from August 1993, and UNHCR began recruiting staff directly for the social service programmes in the camps. Some of the CFSI staff joked in private about the situation '*When CFSI was asked to kneel down, the agency management forced its staff to crawl, even, then the master was not pleased*'.

Davis (1991) explained about the Vietnamese asylum seekers in Hong Kong by saying that "the role of voluntary organisation, however, was unclear. It was undoubtedly not an agent of significant change, but met the principal interest of the Hong Kong Government in ensuring that something was being 'seen to be done' thereby helping people - locally, regionally and internationally - to lose sight of the fundamental issues" (Davis, 1991).

However, now it is clear that the Hong Kong government and UNHCR saw the role of the voluntary organisations as that of another set of tools in their hands in 'managing' the refugees. The voluntary agencies were required as far as it suited the UK-Hong Kong government and UNHCRs interests', (incidentally both their interests were the same) and not the interest of the asylum seekers.

It appears that a carefully planned social service intervention could have reduced the negative consequences of the process of ethnocide. But the dilemma of the social service agencies was often that the resources for such intervention had to come from the agencies who perpetuated the process of ethnocide as part of their wider plan to control the cultural groups such as the asylum seekers to fit into their socio-political objectives.

9 Solving the Refugee Problem or a Planned Ethnocide?

'Refugee problem in Hong Kong is solved' is a euphemism used by the refugee manages to refer to the success of their planned process of ethnocide. The data indicated the possibility of the displaced asylum seekers facing serious socio-cultural consequences due to detention. A large number of children grew up in the detention centres deprived of cultural and social stimulation and adequate opportunities. The cumulative process of such deprivation could be summed up as ethnocide. This is not an accidental phenomenon, but a product of a well-planned and well-executed scheme by the British government in Hong Kong.

Though, one of the major contribution of this book is a major discourse on the phenomenon of ethnocide, this study also posed unique theoretical and methodological issues related with anthropological fieldwork. Issues such as scientific approach and issues of neutrality and objectivity. In a situation of highly polarised social interests, any intervention, whether fieldwork for data collection or humanitarian intervention become value loaded. In such overwhelming situation, the question arises whether the field worker has to take sides. The only objective decision he/she can make is the degree of subjectivity and partiality.

This chapter presents a summary of main findings of the research carried out among the Vietnamese refugees in Hong Kong. In nutshell, the key variables that contributed to the process of ethnocide in the refugee detention centres were, closed camps, limited personal space, use of disproportionate violence by camp management, media censorship, constant movement of asylum seekers from one camp to another and within the camp itself; discouraging the use of names, reduction of social service facilities, prolonged period of forced inaction, curtailing cultural and religious activities, discouraging community participation, control of personal communication channels, constant media portrayal of asylees as violent populace, control over food distribution, and by maintaining an 'informer' network.

Methods of Ethnocide

Understanding the methods of ethnocide used in Hong Kong would provide a useful tool for human right activists to revitalise humanitarian intervention strategies and to develop appropriate policies. The core of ethnocide is the effort of the authorities, often with state sanction to distort the individual and collective human sprit of asylum seekers through well planned strategies of total control. In the Hong Kong refugee detention centres the camp authorities perpetuated ethnocide through the following methods.

Total control

The key aspect of ethnocide is an effort of the dominant group to exercise total control in all spheres of life of the contact group. Whenever additional procedures and plans are initiated, the core objective of such plan is to gain more control over another additional sphere of life of the contact group or to consolidate the power they already have.

Rewarding the bureaucracy

A highly efficient bureaucracy is the cornerstone of the success of ethnocide. The more a bureaucrat involved in refugee work says that they are merely doing a difficult job, it is more likely that they are demanding a proper reward. It is not an accident that almost all the top bureaucrats of the colonial government involved in the refugee work were rewarded with lucrative posts in post colonial Hong Kong Government.

Cultivating bureaucratic alliances

Cultivating bureaucratic alliances help each agency to tide over occasional unpleasant flare-ups and administrative goof-ups, which require shielding from other bureaucrats.

Cultivated channels of communication with International human right activists

In any situation of ethnocide there will be a few dedicated activists who could become a 'nuisance' for the administrators. The Hong Kong refugee management regime successfully neutralised such groups and agencies like the local branch of the Amnesty International (AI) by cultivating strategic channels of communication. The refugee bureaucracy regime managed to silence these groups in two ways. One, they successfully exploited the conceptual poverty of AI in dealing with rights of the refugees detained in the camps. Secondly, they created an illusion among the local AI leadership that they have access to the camps and to the top bureaucrats at any time. It was true that the bureaucrats were ever willing to wine and dine the AI local leaders, but they seldom allowed the AI leaders to visit the camps independently or to talk to the refugees.

Closed camps

Controlling the free movement of individuals and communities is the cornerstone of ethnocide. It provides a social foundation for the authorities to build on other means of social control. Restriction of movements could be brought in and justified in various ways. Security to the detainees, security of the local population, legal, political and administrative reasons are also often invoked by the authorities to justify administrative detention.

Limited personal space

Personal space is a symbol of personal status and power. Limiting the personal space enjoyed by the target population is another key aspect of total control. In refugee camps, the camp authorities decide the nature of personal space each refugee can enjoy to sleep, to walk around and to socialise with other refugees.

Use of disproportionate force

Even on the smallest provocation was retaliated with maximum force. In the modern history of Hong Kong, the colonial government sent armoured carriers only to the refugee detention centres.

Inaction on inter group violence

Deliberate inaction on inter group violence. Some times violence were abetted and facilitated in the camps by the camp management.

Media censorship

Media censorship brings two benefits. One, the authorities' gets a chance to define the issues and to shape public opinion according to their own convenience. Secondly, in a situation of total censorship of media, further confusion is created, which is invariably to the advantage of the concerned authorities. Most interestingly, in Hong Kong the UNHCR enforced a ban on the media.

Meaning of detention

There are different meanings of detention for various actors in this social process. At the beginning several of them were relieved to reach a 'safe place', a first potential step towards a better future. But they experienced the first shock when they realised that they were to be detained and would not automatically get a ticket to go to the United States as was the practice for the past 17 years.

The asylum seekers began experiencing the real meaning of incarceration only after their detention begins. The meaning of detention begins to sink in when medical attention is required and they are unable to access it immediately, or when they have to send letters, or bury their dead, or offer prayers to their ancestors, or teach their young ones the Vietnamese way of life. In many little ways the meaning of detention starts to infiltrate their minds. The feeling of loss and powerlessness to influence the course of events, which shape their lives in the detention centres and the possibility of escape seems very remote.

In the detention centres, they experienced violence in every aspect of their lives. The meaning of existence was ridiculed; social status was lowered or completely lost. The administrators and the service agency staff treated everybody alike in the camps, irrespective of their social status back in Vietnam. In the camps there was no difference in the social status between a fisherman, farmer or a pilot.

The camp life altered cultural norms, traditions and the function of language. Family structures and patterns, social norms and familiar support networks were severely disturbed. Any attempt to recreate support network was suppressed. Contacts with various social institutions, ownership and work were restricted. Most importantly, all civil freedoms were curtailed. Change of perception about self had an impact on health and identity leading to lack of self-confidence, and well being.

Social consequences

Camp administrators effectively developed several strategies to 'manage' the asylum seekers. Recurrent moving of asylum seekers from one camp to another, even within the camp from one location to another location, reallocation of bed space, isolation of so called 'trouble makers', domestic intelligence gathering network, forming alliance with the criminal elements, indiscriminate use of tear gas, surveillance cameras, barbed wires were means of control. Further, the asylum seekers were referred to by numbers rather than their names, which to them was very dehumanising.

Apparently the British administrators in Hong Kong managed to get away with the severe human rights violations of the Vietnamese asylum seekers. Colonial legacy of the administration is the only explanation for this naked violation of human rights with impunity.

Cultural consequences

Cultural transmission, transmission of social norms, values, belief, organisation of society, family patterns, pattern of child bearing, attitude towards authority, work pattern, and patterns of social associations were severely disturbed or altered in the camps. A generation of youngsters grew up with cultural handicap that led to severe maladjustment with their future environment. Young children perceived the diminished role of one's own language for survival in the camps. 'Age bands' were common in the camps undermining parental authority. High number of teenage pregnancy was a symptom of youngsters discovering power in a powerless situation.

There are serious implications on mental health and social adaptation capabilities of the population under detention, even after their ordeal of detention is over. The most important consequence is the loss of social life, loss of supportive social network, and means to influence the course of one's own life. Even though the asylum seekers detained in Hong Kong detention centres showed considerable resilience in coping with the conditions, however, this fragile equilibrium could be momentary. In conclusion, the detention centre experience is a conflict between the asylum seeker's attempt to recreate a social life and supportive network in the camps and the camp administrators attempt to destroy any such supportive mechanisms.

Politics of humanitarianism

The study on Vietnamese asylum seekers detained in Hong Kong gives ample clues, to suspect the political motivation of humanitarianism. Probably, the humanitarian response to the asylum seekers began with all the noble intentions of altruism and human considerations. However, in the long run this concern transformed to suit the needs of political interests of the administration. With a massive resource base they maybe able to detain a large number of asylum seekers for long periods of time. Nevertheless, the process of detention is clearly at the expense of serious socio-cultural and psychological consequence on the children, disabled, elderly and others. International response to any refugee crisis may be directly related to the political or diplomatic mileage a country can derive by being a player init. There are several group of refugees displaced in many Asian countries (Table 10.1), but none of them received any particular attention, unlike the attention enjoyed by the Vietnamese refugees. This in itself is a clear example of the role of politics in determining the factors associated with the refugee adaptation to the host society. The British Crown Colony bureaucrats might be able to indulge in self congratulation about the way they are handled the crisis, by arguing that the later policy was a 'deterrent' for people coming out of Vietnam to Hong Kong seeking asylum.

Success and failure of all the initiatives have to be measured against the basic principles of Human Rights Covenants. The measure of success of any durable solutions should be based on the level of the solution's adherence to these principles.

Detention of the asylees in Hong Kong and the subsequent outcome - ethnocide- was politically motivated for the political convenience of the UK-Hong Kong government. So all the asylees were considered to be political prisoners. Even Amnesty International, the self proclaimed champion of human rights (a British Human Rights organisation), hid behind the excuse of 'our mandate is limited'. Or were they not comfortable in exposing the Human Rights violations of the political prisoners of a British Crown Colony? The role of the Branch office of the UNHCR in protecting the rights of the Vietnamese asylum seekers in Hong Kong in recent years is also questionable. They were more eager to please the interests of the developed West (one who funded the programme) rather than giving attention to the rights and privileges of abandoned asylum seeking children detained in Hong Kong camps.

David Cox sums up the refugee experience in Asia as, 'To a large degree, local social work agencies and staff in Asia appear to be cushioned against the refugee situations. The refugees are mainly in camps, aid is largely international, the goal is settlement overseas or repatriation, and at times there appears to be some antipathy towards the refugees. Refugees are seen to be an international rather than local concern, and that can easily mean they become no one's concern' (Cox 1991).

Hong Kong is a typical example of such a situation in Asia. Vietnamese asylum seekers in Hong Kong is an international problem, the international community can't leave the unfinished agenda of asylum seekers to Hong Kong people alone to solve. There is a clear case against UK-Hong Kong government in violating the human rights of Vietnamese asylum seekers in general, and women and children in particular.

Theoretical and methodological implications

A lot more has to be desired in the area of refugee theorising and developing models in explaining the socio-cultural process taking place in refugee detention camps like Hong Kong. A highly transient community and a reluctant camp administration render data collection process extremely difficult. The researcher managed to collect data only because he had access to the camps as a camp service agency staff. An independent researcher, in such situation may be forced to compromise to the interests of the camp administrators. Often the camp residents view such an outsider with suspicion and he or she may take a long time to build up rapport and identify the key informants.

Limitation of the concept ethnocide in understanding detention camps

The concept of ethnocide is not presented as a grand theory to understand the asylum seeker detention phenomena, but it could act more or less as an indicator to understand the phenomena. Ethnocide by itself may not be able to explain the complexity and the direction of changes taking place in the detention camps. A mature theory to explain the phenomenon of asylum seeker detention in Hong Kong or elsewhere should be strong enough in explaining the following issues comprehensively.
a) The intentional context
b) The local context
c)   The day to day context of camp life
d) The camp management issues
e) The role of humanitarian service and UNHCR intervention
f)   The social and political context which generates refugees
g) The personal context of asylum seekers
   Perhaps until such a grand theoretical framework evolves the concept of ethnocide along with other concept such as Goffman's concept of total institution, presented in a broad human rights perspective may adequately describe the phenomenon under study. This methodological poverty should not be neglected as lack of an intellectual rigor, but should be understood in the context of the complexity of social phenomena under study, and the methodological difficulty in developing a data collection strategy in such complex social process.

In the preceding chapters, a genuine attempt has been made to develop an ethnographic profile of the Vietnamese asylum seekers detained in Hong Kong detention centres. This may be a contribution to the existing knowledge on the conditions of refugees in the camps. Also, I hope that in future when some researchers enquire into the history of Vietnamese refugee process, this account may be helpful for them to understand the situation in a better way.

Table 9.1   Number of refugees in Asia, by country or area of asylum and origin, 1985-1992

Country or area of asylum	Area of origin	Numbers
Australia	Indochina	97 000
Bangladesh	Burma	300 000
China	Vietnam	279 750 - 280 500
Hong Kong	Vietnam	49 500
India	Afghanistan	5 846 - 5 500
	Iran	1 215 - 500
	Bangladesh (CHT)	50 000
	Srilanka	260 000
	Tibet	100 000
	Other	92 - 3 500
Nepal	Tibet	15 000
Indonesia	Indochinese	9 453 - 4 500
Iran	Afghanistan	1 800 000- 2 350 000
	Other	100 000 500 000
Japan	Indochina	1 290- 8 400
Lao	Cambodia	1 200
Macau	Indochina	727 - 370
Malaysia	Indochina	8 853 - 20 500
New Zealand	Indochina	4 700
Pakistan	Afghanistan	2 500 000 - 3 275 700
Papa New Guinea	Indonesia	10 946 7 700
Philippines	Indochina	14 867 26 650
Thailand	Cambodia	41 619 - 17 230
	Lao(PDR)	82 094- 68 741
	Vietnam	4 726- 13 974
Vietnam	Cambodia	21 000 15 000

(Compiled from various sources)

Bibliography

ADELMAN, H. (1979) *The Holocaust and the indo china refugees*, View point, Winter.

ADELMAN, H (1980) *A comparison of the Canadian and American Approach to Refugees*, Citizens Applied Research Institute, George Mason University, Fairfax VA.

ADELMAN, H (1980) Public education and the Indochinese refugees. *Journal of Refugee Resettlement*, Washington DC.

ADELMAN, H (1980) Refugee sponsorship and backlash, *The Indochinese refugee movement into Canada* (Ed.H Adelman), Copp Clark, Toronto.

ADELMAN, H. (1980) *A comparison of the Canadian and American Approach to Refugees*, Citizens Applied Research Institute, George Mason University, Fairfax VA.

ADELMAN, H. (ed) (1980) *The indo-Chinese refugee Movement into Canada*, Copp Clark, Toronto.

ADELMAN, H. (1982) *Canada and Indo-Chinese Refugees*, Weigl Educational Publishers.

ADELMAN, H. (1983) Palestinian refugees: Defining the humanitarianism problem, *In World Refugee Survey*, Refugee Policy Group, Washington DC.

ADELMAN, H. (1986) Palestinian refugees and politics, *Middle East Focus* (Guest editor), Vol. 9, no.2.

ADELMAN, H. (1988) Refugee or asylum: a philosophical perspective, *Journal of Refugee Studies*, vol.1, no. 1, pp. 7-19.

ADELMAN, H. AND LANPHIER, M. et al. (1984) *Unaccompanied Children in emergencies: the Canadian Experience*, York University, Toronto.

ADEPOJU, A. (1982) The dimension of refugee problem in Africa, *African Affairs*, Vol. 81, no. 33.

ADEPOJU, A. (1985) Refugees in Africa: problems and prospects, in *Causes and Consequences of Refugee Migrations in third world* (Ed. J. Rogge), Manitoba University, Canada.

AGATHANGELOU, A.M. (1988) Refugees and services in Britain, *Reports for the British Refugee Council*.

ALEXANDER Casello (1989) The refugees from Vietnam: Rethinking the issue, *The World Today Aug/Sept 1989*.

ALLODI, F (1982) Psychiatric sequel of torture, and implications for treatment, *World Medical Journal*, pp. 71-5

ALLODI, F. (1980) The psychiatric effects in children and families of victims of political persecution and torture, *Danish Medical Bulletin*, Vol. 27. no. 5, pp. 229-32.

ALLODI, F. AND COWGILL, G. (1982) Ethical and Psychiatric aspects of torture: a Canadian study, *Canadian Journal of Psychiatry*, vol. 27. pp. 98-102.

ALLODI, F. AND RANDALL, G. (1985) Physical and psychiatric aspects of torture: two medical studies, In the *Breaking of Bodies and Minds: Torture, Psychiatric Abuse and Mental health Professionals* (Ed. E. Stover and E. Nightingale), W.H. Freeman and Company, New York.

ALLODI, F. AND ROJAS, A. (1985). The health and adaptation of victims of political violence in Latin America (Psychiatric effects of torture and disappearance), In Psychiatry: the state of the Art (ed. P. Pichot, P. Berner, R. Wolf and K. Thau), *Proceedings of the VII World Congress of Psychiatry, Vienna*, 11-16 July 1983. Plenum Press, New York.

AMNESTY INTERNATIONAL (1988) ASA 19/4/88   UA 227/88 Hong Kong: Ill-treatment of Vietnamese refugees in Hong Kong detention centre.

AMNESTY INTERNATIONAL (1989) ASA 19/1/89   UA 288/89 - Hong Kong: Ill-treatment of Vietnamese asylum-seekers at Sek Kong Detention Centre.

AMNESTY INTERNATIONAL (1989) ASA 19/2/89   UA 378/89 - Hong Kong: Fear of refoulement: Yang Yang.

AMNESTY INTERNATIONAL (1990)   Memorandum to the Governments of Hong Kong and the United Kingdom regarding the protection of Vietnamese asylum seekers in Hong Kong. ASA 19/01/90.

AMNESTY INTERNATIONAL (1990) ASA 19/1/90   Memorandum to the governments of Hong Kong and the United Kingdom regarding the protection of Vietnamese asylum seekers in Hong Kong.

AMNESTY INTERNATIONAL (1990) ASA 19/2/90   *AI News Release*: Vietnamese asylum seekers denied basic rights by Hong Kong and Britain, says full Amnesty International report.

AMNESTY INTERNATIONAL (1990) ASA 19/5/90   Hong Kong: Protection of Vietnamese asylum-seekers: developments since December 1989.

AMNESTY INTERNATIONAL (1990) ASA 19/6/90   *AI News Release*: Hong Kong refugee screening process still flawed, Amnesty International says.

AMNESTY INTERNATIONAL (1991) ACT 77/1/91   Women in the front line: human rights violations against Women.

AMNESTY INTERNATIONAL (1992) ASA 19/1/92   EXTRA 76/92 - Hong Kong: fear of forcible return (refoulement): Liu Yijun, Lin Lin.

AMNESTY INTERNATIONAL (1992) ASA 19/3/92 , ASA 19/01/92, 4 September) - Hong Kong: fear of forcible return (refoulement): Liu Yijun, Lin Lin.

AMNESTY INTERNATIONAL (1994)   Hong Kong : arbitrary detention of Vietnamese asylum seekers (ASA 19/04/94).

AMNESTY INTERNATIONAL (1994) ASA 19/1/94   Hong Kong and human rights: flaws in the system: a call for institutional reform to protect human rights.

AMNESTY INTERNATIONAL (1994) ASA 19/2/94   Hong Kong and human rights: flaws in the system: a call for institutional reform to protect human rights: summary of Amnesty International's report.

AMNESTY INTERNATIONAL (1994) ASA 19/4/94   Hong Kong: Arbitrary detention of Vietnamese asylum-seekers.

AMNESTY INTERNATIONAL (1995) ASA 19/1/95   Hong Kong: Safeguards for human rights: Amnesty International's concerns.

AMNESTY INTERNATIONAL (1997) ASA 19/4/97   Hong Kong: Human rights, law and autonomy: the risks of Transition.

AMNESTY INTERNATIONAL Annual Reports (1989, 1990, 1991, 1992, 1993, 1994, 1995, 1996, 1997).

ANDREW Pearse and Mathias Setifel (1979) Inquiry into participation a research approach, UNRISD/79/C.14 Geneva.

ARMSTRONG (1987) Refugee resettlement schemes in Tanzania. Land Reform, land Settlement and Co-operatives, Rome.

ARMSTRONG (1988) Refugee wellbeing in settlements: an examination of the Tanzanian case. Journal of Refugee Studies, vol. 1, no.1, pp 57-73.

ASIA WATCH (1991) Indefinite Detention and Mandatory Repatriation. The Incarceration of Vietnamese in Hong Kong Vol. No.3 Issue No 24. New York.

ASIA WATCH (1992) Refugees at risk: forced Repatriation of Vietnamese from Hong Kong. Asia Watch 4 pp 1-11 1992.

BABAR, T. (1980) Regional instruments relating to the status of refuges. Research Center, Hague academy of International Law, The Hague.

BABAR, T. (1981) Protection of refugees in South Asia. Swedish Institute of International Law, Upsala.

BACH, Robert L (1990) Transforming socialist emigration: lessons from Cuba and Vietnam. *Paper presented at 12th Annual National Legal Conference of Center for Migration Studies*, April 1989, Washington DC.

BAKER, Pam (1996) Submission to the UNHCR on behalf of 11 asylum-seekers, and their families, who were interviewed by security personnel from Security Branch (Hong Kong) and / or Defence Liaison Office of the United States Consulate. Publisher: Pam Baker & Co.

BALE Chris (1990) Vietnamese Boat People, *The Other Hong Kong Report* (Ed.Richard Y.C.Wong, Joseph Y.S. Cheng), The Chinese University Press.

BARNES-DEAN, V. L. (1985) Chapter in Crisis in Uganda (Ed. P. Wiebe C. P. Dodge), Pergamon Press, New York/ London.

BASCOM, J. (1986) Self-settling refugees : strategies for survival and success. *The rural Sociologist*, July.

BASIL, Fernando J. (1991) Asian refugees: A search for solutions. IA, CCA. Hong Kong.

BEIGEL, A., and BERREN, M.R (1985) Human induced disasters, *Psychiatric Annals*, 15, 143-150.

BEISER, M AND FLEMING, J. A. E. (1986) Measuring psychiatric disorder among Southeast Asian refugees. *Psychological Medicine*, vol, 16, pp. 627-39.

BEISER, M. (1985) A study of depression among traditional Africans, urban north Americans and Southeast Asian refugees, In *Culture and Diagnosis* (Ed. B. Good and A. Kleinman), University of California Press, Berkeley.

BEISER, M. (1987) Changing time perspective and mental health among Southeast Asian refugees, In *Culture, Medicine and Psychiatry*, vol.II, pp. 437-64.

BEISER, M. (1988) Influence of time, ethnicity and attachment on depression in southeast Asian refugees, *American Journal of Psychiatry*, vol. 145, no. 1, pp. 4651.

BERREN, M.R., BEIGEL, A., and GHERTNER, S.(1980) A typology for the classification disasters, *Community Mental Health journal*, 16, 103-111.

BERRY, J.W (1991) Managing the process of acculturation for problem prevention, Mental health services for refugees, NIMH, Maryland.

BERRY, J.W (1991) *Refugee adaptation in settlement countries: An overview with an emphasis on primary prevention, in Refugee Children, Theory, Research and Services,* Ed. Fredrick C. Ahearn, Jr and Jean Athey, The John Hopkins University Press.

BERRY, J.W. (1990) Acculturation and Adaptation: A general framework, In *Mental health of Immigrants and Refugees Proceedings of a Conference,* Ed: Wayne H. Hotzman and Thomas H. Borneman, Hogg Foundation for Mental Health The University of Texas, Austin.

BERRY, W. John (1990) Acculturation and Adaptation: a General Framework in Mental Health of Immigrants and Refugees, (Ed.) Wayne H. Holtzman Thomas H. Bornemann, Hogg foundation for Mental Health, The University of Texas.

BERRY, W. John (1991a) *Refugee Adaptation n Settlement Countries: An overview with an Emphasis on Primary Prevention in Refugee Children Theory Research and Services* (Ed.) Frederick L. Ahearn and Jean L. Athey, Johns Hopkins University Press.

BOAVIDA, Joao (1991) Bereavement:.Past versus present, RPN Refugee Study Centre, Oxford. UK

BOLLAG, U. (1982) Prisoners of armed conflict: Nicaragua an ICRC survey, *Disasters*, vol. 6, pp. 110-15.

BOLLAG, U. (1985) Utilization of local first aiders in the provision of health care for prisoners by the International Committee of the Red Cross in Nicaragua, *Journal of Community Health*, vot.10, pp. 17-21.

BONNERJEA, L. (1985) *Shaming the world: The needs of women refugees*, WUS/CHANGE, London.

BOSHYK, Y. (1982) *Displaced Persons and Political Refugees, 1945-54: A Selected Bibliography.*

BOUSQUET, G. L. (1987) Living in a state of limbo: a case study of the Vietnamese refugees in camps in Hong Kong, In *People in Upheaval* (Ed. E.Colson and S.Morgan), Center for Migration Studies, New York. pp 34-53.

BRITISH REFUGEE COUNCIL (1989) *Forced repatriation of Vietnamese from Hong Kong.* The Refugee Council.

BUCHIGNANI, N. L. (1980) The economic adaptation of Southeast Asian refugees in Canada. In *Southeast Asian Exodus* (Ed. E. Tepper), pp. 191-204. Canadian Asian Studies Association, Ottawa.

BUCHIGNANI, N. L. AND INDRA, D. (1985) *Continuous Journey: A social History of South Asians in Canada*, McClelland and Stewart, Toronto.

BUI, Diana D. (1990) *Hong Kong: the other story. The situation of Vietnamese women and children in Hong Kong's detention centres*, Indochina Resource Action Centre [d] 1628 Sixteenth Street, N.W., 3rd Floor Washington, D.C. 20009.

BUI, Q. L. (1978) *Report on Indo-Chinese refugees*, Depute Mayor's Office, San Francisco CA.

BUI, Q., CAPLAN, N. AND WHITMORE, J (1985) Economic adaptation among recently arrived Southeast Asian refugees, In *Economic Outlook* USA, Institute for Social Research, University of Michigan, Ann Arbor MI.

BUI, Q., CAPLAN, N. AND WHITMORE, J (1985) *Scholastic Achievement Among the Children of Southeast Asian Refugees*, ISR final report, March, The Spencer Foundation, Chicago.

BUI, Q., CAPLAN, N. AND WHITMORE, J. (1985) Southeast Asian refugees self-sufficiency study, Department of Health and Human Services, Washington DC, January.

BUSTOS, E. (1986) Latin American youth in exile: is it a lost generation? Paper presented at *International Seminar of the Centers that Attend Refugees, Frankfurt, May.

BUSTOS, E. (1986) Some considerations on psychotherapy with tortured refugees, Lecture at the 5th International Seminar on Rehabilitation of Exiled Torture Victims and their Families, RCT Copenhagen, May.

CAMMACK, D. R. AND ROK, A. (1986) Lesotho, Botswana, Swaziland: Captive States, In *Destructive Engagement: Southern Africa at War* (Ed. D. Martin and P. Johnson), Zimbabwe Publishing House.

CANADIAN INSTITUTE OF UKRAINIAN STUDIES (1982) Boshyk, Y. and Balan, B. Political Refugees and Displaced Persons, 1945-54: a selected bibliography and guide to research with special reference to Ukrainians, Research Report No. 2.

CANADIAN INSTITUTE OF UKRAINIAN STUDIES (1984) Petryshyn, W. R. and Chomiak, N. Political Writings of Post-world War Two Ukrainian Émigrés: annotated bibliography and guide to research, Research Report No. 4.

CELS, J. (1987) New developments in the protection of refugees and asylum seekers in Europe. In *Human Rights and Foreign policy* (Ed.D.Hill), MacMillan, London.

CELS, J.(1986) A liberal and humane policy for refugees and Asylum seekers: Still a Realistic policy Option ? *Report for the European Consultation on Refugees and Exiles*, December.

CENTLIVERS, P.(1988) The Afghan refugees in Pakistan: an ambiguous identity. *Journal of refugee studies*, Vol 1.no.2.

CHAN, Kwok B. and LOVERIDGE, David (1987) Refugees "in transit": Vietnamese in a refugee camp in Hong Kong, *International Migration Review,* vol.21 pp. 745-759.

CHAN, Kwok Bun (1990) Hong Kong's response to the Vietnamese refugees: a study in humanitarianism, ambivalence and hostility, *Southeast Asian Journal of Social Science*, special Issue, Focus on Indo-Chinese refugees 15 years later, vol.18 p 94-110.

CHAN, Wing-tai (1989) Hong Kong Government policy on Vietnamese refugees: a human rights perspective, Department of Social and Public Administration, City Polytechnic of Hong Kong.

CHAN, Yuk-chun, Eikie.(1990) A study of the policy-making process of the liberalization policy for the Vietnamese refugees. Department of Public and Social Administration, City Polytechnic of Hong Kong.

CHAN, K.B (1984) Indo-Chinese refugees and social support: The theoretical importance of the family and social network in research and social intervention, In *Refugees Resettlement: Southeast Asians in Transition* (Ed.R.C.Nann, P.J.Johnson and M. Beiser), pp.125-31. University of British Columbia, Canada.

CHAN, K.B (1986) Cultures, values and social structure of the people of Indochina. *Forces*, no.73.pp.669.

CHAN, K.B (1987) Uprooting, loss and adaptation: the resettlement of Indo-Chinese refugees in Canada, Canadian Public Health association, Ottawa,.

CHAN, K.B (1987) Looking ahead: towards a framework for research on Indo-Chinese Canadians, In *Uprooting, Loss and Adaptation*, pp. 171-5.

CHAN, K.B (1987) Unemployment, social support and coping: The psychological response of Indochinese refugees to economic marginality, In *Uprooting, Loss and Adaptation*, pp. 116-31.

CHAN, K.B (1988) Perceptions of Chinese and Indo-Chinese community leaders in Montreal, Canada, *Canadian Ethnic Studies* (special issue).

CHAN, K.B. AND INDRA, D.(1987) *Uprooting, Loss and adaptation: The Resettlement of Indo-Chinese Refugees in Canada*, The Canadian Public Health Association, Ottawa.

CHAN, K.B. AND LAM L. (1983) Structures and values of the Chinese family in Vietnam, In the *South East Asian Environment* (ed.D.Webster), University of Ottawa Press, Ottawa, pp.206-20.

CHAN, K.B. AND LAM L (1983) Resettlement of Vietnamese-Chinese refugees in Montreal: some socio-psychological problems and dilemmas. *Canadian Ethnic studies*, vol.15, no 1, pp.1-17.

CHAN, K.B. AND LAM L. (1987) Community, kinship and family in Chinese Vietnamese society: some enduring values and patterns of interaction, In *Uprooting, Loss, and Adaptation*, pp.27-41.

CHAN, K.B. AND LAM L (1987) Psychological problems of Chinese Vietnamese refugees in Quebec, In *Uprooting, Loss, and Adaption*, pp.27-41.

CHAN, K.B. AND LOVERIDGE, D. (1987) Prelude to resettlement: a clinical view of the transit camp experience of Vietnamese refugees, In *Adaptation Linguistic et Culturelle*, pp.5-23.

CHAN,K.B. AND LOVERIDGE, D. (1988) Refugees in transit: Vietnamese in a refugee camp in Hong Kong. *International Migration Review*, vol.21, fall (special issue), pp. 745-59.

CHAN, K.B.(1983). Mental health needs of Indo-Chinese refugees: towards a national refugee resettlement policy and strategy in Canada, In *Community Mental Health Action: Primary Prevention Programming in Canada* (Ed. D.Paul Lumsden), pp.259-69, Canadian Public Health Association, Ottawa.

CHANTAVANICH, S. (1988) Japan and the Indo-Chinese refugees, In *Indo-Chinese Refugees: Asylum and Resettlement* (Ed. S. Chantavanich and Reynolds), Institute of Asian Studies, Chulalongkorn University, Bangkok.

CHANTAVANICH, S. (1988) Introduction. In *Indo-Chinese Refugees: Asylum and Resettlement* (Ed.S. Chantavanich and Reynolds), Institute of Asian Studies, Chulalongkorn University, Bangkok (In Thai).

CHENG Ka-man, Francis (1990) A political perspective in the study of the issue of Vietnamese refugees and boat people: With particular reference to the Mandatory Repatriation Policy, Department of Public and Social Administration, City Polytechnic of Hong Kong.

CHENG, Kam-yuk (1990) A study on the Hong Kong government's 1988 open camp policy for Vietnamese boat people. Department of Social and public Administration, City Polytechnic of Hong Kong.

CHEUNG, Siu-yin (1989) An analysis of Public attitude towards liberalization policy of Vietnamese refugees and social impacts of the policy. Department of Public and Social Administration, City Polytechnic of Hong Kong.

CHONGVATANA, N. (1985) Indo-Chinese refugees in Thailand and Family planning, *Journal of Social science*, vol 22, no. 1.pp.39-59.

CHONGVATANA, N. (1984) Socio-economic and Demographic Background and Family Planning: A research Report. Institute of Population Studies, Chulalongkorn University, Bangkok.

CHONGVATANA, N. AND LAVEBY, W.R. (1984) Knowledge and practice of contraception in two Indo-Chinese refugee camps, Population Studies Center Research Report, No.84-61, University of Michigan.

CHRISTENSEN, H. (1983) Afghan refugees in Pakistan: from emergency towards self reliance, A report on the food relief situation and related socio-economic aspects, UNRISD Report No. 84.2, Geneva.

CHRISTENSEN, H. (1983) Sustaining Afghan refugees in Pakistan, Report on the food situation and related social aspects. UNRISD Report No.84.2.Geneva.

CHRISTENSEN, H. (1984) On sources and source evaluation, *Journal of Eastern African Research and Development*,vol,14.

CHRISTENSEN, H. (1985) Transfer to wilderness. Current status of and assistance to African refugees, History and settlement of Burundian refugees in Tanzania, UNRISD report No.85.4, Geneva.

CHRISTENSEN, H.((1982) Survival strategies for and by camp refugees, Report on a six week exploratory sociological field study into the food situation of refugees in camps in Somalia, UNRISD Report No.84.2, Geneva, Reprinted in *Horn of Africa*, vol.5, no.4.

CHRISTENSEN,H.(1978) The progress of refugee Settlement in Africa. Dissertation, Institute of Cultural Sociology, University of Copenhagen, International University Exchange Fund, Geneva.

CHRISTENSEN, H.(1983) The food situation of Afghanistan refugees in Pakistan, *Refugees Magazine*, no.2.

CHRISTNSEN, H., AGUAYO, S., O'DOGHERTY, L AND VARESE, S. (1987) Social and cultural conditions and prospects of Guatemalian refuges in Mexico, UNRISD and El Colegio Report No.87.1.Geneva.

CLARK. D, JORDAN. A, PATERSON. C, SAMUELS. H. (1990) '*Its All a Matter of Luck*', The Vietnamese Refugee Screening Process in Hong Kong.

CLARK, Lance (1987) Promoting Refugee Participation in Assistance Projects, Refugee Policy Group, Washington DC.

CLARK, Lance (1987) Promoting Refugee Participation in Assistance Projects, Refugee Policy Group, Washington DC.

CLASTRES, Pierre (1974) On Ethnocide, *Homme*; 14, 3-4 Jul-December 101-110 France.

COLSON, E. AND SCUDDER, T. (1982) From welfare to development: A conceptual framework of the analysis of dislocated people, In *Involuntary Migration and Resettlement* (eds. A. Hansen and A. Oliver-Smith), pp.267-87, Boulder, Westview Press.

COLSON, E. AND MORGAN, S. eds (1987) People in Upheaval, Center for Migration Studies, New York.

COLSON, E. (1987) Migrants and their hosts, Introduction to People in Upheaval (Ed. S. Morgan and E. Colson), pp.1-16, Center for Migration studies, New York.

COLSON, E. (1971) *The social consequences of Resettlement*. Manchester University Press.

COMERFORD, Suzy (1991) Campaign to end detention of Vietnamese children and families in Hong Kong; background information sheets on RCHK and the detention situation, Refugee Concern, Hong Kong

COMMUNITY AND FAMILY SERVICES (1991) Briefing packet, Community development work, Hong Kong.

COMMUNITY AND FAMILY SERVICES (1992) Social development project, Project description, Hong Kong.

COMMUNITY AND FAMILY SERVICES INTERNATIONAL (1993) Women in detention : the Vietnamese in Hong Kong, Executive summary of the June 1993 assessment, Refugee Participation Network (RPN), 15 pp. 24 - 25

CONNOR, K. M. CHAMPAGNE, D. AND SHRODER, J. F (1981) Background to the Afghan Crisis, Center for Afghanistan Studies, University of Nebraska-Omaha.

CONNOR, K. M. (1985) An analysis of the 'Push' factors in the Afghan refugee situation: are refugees always involuntary migrants? Paper presented at the University of Wisconsin Conference on South Asia, Autumn.

CONNOR, K. M. (1982) Afghan refugees in Pakistan: the characteristics of self- settled versus camp refugees, Paper presented to the Association of American Geographers, April.

CONNOR, K. M. (1982) Educational needs of Afghan refugees in Pakistan, Paper presented at third World Conference, autumn.

CONNOR, K. M. (1982). Afghan refugees in United States: A spatial analysis. Paper presented to the Association of American Geographers.

CONNOR, K. M. (1985) Afghan refugees in Peshawar, *Afghanistan Forum*, vol.13, March.

CONNOR, K. M. (1986) *Rationale for the movement of Afghan refugees to Pakistan in Afghan Resistance: the Politics of Survival* (Ed.G.M.Farr and J.G. Merriam), Westview Press, Boulder CO.

CONNOR, K. M. (1987) An analysis of residential choice among self-settled refugees from Afghanistan in Peshawar, Pakistan, Department of Geography, University of Nebraska-Lincoln.

CONNOR, K. M. (1981) The role of food in the process of refugee acculturation, Paper presented to the University of Wisconsin Conference on South Asia, November.

COX, David (1990) Children and Migration: A Social workers perspective, International symposium proceedings, Children and Migration, ISS Hong Kong

COX, David (1991) Patterns of Migration in the Asian Pacific Region, in Sandra Sewell and Anthony Kelly, *Social Problems in Asia Pacific Region*, Boolarong Publication, Brisbane, Australia.

COX, D. R (1979) Australia's immigration policy and refugees, In *Refugees, Resources, Reunion* (ed.R. Birrell et al.) Victoria publishers, Melbourne.

COX, D. R (1981) Refugee settlement: an Australian case study, In *Refugees: Challenge to the Future* (Ed.C.A. Price) Canberra Academy of Social Sciences in Australia.

COX, D. R (1982) Professional refugees in Australia: the employment related experience of professionally -qualified refuges from Southeast Asia, Department of Social Studies, University of Melbourne.

COX, D. R (1983) Professionally qualified refugees from Vietnam, *Australian Journal of Social Issues*, vol.18, no.4.

COX, D. R (1983) Refugee settlement in Australia: review of an era, *International Migration*, vol.21, no.3.

COX, D. R (1984) A developmental approach to African refugees, ICARA II Briefing Paper No. 1. June.

COX, D. R (1984) Africa's refugee crisis: new directions for assistance, aid and development, BRC policy statement. Second International Conference of Assistance to Refugees in Africa, June.

COX, D. R (1984) British Government aid to African refugees, ICARA II Briefing Paper No.4, June.

COX, D. R (1984) The politics of repatriation: Ethiopian refugees in Djibouti, 1977 -1983, *Review of African Political Economy*, no.30.

COX, D. R (1985) Welfare services for migrants: can they be better planned? International Migration, vol.23, no. 1, pp.73-95.

COX, D. R (1986) Australia: a record of generosity, *Refugees*, pp.17-20, UNHCR, CRISP, J (1983) The British Refugee Council: research and resources on African refugees, African Research and Documentation, no.32.

COX, D. R. (1975) The role of ethnic groups in migrant welfare, In *Welfare of Migrants*. Australian Government Printing service, Canberra.

CRAVENS RICHARD B. AND THOMAS H. BORNEMANN (1990) Refugee camps in countries of first asylum and the North American resettlement process, in *Mental health of immigrants and refugees*, University of Texas.

CRISP, J. AND VAN HEAR, N. (1986) Refugee: Dynamics of displacement, A report for the independent commission on International Humanitarian issues.

CRISP, J. AND D'SOUZA, F. (1985) The Refugee Dilemma, Minority Rights Group, British Refugee Council.

CRISP, J. AND NETTLETON, C. (1984) Refugee Report, British Refugee Council.

DALEY, P. (1984) The Rural Settlement of African Refugees with Special Reference to Sudan and Tanzania, Unpublished M.A. thesis, SOAS, London.

DANIEL, Wolf (1990) A subtle form of in humanity: Screening of the Boat people in Hong Kong, *International Journal of Refugee Law,* special Issue, Oxford University Press.

DAVIS, Leonard (1990) Mandatory repatriation is not the answer to Hong Kong's problem Refuge, vol.9, p.10-11.

DAVIS, Leonard. (1989) Hong Kong and the Indo-Chinese refugees, Inst. of Asian Studies, Chulalongkorn University, Bangkok.

DAVIS, LEONARD. (1991) Hong Kong and the Asylum seekers from Vietnam. Macmillan.

DESBARATS, J. AND HOLLAND, L. (1983) Indo-Chinese settlement patterns in Orange County, *Amerasia journal*, vol, pp. 23-46.

DESBARATS, J. AND JACKSON, K.D. (1985) Vietnam, 1975-1983: the cruel peace, *Washington Quarterly*, vol, pp.169-82.

DESBARATS, J. (1984) Reply to commentary on Indo-Chinese settlement patterns in Orange County, *Amerasia Journal*, vol.14, pp.133-40.

DEWAALA, A. (1987) Famine that kills: Darfur 1984-85, Report for Save the Children Fund, London.

DONNELLY, Nancy D. (1992) The impossible situation of Vietnamese in Hong Kong's detention centres, Selected Papers on Refugee Issues / Pamela DeVoe (ed.) pp. 120 - 132, *American Anthropological Association,* Washington DC. 20009, USA.

DOWNING, B. T. AND DWYER, S. (1981) Hmong refugees in an American city : a case study in Language and Linguistics, also in Minne TESOl Journal,vol.2 (1982),pp.17-31.

DOWNING, B.T (1982) Vietnamese learning Swedish and Hmong Learning French: a comparison of language policies and programmes, In The Hmong in West: Observations and Reports (ed.B.T. Downing and D.P.Olney), pp.249-67, Center for Urban and Regional Affairs, Minneapolis.

DOWNING, B.T (1984) Hmong resettlement in the Twin Cities, CURA Reporter, University of Minnesota.

DOWNING, B.T (1984) The Hmong resettlement study: a site report, Fort Smith, Arkanas, Office of Refugee Resettlement, Social Security Administration, US Department of Health and Human Services.

DOWNING, B.T (1984) The Hmong resettlement study: site report, Minneapolis St Paul, Minnesota, Office of Refugee Resettlement, Social Security Administration, US Department of Health and Human Services.

DOWNING, B.T (1984) The learning of English by Hmong refugees: a review of research, ERIC document UD023421, ERIC Clearing house on Urban Education.

DOWNING, B.T (1986) The Hmong resettlement study symposium: language issues, In *The Hmong in Transition* (ed. G.L. Hendricks, B.T. Downing and A.S. Deinard), pp 187-93. Center for Migration Studies of New York and Center for Urban and Regional Affairs.

DOWNING, B.T. (1981) Ethnic mother-tounge schools in Minnesota, USA: a study in language maintence, In AILA81: Proceedings I (ed.B.Sigurd and J. Svartik), pp.494-45 (abstract), University of Lund, Sweden.

DOWNING, B.T. AND OLNEY, D.P. (1982) *The Hmong in the West: Observations and Reports* (editors), Centre for Urban and Regional Affairs, Minneapolis.

DOWNING, B.T. AND WHEATON FULLER, J.(1984) Hmong names: Changes and variation in a bilingual context, In papers from the 10th Minnesota Regional Conference on Language and Linguistics (Ed. N. Stenson), pp. 39-50.

DRUKE, L. (1987) Causes of refugee problems and the international response, In Proceedings of the conference 'Human Rights and the Protection of refugees under International Law', Canadian human rights foundation, 29 November-2 December,1987, Montreal.

DUDA, G.R. AND SCHOENMEIER, H.W. AND PEZARO, A (1985) Vocational Training and Trade promotion for the refugee Settlement in El Suki. Socio Psychological Research Centre on Development Planning, University of the Saar.

DUDA, G.R. (1985) Vocational training and Trade Promotion for the Refugee Settlement in Kashm-El-Girba, Socio-Psychological Research Center on Development Planning, University of the Saar.

DZIEGIEL, L (1981) Rural community of contemporary Iraqi Kurdishtan facing modernisation. Study Materials, no.7. Institute of Tropical and Subtropical Agriculture and Forestry, Agricultural Academy in Krakow, Poland.

ESPESO, E.M. (1984) A study of the nature of volunteer jobs, corresponding practices and office policies and benefits derived by refugee volunteer workers, PRPC.

ESPESO, E.M. (1984) A study of the refugees' awareness, impression and participation in vocational training programs in PRPC.

ESPESO, E.M. (1984) Community Organisation: a study of leadership patterns in refugee neighbourhoods, PRPC.

ESPESO, E.M. (1985) Traditional health and burial practices of Indo-Chinese refugees, PRPC.

FAN, Rita (1990) Hong Kong and the Vietnamese boat people: a Hong Kong perspective.

FARMER, R. S. J. (1985) Refugee resettlement issues in New Zealand, *New Zeland Population Review*, vol.11.pp.216-28.

FASIC (1981) A Social - Psychological Study of Twenty five Returning Families, Presented at a seminar on Latin American Exiles entitled 'Mental health and Exile'.

FASS, S.M (1986) Innovations in the struggle for self-reliance: the Hmong experience in the United states, *International Migration Review*, Vol.20, no.2, pp.351-76.

FASS, S.M. (1985) Through a glass darkly: Cause and effect in refugee resettlement policies, *Journal of Policy Analysis and Management*, vol.4, no.3, pp.554-72.

FEINBERG, Michael (1993) The detention of asylum seekers:an unjust and unworkable policy.

FERRIS, Elizabeth G. (1989) The churches, refugees and politics, In *Refugees and International Relations,* Loescher, G. and Monahan, L. [eds] pp 159-177, Oxford University Press.

FERRIS, E.G (1985) Central America: the political impact of refugees, *The World Today,* vol. 41, no.5.

FERRIS, E.G (1985) *Refugees in the World Politics* (editor), Praeger, New York.

FERRIS, E.G (1985) Regional response to Central American refugees, In *Refugees in World Politics* (Ed.E.G.Ferris), Praeger, New York.

FERRIS, E.G (1987) *Central American Refugees and the Politics of Protection,* Praeger, New York.

FERRIS, E.G.(1984) The politics of asylum: Mexico and the Central American refugees, *Journal of Inter American and World Affairs,* vol.26, no.3, pp.357-84.

FOZZARD, Shirley (1986) Life in limbo: the experience of Vietnamese refugees in the closed centres of Hong Kong Seminar paper RSP 21, St Giles, Oxford.

FOZZARD, Shirley (1986) The closed camps as a total institution, RSP 21, St. Giles, Oxford.

FOZZARD, Shirley (1986) Life in limbo: the experiences of Vietnamese refugees in the closed centres of Hong Kong, RSP 21, St Giles, Oxford.

FOZZARD, Shirley (1988) Rethinking refugee problems: Life in limbo -Vietnamese refugees in the closed centres of Hong Kong, *Third World Affairs,* 1987, pp348-351.

FREDERICK, L. AHEARN JR. AND JEAN L. Athey (Ed.1991) *Refugee Children Theory, Research, and Services,* Johns Hopkins University Press.

FREDERICK, C. (1980) Effects of natural vs. human induced violence upon victims, *Evaluation and Change,* Special issue, 71-75.

GEORGE, E. Immerwahr (1983) Refugees and Refuges, In Vatsala Narain, C.P. Prakasam (Ed) *Population policy perspectives in Developing countries,* Himalaya Publishing House, Bombay.

GIBNEY, M. (1986) The 1980 Refugee Act: a humanitarian standard, *Gonzaga Law Review,* vol.21, pp.585-602.

GNEERRE, Maurizio (1987) Minorities, Equality and State, *Development,* 1987, 1, 79-81.

GOFFMAN (1961) Mental asylums, Pengin Books.

GOFFMAN, Erving (1968) Asylums: *Essays on the social situation of mental patients and other inmates,* Harmondswoth Middlesex Penguin.

GOULD, W. (1974) Refugees in Tropical Africa, *International Migration Review,* vol.8, no.3.

HADLEY, ROGER et al (1987) *A community social workers handbook,* Tavistock Publications Ltd. London.

HAINES, D.W.(1985) Refugees in the United States: *A Reference Handbook* (editor), Greenwood Press.

HANKS, J.R. (1987) Fieldwork at Home: Issues in the study of resettled refugees, Paper presented to the American Anthropological Association.

HANSEN, A. (1979) Managing refugees: Zambia's response to Angolan refugees 1966-1977, *Disasters,* vol.3, no.4, pp.375-80.

HANSEN, A. (1979) Once the running stops: assimilation of Angolan refugees into Zambian border villages, *Disaster,* vol.3 no. 4, pp 369-74.

HANSEN, A. (1981) Refugee dynamics: Angolans in Zambia 1966 to 1972. *International Migration Review,* vol.15, no 53/54, pp.175-94.

HANSEN, A. (1982). Self -settled rural refugees in Africa: The case of Angolans in Zambian villages, In *Involuntary Migration and Resettlement: the Problems and Responses of Dislocated Peoples* (editors), Westview Press, Boulder CO.

HANSEN, A. (1977) Once the Running Stops: the Social and Economic Incorporation of Angoloan Refugee into Zambian Border Villages, Ph.D. Dissertation, Cornell University, Ithaca NY.

HARELL-BOUND, B. AND DUNBAR-ORTIZ, R. (1987) Who protects the human rights of refugees? *Africa Today*, 1st/2nd Quarter.

HARRELL-BOUND, B. (1982) Ugandan refugees in the Sudan, UFSI Reports, three-part series, nos. 48, 49, 50.

HARRELL-BOUND, B. (1986) *Imposing Aid: Emergency Assistance to Refugees*, Oxford University Press.

HARROD, J. *The Refugee Child: A Resource Report*, Geneva, Secretariat of the international year of the child.

HARTCUP, A.(1985) Vietnamese Refugees in Hong Kong, *Contemporary Review*, vol. 247, no. 1439.

HASTEDT, G. (1984) Predicting refugee flows: the response patterns of receiving states, Paper presented at International Studies Association Meeting, Atlanta GA.

HATHAWAY, J.C (1984) The evolution of refugee status in international law: 1920-1950, *International and Comparative Law Quarterly*, vol. 3, pp. 348-80.

HATHAWAY, J.C. (1980) Persecution by economic proscription: a new refugee dilemma, *Chitty's Law Journal*, vol.28, pp.190-3.

HAWKE, Jan (1991) The spatial patterning of disease: a study of morbidity in a Vietnamese detention centre in Hong Kong, RSP.

HELTON, Arthur C. (1990) The comprehensive plan of action for Indochinese refugees: an experiment in refugee protection and control, *New York Law School Journal of Human Rights*, 8:11-48, Fall.

HENDRICKS, G.L. AND RICHARDSON, B. (1982) Hmong in the workplace, In *The Hmong in the West*: Observations and Report (ed.B.T. downing and D.P. Olney), pp.387-401, Center for Urban and Regional Affairs, University of Minnesota.

HENDRICKS, G.L. (1979) Indochinese students in higher education: a case study report, Proceedings of the First Annual Conference on Indochinese refugees, George Mason University, Fairfax VA.

HENDRICKS, G.L (1981) Indochinese Refugee Settlement Pattern in Minnesota, Center for Urban and Regional Affairs, University of Minnesota.

HENDRICKS, G.L. (1979) The shaping of ethnic self–identity among Indochinese refugees, *The Journal of Ethnic Studies*, vol. 7, pp.25-41.

HENDRICKS, G.L., DOWNING, B.T. AND DEINARD, A.S. (1986) The Hmong in Transition (editors), Center for Migration studies, Staten Island NY.

HENDRICKS, G.L. AND SKINNER, K.A. (1977) A new minority: Indochinese refugees in higher education, OSA Research Bulletin, vol.18. University of Minnesota Office for Student Affairs, Minneapolis.

HIRSCHON, R. (1988) Heirs of the Greek Catastrophe: The social life of Asia Minor Refugees in Piraeus, Oxford University Press.

HITCHCOX, Linda (1990) Repatriation: solution or expedient? The Vietnamese asylum seekers in Hong Kong, *Southeast Asian Journal of Social Science*, special Issue, Focus on Indochinese refugees 15 years later, vol.18, p. 111-131.

HITCHCOX, Linda (1991) Population movements from Vietnam, *Oxford International Review*, vol.3 pp9-12.

HITCHOX, Linda (1990) *Vietnamese Refugees in Southeast Asian camps*, Oxford, Macmillan series, London.

HO, Fu-kuen. (1989) An analysis of the Hong Kong Government's tactics on the issue of Vietnamese refugees with reference to Charles Lindblom's model of disjointed incrementalism, Department of Public and Social Administration, City Polytechnic of Hong Kong.

HOANG, LAM (1997) Each has a dream, Experience of a volunteer at Pillar Point Refugee Centre, Duke University.

HOCH, P.K. (1983) The reception of Central European refugee physicists of the 1930s: USSR, UK, USA, *Annals of Science*, vol.40, pp.217-46.

HOLOCOMB, B.K. AND CLAY, J.W. (1985) Politics and the Ethiopian famine: report of a 1985 investigation trip, Special Report No.20, *Cultural Survival*, Cambridge, MA.

HOLOCOMB, B.K.(undated) Somali refugees or refugees in Somalia: the Oromo flight from Ethiopia, *Cultural Survival Quarterly,* Cambridge MA.

Hong Kong Government (1983) CAP 115 Immigration (Vietnamese Refugee Centers) (Open Center) Rules.

Hong Kong Government (1988) December, Hong Kong's Centers for Vietnamese Refugees.

Hong Kong Government (1992) Fact Sheet, Vietnamese Migrants in Hong Kong.

Hong Kong Government (1992) October, Status Determination Procedures.

Hong Kong Government (1992) September, The Vietnamese Migrants Problem in Hong Kong, The Hong Kong Government View.

HUGO, G. (1983) Postwar involuntary migrations from within and between Southeast Asian countries: a review. Paper prepared for symposium on the problems and consequences of refugee migration in the developing world, Population Commission of the International Geographical Union, Manitoba, Canada, 29 August-1 September 1983.

HUGO, G. (1986) Differences and similarities between forced and voluntary migration in Asia and some policy implications, Paper presented to International Seminar on People Affected by Uprootedness, UNRISD, Geneva, 5-7 May 1986.

HUGO, G. (1987) Postwar refugee migration in Southeast Asia: patterns, problems and policy consequences, In *Problems and consequences of Refugee Migration in the Developing World* (Ed.J.R.Rogge). Center for Migration Studies, New York.

HUU DINH NGUYEN and FREEMAN, James M. (1992) Disrupted childhood : unaccompanied minors in southeast Asian refugee camps, Summary of fact-finding trip to Hong Kong, Philippines, Thailand, Malaysia, Singapore, Indonesia, 14 Dec 1991 - 14 Jan 1992. Aid to Refugee Children without Parents, Inc.

HUYNH, Dinh Te (1987) Vietnamese Culture, San Diego State University, San Deiego.

HYNDMAN, P. (1982) Asylum and non-refoulment- are these obligations owed to refugees under international law? *Philippine Law Journal*, vol.57, pp.43-77.

HYNDMAN, P (1985) Refugees and Human Rights. In seminar papers, Prospects for the Establishment of an Inter-governmental south Pacific Human Rights Commission, pp. 248-61.

HYNDMAN, P. (1986) Refugees under international law with a reference to the concept of asylum, *Australian Law Journal*, vol.60, pp.34-41.

HYNDMAN, P. (1987) The 1951 Convention definition of refugee: an appraisal with particular reference to the case of Sri Lankan Tamil applicants, *Human Rights Quarterly*, vol.9, no.1, pp.49 -73.

HYNDMAN, P. (1981) An appraisal of the development of the protection afforded to refugees under international law, *Journal of the Law Association of Asia and Western Pacific*, vol. 1, no3 (N.S.) pp. 229-84 International Journal of Refugee Law, special issue, pp. 144-160.

JOAO, Boavida (1991) Bereavement Past Versus Present, *Refugee participation network*, 10, May, UK.

KARBIW, Stanly (1983) *The History of Vietnam war*, Oxford University Press.

KAY, D. (1987) *Chileans in Exile: Private Struggle, Public Lives*, Macmillan, London.

KHAN, S.Z. (1985) Humanitarian Assistance Programme for Afghan Refuges in NWFP.

KIBREAB, G. (1983) Reflections on the African Refugee Problem, SIAS, Africa World Press, New Jersey.

KNUDSEN, John (1990) Prisoners of International politics: Vietnamese refugees coping with transit life, *Southeast Asian Journal of Social Science* Vol. 18. No 1.

KNUDSEN, John (1992) 'To destroy you is no loss' : Hong Kong 1991 - 92, Selected Papers on Refugee Issues, Pamela, D. (ed.) pp. 133 - 145.

KNUDSEN, John (1990) Prisoners of international politics: Vietnamese refugees coping with transit life, *Southeast Asian Journal of Social Science*, special focus on Indo-chinese refugees 15 years later, vol.18, p153-165.

KNUDSEN, John (1992) Chicken Wings : Refugee Stories From a Concrete Hell, Magnat Forlag

KOEHN, P. (1984) The 1974 revolution and its aftermath: implications for refugee outcomes, In *Ethiopian Refugees in the United States*, pp.13-19, Ethiopian Community Development Council, Arlington VA.

KOEHN, P. (1983) The migration of post revolution exiles to the United States; determinant factors and policy implications in the Ethiopian case, Presented to the 26th Annual Meetings of the African Studies Association, Boston, 10 December 1983.

KOEHN, P. (1985) Pre and post revolution emigres and non-returnees: Ethiopian Iranian comparisons. Paper presented at the Joint Annual Meeting of the African and Middle Eastern Studies Associations, New Orleans, 25 November 1985.

KUNZ E.F (1981) Exile, resettlement and refugee theory, *International Migration Review 15*, 42-51.

KWAN, Kam-hung Stephanie (1989) The Hong Kong Government's 1988 screening policy for Vietnamese boat people: origination, implementation and implications, Department of Social and Public Administration, City Polytechnic of Hong Kong.

LAM, L (1982) Vietnamese -Chinese refugees in Montreal: family values and structures, In *Southeast Asian Environment* (Ed.D.Webster), University of Ottawa Press.

LANPHIER, C.M (1982) Dilemma of decentralization: voluntary agencies and refugee resettlement in United States and Canada, In *South-East Asian Context* (Ed.D.Webster), Canadian Asian Studies Association, Ottawa.

LANPHIER, C.M (1982) Sponsorship of refugees in Canada, In *International Catholic Migration Commission Bulletin*, pp.18-36.

LANPHIER, C.M (1983) *Recent resettlement of Southeast Asian Refugees in France*, Refuge, February, pp.6-7.

LANPHIER, C.M (1983) Refugee resettlement: Models in action, *International Migration Review*, vol.17, pp.4-33.

LANPHIER, C.M (1983) Resettlement of Southeast Asians and the Canadian Church, *Canadian Catholic Review*, vol.2 pp.13 -16.

LANPHIER, C.M (1984) Model for resettlement services in Canada, Paper presented to the Symposium on Resettlement services, Canadian Employment and Immigration commission, March.

LANPHIER, C.M (1985) Resettlement as mass movement: governmental policy implications: United States, Canada and France, In Symposium on Indo-Chinese Refugee Resettlements: Proceedings (ed.M. Beiser et al), Mental Health Research Unit, University of British Columbia, Vancouver.

LANPHIER, C.M (1987) Indo- Chinese resettlement: costs and adaptation: Canada, United States and France, In *Refugees: A Third World Dilemma* (Ed.J.Rogge), pp.299-308, Rowman and Littlefield, Totowa NJ.

LANPHIER, C.M.(1981) Canada's response to refugees, *International Migration Review*, vol.15, no.1 pp.113-30.

LANPHIER, C.M (1984) Model for resettlement services in Canada, Paper presented to the Symposium on Resettlement services, Canadian Employment and Immigration commission, March.

LANPHIER, C.M (1985) Resettlement as mass movement: governmental policy implications: United States, Canada and France, In Symposium on Indo-Chinese Refugee Resettlements: Proceedings (ed.M. Beiser et al), Mental Health Research Unit, University of British Columbia, Vancouver.

LANPHIER, C.M (1988) NGOs and refugees : Bureaucratization and politicization, In *Refugees in the Era of Total War* (Ed.A.Bramwell), Unwin Hyman, London.

LANPHIER, C.M., ADELMAN, H., MAY, C. AND LAM, L. (1984) Unaccompanied Minors in Canada, Refugee Resettlement Project, York University.

LANPHIER, C.M., KALBACH,W., RICHMOND, A.H. AND RHYNE, D. (1983) Ethnogenerational Factors in Socio-Economic Achievement in Toronto: The Second Generation during the 1970s, Ethnic Research proramme, York University.

LAWYERS COMMITTEE FOR HUMAN RIGHTS (1992) Hong Kong's refugee status review board : problems in status determination for Vietnamese asylum seekers, A briefing paper, Lawyers Committee New York, NY 10001, USA.

LEE, L.T. (1984) The UN group of governmental experts on international co operation to avert new flows of refugees, *American Journal of International Law*, vol.78,no.2, pp. 480.

LEWINS, F.W. (1984) The significance of factors influencing early Vietnamese settlement in Australia. *Journal for Inter- cultural studies*, vol.5,no.2.

LEWINS, F.W. AND LY, J. (1985) *The First Wave: The Settlement of Australia's First Vietnamese refugees*, George Allen and Unwin, Sydney.

LOESCHER, G. AND LOESCHER, A.D. (1982) *The World's Refugees: A Test of Humanity*, Harcourt Brace Jovanovih, New York, London.

LOESCHER, G. AND SCANLAN, J. (1982) Mass asylum and human rights in American foreign policy, *Human Rights Quarterly*, Spring, pp. 39 - 56.

LOESCHER, G. AND SCANLAN, J. (1983) *The Global Refugee Problem: US and World response*, The Annals of the American Academy of political and Social Science, Sage Publications, Beverly Hills / London.

LOESCHER, G. AND SCANLAN, J (1984) Human rights and US foreign policy and Haitian refugees, *Journal of Inter - American Studies and World Affairs*, August.

LOESCHER, G. AND SCANLAN, J (1984) Human rights, power politics and the international refugee regime: the case of US treatment of Caribbean Basin refugees, World Order Studies Occasional Paper Series No. 14, Center of International Studies, Princeton University.

LOESCHER, G. AND SCANLAN, J (1984) US foreign policy and its impact on refugee follow from Haiti, Occasional Papers No.42. N.Y.U. Center of Latin American and Caribbean Studies.

LOESCHER, G. AND SCANLAN, J (1986) Calculated Kindness: Refugees and America's Half - open Door, 1945 to the Present, The Free Press, Macmillan.

LOESCHER, G. AND SCANLAN, J. (1981) 'Mass asylum' and the US policy in the Caribbean Basin, *The World Today*, October, pp. 387 -95.

LOESCHER, GIL (1993) *Mass migration as a global security problem*, World Refugee Survey.

LOESCHER, GIL (1993) *Beyond Charity: International Cooperation and the Global Refugee Crisis*, New York: Oxford University Press, 1993.

LOESCHER, G. (1987) Refugees: *The International Agenda*, Oxford University Press, Oxford.

LOESCHER, G. (1987) Refugees and foreign policy, In *Human rights and Foreign Policy*, Collier Macmillan, London.

LOESCHER, G. AND CELS, J. (1987) The refugee determination procedure in Belgium and the role of the United Nations High Commissioner for Refugees, In *Refuges in the Age of Total War: Europe and the Middle East* (Ed. Bramwell), Unwin Hyman, London.

LOUGHRY, Maryanne and ESQUILLO, Ruth (1994) In whose best interest? Refugee camp workers comment on the treatment of Vietnamese unaccompanied minors under the Comprehensive Plan of Action Jesuit Refugee Service, Asia Pacific.

LOUGHRY, Maryanne, McCALLIN, Margaret and BENNETT, Gwen (1993) Women in detention: The Vietnamese in Hong Kong, a women's perspective on detention. Executive summary and Report Community and Family Services International (CFSI).

LOVERIDGE, David (1985) Separation and loss: a continuing theme in the lives of the Vietnamese refugees in Hong Kong.

LUCIUK, L.Y. (1986) Home ward-oriented activism among Ukrainian refugees, then and now: a case study, Paper presented to the World Congress of Sociology, New Delhi, India.

LUCIUK, L.Y. (1986) Unintended consequences in refugee resettlement: Post -War Ukrainian refugee migration to Canada, International Migration Review, vol.20, no.74, pp.476 -82.

LUCIUK, L.Y. (1987) Reverse flow: refugees from the Soviet Zone in Germany, 1945 -1947, Paper presented at 'Forcible Repatriation after World War II: an International Symposium', University of Oxford.

LUCIUK, L.Y. (1987) Searching for Place: Ukrainian Refugee Migration to Canada after World War II. Ph. D dissertation, Department of Geography, University of Alberta, In final revision for Canadian Institute of Ukrainian Studies and the University of Alberta Press.

LUCIUK, L.Y.(1983) Lifeworlds in collision: Ukrainian Canadians encounter the displaced persons, In The Displaced persons Experience: Ukrainian Refugees after world War II - a conference (Ed.W, Isajiw), The Canadian Institute of Ukrainian Studies and The Multicultural History Society of Ontario.

LUCIUK, L.Y., LANPHIER, M. AND ADELMAN, H.(1986) Proceedings of 'Refugee or Asylum - a Choice for Canada ? An International Symposium', York University, June 1986.

MAJKA, L. (1984-5) Quarterly Reports, The State of Refugees / Entrants and the Refugee / Entrant programme in Chicago IL.

MALEY AND SAILKAL, F .H. (1986) Afghan Refugee Relief in Pakistan: Political Context and Practical Problems, Working Paper,Department of Politics, University College, University of New South Wales, MAZUR,R. (1986) Linking popular initiative and aid agencies: the case of refugees, Refugee Issues,vol.3, no.2, pp.1 -19, Refugee Studies Programme (Oxford) and British Refugee Council.

MAYER-RIECKH, Elisabeth (1992) 'Beyond concrete and steel' : power-relations and gender, the case of Vietnamese women in the detention centres in Hong Kong. Research paper in partial fulfilment of requirements for MA in Development Studies, The Hague, Oct. 1992 Institute of Social Studies

McCALLIN, Margaret (1993) 'Living in detention' A review of psychosocial well being of Vietnamese children in Hong Kong Detention centers, ICCB, Geneva.

McCALLIN, Margaret (1993) The psychosocial well-being of Vietnamese minors in the Philippine: a comparison with Hong Kong, International Catholic Child Bureau.

McCALLIN, Margaret (1992) Living in detention : a review of the psychosocial well-being of Vietnamese children in the Hong Kong detention centres, International Catholic Child Bureau Geneva.

MCCALLIN, M. (1987) The non- material needs of refugee children, Third World Affairs.

McDONALD, Carole (1993) The CPA and the children: a personal perspective, *International Journal of Refugee Law*, v. 5 (4), pp. 580 -584.

McPHERSON, C. (1984) Turkic refugees 1984: a demographic and comparative study on the Turkic refugees (Uzbeks, Kazakhs, Kirghiz,Turkmen and Tadzhik) in Pakistan and Turkey, National Institute of Population Studies in Pakistan.

McSPADDEN, L.A. (1985) Independence and Dependence: Conflict in the Resettlement of Ethiopian Refugees, Paper presented at the American Anthropological Association meeting, Washington DC, Migration Policy Program, Publication #2.

MINEAR, LARRY AND THOMAS G. WEISS. (1995) *Mercy Under Fire*, Boulder: Westview.

MINERS, J. Norman (1990) Constitution and Administration, In the other Hong Kong report (Eds Richard Y.C. Wong, Joseph Y.S. Cheng), The Chinese University Press.

MOORE, Thomas R. (1979) SIL and the 'New-Found Tribe': The Amarakaeri Experience, *Dialectical Anthropology*, 4, 2, July, 113-125, New York.

MORSINK, H.J.A. (1972) Appraisal of the social viability of four refugee settlement schemes in Southern Tanzania, Division of Social Affairs, UN office at Geneva.

MUNCY, S. (1985) CMHFS: A program description, *A Journal of Refugee Resettlement*, 1, 43-45.

MUNCY, S. (1992) Vietnamese paraprofessionals in child welfare, In *The Psychological Well-Being of Refugee Children: Research, Practice and Policy Issues*, McCallin, Margaret (ed.) pp. 215 - 225, International Catholic Child Bureau CH-1202 Geneva, Switzerland

MUSHKAT, Roda (1993) Implementation of the CPA in Hong Kong: compatibility with international standards, *International Journal of Refugee Law*, v. 5 (4) pp. 559 -579.

NAIDOO, J. (1985) The adaptation of Salvadorean refugees in Canada, *Multiculturalism*, vol.9, no.1, pp.258.

NATIONAL INSTITUTE OF MENTAL HEALTH (1991) Mental Health Services for Refugees, US Department of Health and Huam Services, Maryland.

NGO, Q.H. (1986) Report on the economic and social protection of refugees in France, Presented at International round table on 'Problems arising from migratory movements of refugees, migrants and ethnic minorities', Athens, October.

NGO, Q.H. (1986) Report on humanitarian action for refugees, Presented to International Congress on Peace and Humanitarian Actions, organised by International Institute of Humanitarian Law, San Remo, September.

NGO, Q.H. (1987) Report on principles and practice of asylum in France, in the Federal Republic of Germany and in the United Kingdom, For the Council of Europe.

NGO, Q.H. (1986) Report on refugees and asylum-seekers in Europe, presented to study session on 'Human Rights Policies in Europe: it's Instruments and Effects', organized by Youth and Student Movements for the United Nations (ISMUN), Strasborg, January.

NGOLLE, E.N. (1986) The political status of the UNHCR and patterns in its assistance to Third World refugees, *Cameron Review of International Relations*, December / January.

NICHOLS, B. (1988) *The Uneasy Alliance: Religion, Refugee Work and US foreign policy*, Oxford University Press, New York / Oxford.

NICHOLS, B.(1986) Favor in the wilderness: sanctuary politics and shaping of America's refugee policy, *Refugee Issues*, vol. 2, no.4. Refugee Studies Programme (Oxford) and British Refugee Council.

NIMMONS, N.L. (1987) Refugee Women: The ethno-cultural double back Effects of Violence and Abuse. Paper presented to the Canadian Council for Refugees Spring Conference, Montreal, Quebec, 4 May.

NINDI, B. (1985) Problems of social science research in developing societies with examples from a survey of Zairean refugees in Tanzania, *Social Science Research Review*, vol.1, no.1, pp.53-67.

NOWAK, M. (1984) *Tibetan Refugees: Youth and New Generation of Meaning*, Rutgers University Press, New Brunswick NJ.

OXFAM (1986) How Hong Kong Cares for Vietnamese Refugees.

PAK POY, Patricia (1991) Ethics: ethical ambiguities in refugee assistance, *Refugee Participation Network*, No. 11 pp. 30 - 31.

PALACIO, J.O. (1985) A survey of Central American refugees/ migrants in four urban communities in Belize, Submitted to Center for Immigration policy and Refugee Assistance, Georgetown University.

PASK, D. (1982) Issues in child welfare: the refugee children at 6 -11, Colloquium of Child Welfare Research (Ed.C.Bagley), University of Calgary.

PHILPOT, Terry (1980) A harbour of hope, *Nursing Mirror,* v.151 (25), pp. 24-27.

PIROUET, L. (1979) Urban refugees in Nairobi: small numbers, large problems, Paper presented to ASAUK Conference, London.

PRESTON, R.A.(1988) Educational needs and development for Irian Jaya refugees, ERV, University of Papua New Guinea, Proceedings of the Fourth Annual Midwest Research-To-Practice Conference in adult and Continuing Education, 10-11 October 1985, pp 10-14, University of Michigan, Ann Arbor.

REFUGEE CONCERN (1991) Defenceless in Detention : Vietnamese Children Living Amidst Increasing Violence in Hong Kong.

REFUGEE CONCERN (1991) The RCHK directory, Hong Kong.

REFUGEE CONCERN HONG KONG (1991) Executive summary: Defenceless in detention, Vietnamese children living amidst violence in Hong Kong, Hong Kong.

REFUGEE CONCERN(1991) Position paper on Unaccompanied minors, Hong Kong.

REPORT FOR THE INDEPENDENT COMMISSION ON INTERNATIONAL HUMANITARIAN ISSUES (1986) Refugees dynamics of displacement, Arena Press, Hong Kong.

REYNOLDS, J. (1984) The reception centre phase of the Vietnamese programme.

REYNOLDS, J. (1986) Refugees from Vietnam in Hong Kong, Resulting from a Refugee Action visit to the camps in Hong Kong, Refugee action publications

RICHMOND, A. (1988) Sociological theories of International Migration: the case of refugees. *Current Sociology,* Vol. 36. No 2. 1988, 6-25.

ROBINSON, Court (1990) Testimony before the Senate Appropriations Committee Subcommittee on Foreign Operations March 1, 1990, US Committee for Refugees Washington DC.

ROBINSON, V. (1986) *Transients, Settlers and Refugees: Asians in Britain*, Clarendon Press, Oxford.

ROBINSON, V. (Ed.1993) The International Refugee Crisis. British and Canadian Responses, Macmillian and Refugee Studies Programme Oxford.

ROE, M.D. (1985) Refugee sanctuary for Central Americans: agenda and efficacy, Paper presented at the 8th National Third World Studies Conference, University of Nebraska, Omaha.

ROGGE, J.R (1978) Comments on a typology for refugees in Africa, *Zambian Geographical Journal*, vols.32 -33, pp.46 -60.

ROGGE, J.R (1981) Africa's resettlement strategies, *International Migration Review*,vol.15, no. 1, pp. 195 -212.

ROGGE, J.R (1982) Refugee migration and resettlement, *In Population Redistribution in Africa* (ed,.J.I.Clarke and L Kosinski), pp.39 -43. Heinneman, London.

ROGGE, J.R (1983) Africa's refugees and Canada, *International perspectives*, September/ October, pp.23 -6.

ROGGE, J.R (1983) Sudanese refugees new roots, The IDRC Report, vol. II, no.4. pp.10 -11. Reprinted in Refugees (UNHCR, Geneva) March 1983), p.7.

ROGGE, J.R (1985) Africa's displaced populations: dependency or self sufficiency? In population and Development projects in Africa (ed. JI. Clarke, M. Khogali and L.Kosinki), pp. 68 -83, Cambridge University Press, Cambridge.

ROGGE, J.R (1985) The Indochinese Diaspora: Where have all the refugees gone? Canadian *Geographer*, vol. 29, no.1, pp. 62-72.

ROGGE, J.R (1985) Too Many, Too Long: Sudan's Twenty-year Refuge Dilemma, Rowman and Allenheld, Totowa NJ.

ROGGE, J.R (1986) Urban refugees: some changing dimensions to Africa's refugee problem, *Migration World*, vol.14,no.4.

ROGGE, J.R. (1977) The geography of refugees: some illustrations from Africa, Professional Geographer, vol.29, pp. 186 -93

ROLFE, C.J.D., ROLFE, C.M. AND HARPER, M. (forthcoming 1988) It can be done:Refugee income generation programmes in developing countries, *Intermediate Technology Publications*, London.

ROSE, P.I. (1981) From South Asia to America: Links in a chain, part ll, *Migration Today*, Vol.9, no.4, pp.22-8.

ROSE, P.I. (1981) Links in a chain (expanded version), *Catholic Mind*, vol.80, no.1361, pp. 2-26.

ROSE, P.I. (1981) Links in a chain: observations of the American refugee programme in Southeast Asia, *Migration Today*, vol.9, no.3, pp.6-28.

ROSE, P.I. (1981) Some thoughts about refugees and the descendants of Theseus, *International Migration Review*,vol.15, spring/summer, pp.8-15.

ROSE, P.I. (1983) The business of caring : refugee workers and voluntary agencies, *Refugee reports*, vol. 4, no.2, pp 1-6. Reprinted in Refugee Resettlement: South East Asians in Transition, pp.133-40, University of British Columbia, Vancouver, 1985.

ROSE, P.I (1984) On the jubilee of the International Rescue Committee, *World Refugee Survey*, p.23, US Committee on Refugees, New York.

ROSE, P.I (1984) Some reflections on refugee policy, Dissent, fall, pp. 484-6. Reprinted in *Refugee Resettlement: Southeast Asians in Transition*, pp. 182-8, University of British Columbia, Vancouver.

ROSE, P.I (1984) The harbor masters: American politics and refugee policy, In *Social Problems and Public Policy* (Ed. Michal Lewis), pp. 273-312. JAI Press, Greenwich.

ROSE, P.I (1985) Documenting the plight of the uprooted: moving pictures of the Hmong. *Migration Today*, vol.13, no.4/5, pp.42-4.

ROSE, P.I (1985) Humanitarian proclivities and the pressure of politics, In *American Refugee Policy: Ethical and Religious Reflections* (Ed. JM. Kitagawa), pp.41-6. Seabury Press, San Francisco.

ROSE, P.I (1985) Long night's journey into day the odyssey of the Indochinese refugees, *Society/Transaction*, vol.13, no.4/5, pp.42-4.

ROSE, P.I (1985) Norodom Sihanouk: the once and would be King, *Migration Today*, vol, 13, no.2, pp.13-17.

ROSE, P.I (1985) The politics and morality of US refugee policy, The Center Magazine, September/October, pp.2-8.

ROSE, P.I (1986) Towards a sociology of exile, *International Migration Review*, vol.19, Winter, pp. 768-73.

ROSE, P.I (1986) Working with Refugees (Ed). Center for Migration Studies, Staten Island NY.

ROSE, P.I (1987) The Cantonese connection, *Migration World*, vol.14, no.4, pp. 24-8. RSP, Oxford, UK.

RUBENBEN, G. Rumbaut (1991) The agony of Exile: A study of migration and adaptation of Indochinese Refugee adults and children, In *Refugee Children theory, research and services* (Ed) Frederick L. Ahearn and Jean L. Athey, John Hopkins, Baltimore.

Saigon Giai Phong (1987) July 4, In Vietnamese.

SALISBURY, James E (1992) 'Long term detainment or forced repatriation of Vietnamese boat people political imprisonment'. Report to Amnesty International and relevant agencies on the Vietnamese boat people / refugee situation in Hong Kong, Hong Kong.

SAMHA, M.A. (1980) Migration of refugees and non- refugees to Amman, Jordan 1948-1977, *Population Bulletin of ECWA*, no 19, pp.47-67.

SEAMAN, T.J. (1985) Voices of Exiles: the views of Asylum Seekers on their Experience of the First year in UK, and on the Welfare services offered to them, Unpublished M.Sc. Thesis, London University (Bedford College).

SEDDON, D.(1987) Morocco at War. In *War and Refugees: The Western Sahara Conflict* (ed. R. Lawless and L. Monahan) Printer Publishers, London.

SHAH, G. (1985) Social work in disaster, *Indian Journal of Social Work*, 45, 462-471.

SMITH, C.D AND HESS, S.(1984) Repression and Exile: a study of Salvadoraan Haitian and Guatemalan refugees in Montreal, Report to the Quebec Minister of Social Affairs.

SMITH,C.D. (1985) *A profile of Central American refugees, McGill Reporter*, vol.17, no.29.

SMITH,C.D. (1985) *Beyond the Plant Report*, Refuge, October.

SMITH,C.D. (1986) Repression and Exile: A study of Latin American Refugees in Montreal, Quebec Ministry of Social Affairs.

SMITH, C.D. (1987) Refugee or asylum: Does Canada have a choice ? *International Migration Review*, Summer.

SMITH, C.D. (1985) Central American refugees in Montreal, McGill Daily, 24 January.

SMITH, C.D. (1986) Trials and errors, the experience of Latin American refugees in Montreal, Refuge, April.

SMYSER, W.R. (1987) *Refugees: extended exile.* Prager and Center for Strategic and International studies, Washington, D.C.

SOMMER, Robert (1959) Refereed in Mental Asylums, Goffman 1961.

SOUTH CHINA MORNING POST (1992) August 25.

SOUTH CHINA MORNING POST (1992) 27th September.

SPOONER, B.C (1981) Refugees in the Horn: Six million dispossessed, *Horn of Africa Journal*, vol.4, no.1.

STAVENHAGEN. R (1987) Ethnocide or ethno development: *The challenge, Development*, 1. 74-78.

STEINBUGLER, Tom (1991) Consultation on screening and unaccompanied minors July 08 - 09, 1991, Bangkok, Thailand, Jesuit Refugee Service Asia Pacific.

STEINGRABER, S. (1987) Resettlement and villagization - Tools of militarization in Southwest Ethiopia, *Cultural Survival Quarterly*, vol.11, no 4, pp 38-45

STEINGRABER, S. (1987) Resettlement in Ethiopia: ecological excuses and environmental consequences, In Spoils of famine : Ethiopian Famine policy and Peasant Agriculture (ed.S. Steingraber, J. Clay, B.K. Holocomp, and P. Niggli), *Cultural Survival Report 25*.

STEINGRABER, S.(1986) Ethiopia's policy of genocide against the anuak of Gambellai, *Cultural Survival Quarterly*, Vol.10,no.3, pp.53-6.

STRAND, Paul J. (1985) *Indochinese refugees in America: problem of adaptation and assimilation*, Duke University Press. Durham.

SUEDFELD, Peter (1977) Environmental Effects on Violent Behavior in Prisons, *The International Journal of Offender Therapy and Comparative Criminology*.

SUEDFELD, Peter (1977) Environmental Effects on violent Behaviour in Prisons, *International Journal of offender Therapy and Comparative Criminology*.

SUKSAMRAN, S. (1985) Hope and expectation of Indochinese refugees, Chulalongkorn University, Bangkok.

SUKSAMRAN, S. (1981). The Khmer Refugee and National Integration, Chulalongkorn University, Bangkok.

SUPANNG Chantavanich and Reynolds, E. Bruce (ed.)(1988) *Indochinese refugees: asylum and resettlement,* Inst. of Asian Studies, Chulalongkorn University, Bangkok, Thailand.

SWORD, K.R. (1986). Their prospects will not be bright: British response to the problem of the Polish Recalcitrants' 1946-49, *Journal of Contemporary History*, vol.21, pp.367-90.

TANDON, Y. (1984). Ugandan refugees in Kenya: a community of enforced self- reliance, Paper presented to the symposium, 'assistance to Refugees: alternative viewpoints' Refugee Studies Programme, University of Oxford.

THOMAS, Joe (1993) Human rights violations and the politics of detention pp. 94 - 100, *Voices*, Sep. DAGA Hong Kong.

THOMAS, Joe (1993) The unfinished agenda of the Vietnamese, pp. 82 - 84, *Voices*, Mar/June DAGA, Hong Kong.

THOMAS, Joe (1995) Population displacement, detention and ethnocide : an ethnographic inquiry into the conditions of Vietnamese asylum seekers detained in Hong Kong (1988 - 1994) Ph.D. thesis, Dept of Anthropology, University of Poona.

TORGRIMSON JOHN (1991) Vietnamese Boat People, In '*The other Hong Kong Report*', ed. Sung, Y.W and Lee, M.K., The Chinese University Press, Hong Kong.

TSANG, Siu-yung, Heidi (1990) The development of Vietnamese boat people issue: A chronic strain too Hong Kong, Department of Public and Social Administration, City Polytechnic of Hong Kong.

TSOI, Mona M., YU, Gabriel K.K. and LIEH-MAK, Felice (1986) Vietnamese refugee children in camps in Hong Kong, *Soc. Sci. Med*, v. 23 (11) pp. 1147-1150. Pergamon Journals Ltd

U.S. COMMITTEE ON REFUGEES (1996) World Refugee Survey (WRS), 1996. Washington.

UN General Assembly (1977) Human rights in the administration of justice: Protection of persons subjected to detention or imprisonment, Geneva.

UN General Assembly (1989) International conference on Indo-Chinese Refugees, Geneva.

UN General Assembly (1989) UN Convention on the Rights of the Children, Geneva.

UNHCR (1976) Handbook on Procedures and Criteria for Determining Refugee Status. Geneva.

UNHCR (1988) Guidelines for working with children in difficult situation, Geneva.

UNHCR (1988) Handbook on Procedures and criteria for determining refugee status, Geneva.

UNHCR (1989) Special procedure for handling unaccompanied minors and other special cases under the comprehensive plan of action. Memorandum to UNHCR Branch offices in Bangkok, Hong Kong, Jakarta, Kuala Lumpur and Manila from I. Khan, Senior legal Adviser for Asia and Oceania, 14 August 1989, 531 THA.

UNHCR (1989) Unaccompanied minors, memorandum to the UNHCR representative B.O. Bangkok, Thailand, from I Khan, Senior legal adviser for Asia Oceania, 12 September 1989, 531.THA.

UNHCR (1990) Collection of international instruments concerning Refugees, Geneva.

UNHCR (1990) Report on Joint mission to Hanoi 12-16, Memorandum to Mr. Robert Van Leeuwen from Christine Mougne, Dated 20th July 1990.

UNHCR (1990) Information for Vietnamese asylum-seekers in Hong Kong, Office of the Chief of the UNHCR Mission in Hong Kong.

UNHCR (1991) Joint press release by UNHCR and ISS, New special committee for unaccompanied minors and other vulnerable persons in Hong Kong's detention centers, 4th April 1991.

UNHCR (1993) *The state of the World Refugees*, Penguin Books, NY.

UNHCR (1996) Update On Regional Developments In Asia And Oceania. Executive Committee Of The High Commissioner's Programme Standing Committee 4th Meeting, EC/46/SC/CRP.44. 19 August 1996

VAN ESTERIK, P. (1981) In-home sponsorship for Southeast Asian refugees: a preliminary assessment, *Journal of Refugee Resettlement*, vol. 1, no. 2, p.1826.

VAN ESTERIK, P.(1980) Cultural factors affecting adjustment of Southeast Asian refugees, In Southeast Asian Exodus: from Tradition to Resettlement, p.151-71. Canadian Asian Studies Association.

VIRMANI, A. (1984) *Watching Trapped Generations*, Refugees, July.

VIVIANI, N. (1980) Australian Government policy on the entry of Vietnamese refugees in 1975.

VIVIANI, N. (1980) The Vietnamese in Australia : new problems in old forms, CSAAR Research paper No.11, Griffith University, Brisbane (Available in Vietnamese).

VIVIANI, N. (1981) Refugee resettlement: a response, In *refugees, the challenge of the future* (Ed. C.A. Price) ANU Press, Academy of Social Science Australia.

VIVIANI, N. (1982) Australian government policies on the entry of Vietnamese: record and responsibility, CSAAR Research Paper No.7, Griffith University, Brisbane.

VIVIANI, N. (1983) Refugees the end of splendid isolation ? In *Independence and Alliance: Australia in World Affairs, 1976 -80* (eds. P.J. Boyce and J.R. Angel) George Allen and Unwin, Sydney.

VIVIANI, N. (1984) The long Journey: Vietnamese migration and settlement in Australia, Melbourne University Press, Carlton.

VIVIANI, N. (1985) The Vietnamese in Australia, In *Immigration and Ethnicity in the 1980s* (eds. I.H. Burnley, S. Encel and G. McCall) Longman Cheshire, Melbourne.

VIVIANI, N. and Lawe-Davis, J. (1980). Australian Government policy on the entry of Vietnamese refugees 1976 to 1978, CSAAR Research Paper No.2. Griffith University, Brisbane.

WAGLEY GOW, A. (1991) Protection of Vietnamese asylum seekers in Hong Kong :Detention, screening and repatriation, Working paper submitted to Sub-Commission on prevention of discrimination and protection of minorities (43rd : 5-30. Aug.1991, Geneva) *Human Rights Advocates, CA. 94705, USA*

WALDRON, S.R (1983) Is there a future for the Ogden refugees ? In Proceedings of the VIIth International Conference of Ethiopian studies (Ed.S. Rubensonon), Uppsala, Sweden, Also published (with J. Waldron) in Cultural Survival, Spring, 1984.

WALDRON, S.R. (1984) Building air castles in Somalia: a refugee construction project analyzed, Paper presented at symposium 'Assistance to refugees: alternative View points', Refugee Studies Programme, Oxford, 26-29 March.

WALDRON, S.R. (1986) Resettlement in Ethiopia: where angles fear to tread, Review essay in Refugee Issues, vol.3, no.2, Refugee Studies Programme (Oxford) and British Refugee Council.

WALDRON, S.R. (1988) Working in the dark: why social anthropological research is essential in refugee administration, *Journal of Refugee Studies*, vol.1, no.2.

WALDRON, S.R.(1982) Somali refugee background characteristics: preliminary result from the Qoriooley camps, Northeast African Studies, vol.4, pp.177-24.

WARBURTON, J. (1992) Community development, CFSI documents, Hong Kong.

WEBB, Stephen (1989) Asian refugees a role for the churches? - report of the CCA/WCC-CICARWS Asian refugee working group meeting 17-19 May 1989, Bangkok, Christian Conference Of Asia (CCA); World Council Of Churches Commission On Inter-Church Aid and Refugee World Services (WCC-CICARWS).

WEIL, GOTSHAL AND MANGES (1993) Submission to the United Nations Working Group on Arbitrary Detention By the Lawyers Committee for Human Rights and the Women's Commission for Refugee Women and Children Behalf of Approximately 40,000 Vietnamese Detainees, including the Families of Pham Ngoc Lam, Vuong Son Bach and Cam Gia Ninh.

WEIS, P. (1954) The international protection of refugees. *American Journal of International Law*, vol.48, pp.193 -221.

WEIS, P. (1956) The international status of refugees and stateless persons, Journal du droit International, pp.4 -69 (English/French).

WEIS, P. (1958) The Hague Agreement relating to the refugee seamen of 23 November 1957, *International and Comparative Law Quarterly.*

WEIS, P. (1960) The concept of refugee in international law, Journal du Droit International, no.4 (English/French).

WEIS, P. (1961) The U.N. Convention relating to the status of stateless persons, *The international and Comparative Law Quarterly*, April.

WEIS, P. (1962) The U.N. Convention on the Reduction of Statelessness, 1961, *The International and Comparative Law Quarterly*, October.

WEIS, P. (1962) The U.N. Convention on the Reduction of Statelessness. Le Monde Diplomatique (Paris) January.

WEIS, P. (1965) *The Convention Relating to the Status of Refuges*, Interpreter Release, vol.42, no.1.

WEIS, P. (1966) Territorial asylum, *Indian Journal of International Law*, vol.6, no.2.

WEIS, P. (1966) The rights of asylum in the context of the protection of human rights in the regional and municipal law, *International Review of the Red Cross*, September.

WEIS, P. (1967) The 1967 Protocol Relating to the status of Refugees and some questions of the Law of Treaties, *British Yearbook of International law*, vol.13.

WEIS, P. (1968) Human rights and refugees, *Interpreter Releases*, vol. 45, no.11.

WEIS, P. (1968) Recent developments in the law of territorial asylum, Revue des droits del' Hommme, vol.1, no.3.

WEIS, P. (1968) Territorial asylum, UNHCR Reports, *Special issue for Human Rights Year.*

WEIS, P. (1968) The office of the United Nations High Commissioner for Refugees and Human Rights, Revue des Droits del'Homme, vol.1, no.2

WEIS, P. (1968) The Universal Declaration of Human Rights, *Pax Romana Journal* (Fribourg), vol.1 (English /French).

WEIS, P. (1969) The United Nations Declaration on Territorial asylum, *The Canadian Yearbook of International Law.*

WEIS, P. (1970) Diplomatique protection of nationals and international protection of human rights, Revue des Droits del' Homme, vol. 4, pp. 643 -78.

WEIS, P. (1970) The Convention of the Organization of African Unity Governing the Specific Aspects of the Refugee Problem in Africa. Revue des Droits del' Homme,vol.3, no.3.

WEIS, P. (1971) Refugees and human rights, *Israel Yearbook on Human Rights*,vol.1, pp.35-50.

WEIS, P. (1973) Refuge Law - a new branch of law. *International Bar Journal*. London.

WEIS, P. (1973) Refugees and Law, World Peace Through Law Center, Washington.

WEIS, P. (1974) The 'de facto' refugees, AWR Bulletin, vol.12, pp.174-85.

WEIS, P. (1975) The right to leave and return in the Middle East, *Israel Yearbook of Human Rights*,vol.5, pp.322 -65.

WEIS, P. (1977) Asylum and Terrorism, Review of the International Commission of Jurists, no.19, pp. 37-43.

WEIS, P. (1979) The Draft United Nations Convention on Territorial Asylum, *British Yearbook of international Law*, vol 50, pp.151-72.

WEIS, P. (1980) Refugees in orbit, Israel *Yearbook on Human Rights*, vol. 10, pp 157-66.

WEIS, P. (1984) Manifestly unfounded claims for asylum or refugee status, AWR Bulletin, vol.21, no.30, pp.15 -18.

WEIS, P. (1984) Statelessness, Report for the Independent Commission on International Humanitarian issues, December.

WEIS, P. (1951) Who is a refugee? *Wiener Library Bulletin*, no 3/4, p 20.

WEIS, P. (1950) A refugee Charter, *Jewish Affairs*,Vol 4, no.10-12.

WEIS, P. (1953) Legal aspects of the Convention of 28 July 1951 relating to the status of refugees, *British Yearbook of International Law*,vol.28, pp.478-89.

WESTERMEYER, J AND WILLIAMS, C. L. (1986) Refugee Mental Health in Resettlement Countries (Ed.) Hemisphere Publishing Corporation, New York.

WESTERMEYER, J., VANG, T.F AND NEIDER, J. (1983) A comparison of refugees using and not using a psychiatric service: an analysis of DSM-III criteria and self rating scales in cross cultural context, *Journal of Operational Psychiatry*, vol.14, pp. 36-41.

WESTERMEYER, J., VANG, T.F. AND LYFONG, G. (1983) Hmong refugees in Minnesota: characteristics and self perceptions, Minnesota Medicine, vol. 66, 431-9.

WESTERMEYER, J. (1986) Planning mental health services for refugees. In Refugee Mental *Health Issues in Resettlement Countries* (Ed.C.L. Williams and J. Westermeyer). Hemisphere Publishing Corporation, New York.

WESTERMEYER, J. (1986) Psychiatric care of refugees, In *Medical Care of Refugees* (Ed. R. H. Sandler), Oxford University Press, New York.

WESTERMEYER, J. (1984) Refugees in Minnesota: sex roles and mental health, *Medical Anthropology*, vol.8, pp.229-45.

WILLIAMS, C.L (1985) The Southeast Asian refugees and community mental health, *Journal of Community Psychology*, vol. 13, pp. 258-68.

WILLIAMS, C.L (1986) Mental health assessment of refugees, In *Refugee Mental Health in Resettlement Countries* (Ed.C.L. Williams and J. Westermeyer), Hemisphere Publishing Corporation, New York.

WILLIAMS, C.L.(1983) Psychiatric problems among adolescent Southeast Asian refugees, *Journal of Nervous and Medical Diseases*, vol. 171, pp. 79-85.

WILSON, K.B. (1985) Refugees-Access and Labelling, *Development and Change*, vol.16, no.3, pp. 429 -50

WILSON, K.B. (1986) Rehousing the Greek Cypriot refugees from 1974 - dependency, assimilation and politicization, In Cyprus 1960- 1985: The first 25 years of Independence (Ed.J. Kpumonlides), Oxford University Press.

WILSON, K.B. (1987) Rehousing the Greek Cypriot Refugees from 1974: A study of Institutional Access and Labeling, DPhil dissertation, University of Sussex.

WILSON, K.B. (1988) Refugees and refugee studies: A label and an agenda, *Journal of Refugee Studies*, vol.1, no.1, pp.1-6.

WILSON, K.B. (1988) Refugees, repatriation, and root causes, *Journal of Refugee Studies* vol.1, no.2.

WOLF, Daniel (1990) A subtle form of inhumanity: screening of the boat people in Hong Kong: *International Journal of Refugee Law*, special issue. pp. 161-172.

WOLF, Daniel (1991) Final betrayal (Criticism of refugee screening process in Hong Kong : 'Records are being distorted, legitimate refugees are being denied status and the result is that people are suffering indefinite detention and face forcible repatriation', Documentary Video record.

WOLF, Daniel and Shep Lowman (1990) Towards a new consensus on the Vietnamese boat people, SAIS Review.10:101-19 Summer/ Fall.

WONG, Ling-fat Stephen, (1989) Analysis of the policy of liberalizing refugee camps, Department of Social and public Administration, City Polytechnic of Hong Kong.

YOSSEF. S. Ben-Porath (1991) The Psychosocial Adjustment in NIMH, Mental Health Services for Refugees, Maryland.

YOUNG, V. Pauline (1956) *Social Structure.*

ZUCKER, N.L AND SCHEINMAN, R.S. (1981) Refugee policy, The New York Times, op.ed., Sunday 24 May 1981, p.E19.

ZUCKER, N.L. (1983) Contemporary American immigration and refugee policy: an overview, In New comers to the United States: Children and Families (Ed. M. frank), pp. 5-14. The Haworth Press, New York.

ZUCKER, N.L. AND ZUCKER, N.F. ((1982) Refugee resettlement in the United States: the role of the voluntary agencies. Translational Legal Problems of Refugees, 1982, *Michigan Yearbook of International Legal Studies* (Ed. D.M. Levy), pp. 155-77. Clark Boardman Company Ltd, New York.

ZUCKER, N.L. AND ZUCKER, N.F. (1981) The voluntary agencies and refugee resettlement in the United States: a report to the Select Commission on Immigration and Refugee Policy, In US *Immigration Policy and the National Interest*, Appendix C to the Staff Report of the Select Commission on Immigration and Refuge Policy, Papers on Refugee, pp.509 -96. Washington DC.

ZUCKER, N.L. AND ZUCKER, N.F. (1987) *The Guarded Gate: The Realty of American Refugee Policy*, Harcourt Brace Jovanovich, San Diego.

International Human Rights Instruments

A. U.N. CHARTER, June 26, 1945, 59 Stat. 1031, T.S. 993, 3 Bevans 1153, entered into force Oct. 24, 1945.

B. THE INTERNATIONAL BILL OF HUMAN RIGHTS

1. Universal Declaration of Human Rights, G.A. res. 217A (III), U.N. Doc A/810 at 71 (1948)
2. International Covenant on Economic, Social and Cultural Rights, G.A. res. 2200A (XXI), 21 U.N. GAOR Supp. (No. 16) at 49, U.N. Doc. A/6316 (1966), 993 U.N.T.S. 3, entered into force Jan. 3, 1976.
3. International Covenant on Civil and Political Rights, G.A. res. 2200A (XXI), 21 U.N. GAOR Supp. (No. 16) at 52, U.N. Doc. A/6316 (1966), 999 U.N.T.S. 171, entered into force Mar. 23, 1976.
4. Optional Protocol to the International Covenant on Civil and Political Rights, G.A. res. 2200A (XXI), 21 U.N. GAOR Supp. (No. 16) at 59, U.N. Doc. A/6316 (1966), 999 U.N.T.S. 302, entered into force March 23, 1976.
5. Second Optional Protocol to the International Covenant on Civil and Political Rights, aiming at the abolition of the death penalty, G.A. res. 44/128, annex, 44 U.N. GAOR Supp. (No. 49) at 207, U.N. Doc. A/44/49 (1989), entered into force July 11, 1991.

C. PREVENTION OF DISCRIMINATION AND PROTECTION OF MINORITIES

1. International Convention on the Elimination of All Forms of Racial Discrimination, 660 U.N.T.S. 195, entered into force Jan. 4, 1969.
2. Declaration on Race and Racial Prejudice, E/CN.4/Sub.2/1982/2/Add.1, annex V (1982).
3. Declaration on Fundamental Principles concerning the Contribution to the Mass Media to Strengthening Peace and International Understanding, to the Promotion of Human Rights and to Countering Racialism, Apartheid and Incitement to War, adopted by the UNESCO General Conference at its twentieth session, Paris, 22 November 1978, UNESCO's Standard-Setting Instruments, IV.C. (1994).
4. Declaration on the Elimination of All Forms of Intolerance and of Discrimination Based on Religion or Belief, G.A. res. 36/55, 36 U.N. GAOR Supp. (No. 51) at 171, U.N. Doc. A/36/684 (1981).
5. Declaration on the Rights of Persons Belonging to National or Ethnic, Religious or Linguistic Minorities, G.A. res. 47/135, annex, 47 U.N. GAOR Supp. (No. 49) at 210, U.N. Doc. A/47/49 (1993).

D. WOMEN'S HUMAN RIGHTS
1. Convention on the Elimination of All Forms of Discrimination against Women, G.A. res. 34/180, 34 U.N. GAOR Supp. (No. 46) at 193, U.N. Doc. A/34/46, entered into force Sept. 3, 1981.
2. Convention on the Political Rights of Women, 193 U.N.T.S. 135, entered into force July 7, 1954.
3. Declaration on the Protection of Women and Children in Emergency and Armed Conflict, G.A. res. 3318 (XXIX), 29 U.N. GAOR Supp. (No. 31) at 146, U.N. Doc. A/9631 (1974).
4. Declaration on the Elimination of Violence Against Women, G.A. res. 48/104, 48 U.N. GAOR Supp. (No. 49) at 217, U.N. Doc. A/48/49 (1993).
5. Beijing Declaration and Platform of Action, A/CONF.177/20 (1995) and A/CONF.177/20/Add.1 (1995).
6. The Human Rights of Women: A Reference Guide to official United Nations Documents

E. SLAVERY AND SLAVERY-LIKE PRACTICES
1. Slavery Convention, 60 L.N.T.S. 253, entered into force March 9, 1927.
2. Protocol amending the Slavery Convention, 182 U.N.T.S. 51, entered into force December 7, 1953.
3. Supplementary Convention on the Abolition of Slavery, the Slave Trade, and Institutions and Practices Similar to Slavery, 226 U.N.T.S. 3, entered into force April 30, 1957.
4. Convention for the Suppression of the Traffic in Persons and of the Exploitation of the Prostitution of Others, 96 U.N.T.S. 271, entered into force July 25, 1951.

F. RIGHTS OF PRISONERS AND DETAINEES
1. Standard Minimum Rules for the Treatment of Prisoners, adopted Aug. 30, 1955, by the First United Nations Congress on the Prevention of Crime and the Treatment of Offenders, U.N. Doc. A/CONF/611, annex I, E.S.C. res. 663C, 24 U.N. ESCOR Supp. (No. 1) at 11, U.N. Doc. E/3048 (1957), amended E.S.C. res. 2076, 62 U.N. ESCOR Supp. (No. 1) at 35, U.N. Doc. E/5988 (1977).
2. Basic Principles for the Treatment of Prisoners, G.A. res. 45/111, annex, 45 U.N. GAOR Supp. (No. 49A) at 200, U.N. Doc. A/45/49 (1990).
3. Body of Principles for the Protection of All Persons under Any Form of Detention or Imprisonment, G.A. res. 43/173, annex, 43 U.N. GAOR Supp. (No. 49) at 298, U.N. Doc. A/43/49 (1988).

G. PROTECTION FROM TORTURE, ILL-TREATMENT AND DISAPPEARANCE
1. Declaration on the Protection of All Persons from Being Subjected to Torture and Other Cruel, Inhuman or Degrading Treatment or Punishment, G.A. res. 3452 (XXX), annex, 30 U.N. GAOR Supp. (No. 34) at 91, U.N. Doc. A/10034 (1975).
2. Convention against Torture and Other Cruel, Inhuman or Degrading Treatment or Punishment, G.A. res. 39/46, annex, 39 U.N. GAOR Supp. (No. 51) at 197, U.N. Doc. A/39/51 (1984), entered into force June 26, 1987.
3. Principles of Medical Ethics relevant to the Role of Health Personnel, particularly Physicians, in the Protection of Prisoners and Detainees against Torture and Other Cruel, Inhuman or Degrading Treatment or Punishment, G.A. res. 37/194, annex, 37 U.N. GAOR Supp. (No. 51) at 211, U.N. Doc. A/37/51 (1982).
4. Declaration on the Protection of All Persons from Enforced Disappearances, G.A. res. 47/133, 47 U.N. GAOR Supp. (No. 49) at 207, U.N. Doc. A/47/49 (1992).

H. HUMAN RIGHTS IN THE ADMINISTRATION OF JUSTICE

1. Code of Conduct for Law Enforcement Officials, G.A. res. 34/169, annex, 34 U.N. GAOR Supp. (No. 46) at 186, U.N. Doc. A/34/46 (1979).
2. Basic Principles on the Use of Force and Firearms by Law Enforcement Officials, Eighth United Nations Congress on the Prevention of Crime and the Treatment of Offenders, Havana, 27 August to 7 September 1990, U.N. Doc. A/CONF.144/28/Rev.1 at 112 (1990).
3. Basic Principles on the Role of Lawyers, Eighth United Nations Congress on the Prevention of Crime and the Treatment of Offenders, Havana, 27 August to 7 September 1990, U.N. Doc.A/CONF.144/28/Rev.1 at 118 (1990).
4. Guidelines on the Role of Prosecutors, Eighth United Nations Congress on the Prevention of Crime and the Treatment of Offenders, Havana, 27 August to 7 September 1990, U.N. Doc. A/CONF.144/28/Rev.1 at 189 (1990).
5. Basic Principles on the Independence of the Judiciary, Seventh United Nations Congress on the Prevention of Crime and the Treatment of Offenders, Milan, 26 August to 6 September 1985, U.N. Doc. A/CONF.121/22/Rev.1 at 59 (1985).
6. United Nations Standard Minimum Rules for Non-custodial Measures (The Tokyo Rules), G.A. res. 45/110, annex, 45 U.N. GAOR Supp. (No. 49A) at 197, U.N. Doc. A/45/49 (1990).
7. Principles on the Effective Prevention and Investigation of Extra-Legal, Arbitrary and Summary Executions, E.S.C. res. 1989/65, annex, 1989 U.N. ESCOR Supp. (No. 1) at 52, U.N. Doc. E/1989/89 (1989).
8. Safeguards Guaranteeing Protection of the Rights of Those Facing the Death Penalty, E.S.C. res. 1984/50, annex, 1984 U.N. ESCOR Supp. (No. 1) at 33, U.N. Doc. E/1984/84 (1984).
9. Declaration of Basic Principles of Justice for Victims of Crime and Abuse of Power, G.A. res. 40/34, annex, 40 U.N. GAOR Supp.(No. 53) at 214, U.N. Doc. A/40/53 (1985).

I. JUVENILES

1. United Nations Rules for the Protection of Juveniles Deprived of their Liberty, G.A. res. 45/113, annex, 45 U.N. GAOR Supp. (No. 49A) at 205, U.N. Doc. A/45/49 (1990).
2. United Nations Guidelines for the Prevention of Juvenile Delinquency (The Riyadh Guidelines), G.A. res. 45/112, annex, 45 U.N. GAOR Supp. (No. 49A) at 201, U.N. Doc. A/45/49 (1990).
3. United Nations Standard Minimum Rules for the Administration of Juvenile Justice ("The Beijing Rules"), G.A. res. 40/33, annex, 40 U.N. GAOR Supp. (No. 53) at 207, U.N. Doc. A/40/53 (1985).

J. RIGHTS OF THE CHILD

1. Declaration of the Rights of the Child, G.A. res. 1386 (XIV), 14 U.N. GAOR Supp. (No. 16) at 19, U.N. Doc. A/4354 (1959).
2. Convention on the Rights of the Child, G.A. res. 44/25, annex, 44 U.N. GAOR Supp. (No. 49) at 167, U.N. Doc. A/44/49 (1989), entered into force Sept. 2, 1990.

K. WORLD CONFERENCES ON HUMAN RIGHTS

1. Vienna Declaration, World Conference on Human Rights , Vienna, 14 25 June 1993, U.N. Doc. A/CONF.157/24 (Part I) at 20 (1993).
2. Proclamation of Teheran, Final Act of the International Conference on Human Rights, Teheran, 22 April to 13 May 1968, U.N. Doc. A/CONF. 32/41 at 3 (1968).

L. FREEDOM OF ASSOCIATION
1. Freedom of Association and Protection of the Right to Organise Convention (ILO No. 87), 68 U.N.T.S. 17, entered into force July 4, 1950.
2. Right to Organise and Collective Bargaining Convention (ILO No. 98), 96 U.N.T.S. 257, entered into force July 18, 1951.
3. Workers' Representatives Convention (ILO No. 135), 883 U.N.T.S. 111, entered into force June 30, 1973. Labour Relations (Public Service) Convention (ILO No. 151), 1218 U.N.T.S. 87, entered into force Feb. 25, 1981.

M. EDUCATION
1. Convention against Discrimination in Education, 429 U.N.T.S. 93, entered into force May 22, 1962.

N. DISABLED PERSONS
1. Declaration on the Rights of Mentally Retarded Persons, G.A. res.2856 (XXVI), 26 U.N. GAOR Supp. (No. 29) at 93, U.N. Doc. A/8429 (1971).
2. Principles for the Protection of Persons with Mental Illnesses and the Improvement of Mental Health Care, G.A. res. 46/119, 46 U.N. GAOR Supp. (No. 49) at 189, U.N. Doc. A/46/49 (1991).
3. Declaration on the Rights of Disabled Persons, G.A. res. 3447. (XXX), 30 U.N. GAOR Supp. (No. 34) at 88, U.N. Doc. A/10034 (1975).

O. REFUGEES AND ASYLUM
1. Convention relating to the Status of Refugees, 189 U.N.T.S. 150, entered into force April 22, 1954.
2. Protocol Relating to the Status of Refugees, 606 U.N.T.S. 267, entered into force Oct. 4, 1967.
3. Statute of the Office of the United Nations High Commissioner for Refugees, G.A. res. 428 (V), annex, 5 U.N. GAOR Supp. (No. 20) at 46, U.N. Doc. A/1775 (1950).
4. Declaration on Territorial Asylum, G.A. res. 2312 (XXII), 22 U.N. GAOR Supp. (No. 16) at 81, U.N. Doc. A/6716 (1967).

P. NATIONALITY, STATELESSNESS AND RIGHTS OF ALIENS
1. Convention on the Reduction of Statelessness, 989 U.N.T.S. 175, entered into force Dec. 13, 1975.
2. Convention relating to the Status of Stateless Persons, 360 U.N.T.S. 117, entered into force June 6, 1960.
3. Declaration on the Human Rights of Individuals Who are not Nationals of the Country in which They Live, G.A. res. 40/144,annex, 40 U.N. GAOR Supp. (No. 53) at 252, U.N. Doc. A/40/53 (1985).

Q. REGIONAL CONVENTIONS
1. African [Banjul] Charter on Human and Peoples' Rights, adopted June 27, 1981, OAU Doc. CAB/LEG/67/3 rev. 5, 21 I.L.M. 58 (1982), entered into force Oct. 21, 1986.
2. African Charter on the Rights and Welfare of the Child, OAU Doc. CAB/LEG/24.9/49 (1990).
3. The Addis Ababa Document on Refugees and Forced Population Displacements in Africa, Adopted by the OAU/UNHCR Symposium on Refugees and Forced Population Displacements in Africa, Addis Ababa, Ethiopia, 8 - 10 September 1994
4. Convention Governing the Specific Aspects of Refugee Problems in Africa, 1001 U.N.T.S. 45, entered into force June 20, 1974.

5. Declaration on a Code of Conduct for Inter-African Relations, Assembly of Heads of State and Government, Thirtieth Ordinary Session, Tunis, Tunisia, 13-15 June 1994.
6. The Dar es Salaam Declaration on Academic Freedom and Social Responsibility of Academics (1990).
7. The Kampala Declaration on Intellectual Freedom and Social Responsibility (1990).
8. The Khartoum Declaration on Africa's Refugee Crisis, September (1990).
9. Charter of the Organizaton of American States, 119 U.N.T.S. 3, entered into force December 13, 1951, amended 721 U.N.T.S. 324, entered into force Feb. 27, 1990.
10. American Declaration of the Rights and Duties of Man, O.A.S. Res. XXX, adopted by the Ninth International Conference of American States (1948), reprinted in Basic Documents Pertaining to Human Rights in the Inter-American System, OEA/Ser.L.V/II.82 doc.6 rev.1 at 17 (1992).
11. American Convention on Human Rights, O.A.S. Treaty Series No. 36, 1144 U.N.T.S. 123 entered into force July 18, 1978, reprinted in Basic Documents Pertaining to Human Rights in the Inter-American System, OEA/Ser.L.V/II.82 doc.6 rev.1 at 25 (1992).
12. Additional Protocol to the American Convention on Human Rights in the Area of Economic, Social and Cultural Rights, O.A.S. Treaty Series No. 69 (1988), signed November 17, 1988, reprinted in Basic Documents Pertaining to Human Rights in the Inter-American System, OEA/Ser.L.V/II.82 doc.6 rev.1 at 67 (1992).
13. Protocol to the American Convention on Human Rights to Abolish the Death Penalty, O.A.S. Treaty Series No. 73 (1990), adopted June 8, 1990, reprinted in Basic Documents Pertaining to Human Rights in the Inter-American System, OEA/Ser.L.V/II.82 doc.6 rev.1 at 80 (1992).
14. Inter-American Convention to Prevent and Punish Torture, O.A.S.Treaty Series No. 67, entered into force Feb. 28, 1987, reprinted in Basic Documents Pertaining to Human Rights in the Inter-American System, OEA/Ser.L.V/II.82 doc.6 rev.1 at 83 (1992).
15. Statute of the Inter-American Commission on Human Rights, O.A.S.Res. 447 (IX-0/79), O.A.S. Off. Rec. OEA/Ser.P/IX.0.2/80, Vol. 1 at 88, Annual Report of the Inter- American Commission on Human Rights, OEA/Ser.L/V/11.50 doc.13 rev. 1 at 10 (1980), reprinted in Basic Documents Pertaining to Human Rights in the Inter-American System, OEA/Ser.L.V/II.82 doc.6 rev.1 at 93 (1992).
16. Regulations of the Inter-American Commission on Human Rights, reprinted in Basic Documents Pertaining to Human Rights in the Inter-American System, OEA/Ser.L.V/II.82 doc.6 rev.1 at 103 (1992).
17. Statute of the Inter-American Court on Human Rights, O.A.S. Res. 448 (IX-0/79), O.A.S. Off. Rec. OEA/Ser.P/IX.0.2/80, Vol. 1 at 98, Annual Report of the Inter- American Court on Human Rights, OEA/Ser.L/V.III.3 doc. 13 corr. 1 at 16 (1980), reprinted in Basic Documents Pertaining to Human Rights in the Inter-American System, OEA/Ser.L.V/II.82 doc.6 rev.1 at 133 (1992).
18. Rules of Procedure of the Inter-American Court on Human Rights, Annual Report of the Inter-American Court of Human Rights, 1991, O.A.S. Doc. OEA/Ser.L/V/III.25 doc.7 at 18 (1992), reprinted in Basic Documents Pertaining to Human Rights in the Inter-American System, OEA/Ser.L.V/II.82 doc.6 rev.1 at 145 (1992).
19. [European] Convention for the Protection of Human Rights and Fundamental Freedoms, 213 U.N.T.S. 222, entered into force Sept. 3, 1953, as amended by Protocols Nos 3, 5, and 8 which entered into force on 21 September 1970, 20 December 1971 and 1 January 1990 respectively.
20. Protocol to the Convention for the Protection of Human Rights and Fundamental Freedoms, 213 U.N.T.S. 262, entered into force May 18, 1954.
21. Protocol No. 2 to the 1950 European Convention for the Protection of Human Rights and Fundamental Freedoms, E.T.S. 44, entered into force Sept. 21, 1970.

22. Protocol No. 3 to the 1950 European Convention for the Protection of Human Rights and Fundamental Freedoms, E.T.S. 45, entered into force Sept. 21, 1970.
23. Protocol No. 4 to the 1950 European Convention for the Protection of Human Rights and Fundamental Freedoms, E.T.S. 46, entered into force May 2, 1968.
24. Protocol No. 5 to the 1950 European Convention for the Protection of Human Rights and Fundamental Freedoms, E.T.S. 44, entered into force Dec. 20, 1971.
25. Protocol No. 6 to the 1950 European Convention for the Protection of Human Rights and Fundamental Freedoms, E.T.S. 114, entered into force March 1, 1985.
26. Protocol No. 7 to the 1950 European Convention for the Protection of Human Rights and Fundamental Freedoms, E.T.S. 117, entered into force Nov. 1, 1988.
27. Protocol No. 8 to the 1950 European Convention for the Protection of Human Rights and Fundamental Freedoms, E.T.S. 118, entered into force Jan.1, 1990.
28. Protocol No. 9 to the 1950 European Convention for the Protection of Human Rights and Fundamental Freedoms, E.T.S. 140, entered into force Oct. 1, 1994.
29. Protocol No. 10 to the 1950 European Convention for the Protection of Human Rights and Fundamental Freedoms, E.T.S. 146, March 25, 1992.
30. Protocol No. 11 to the 1950 European Convention for the Protection of Human Rights and Fundamental Freedoms, E.T.S. 155, May 11, 1994.
31. European Social Charter, 529 U.N.T.S. 89, entered into force Feb.26, 1965.
32. Additional Protocol to the European Social Charter, E.T.S. 128, May 5, 1988, not in force.
33. Protocol Amending the European Social Charter, E.T.S. 142, Oct. 21, 1991, not in force.
34. European Convention for the Prevention of Torture and Inhuman or Degrading Treatment or Punishment, E.T.S. 126, entered into force Feb. 1, 1989.